CREEPERS

CREEPERS

British Horror and Fantasy
in the Twentieth Century

**Edited by
Clive Bloom**

Pluto Press
LONDON • BOULDER, COLORADO

First published 1993 by Pluto Press
345 Archway Road, London N6 5AA
and 5500 Central Avenue
Boulder, Colorado 80301, USA

British Library Cataloguing in Publication Data
A Catalogue record for this book is available from the British Library
ISBN 0 7453 0664 0 hb
ISBN 0 7453 0665 9 pb

Library of Congress Cataloging-in-Publication Data
Creepers : British horror and fantasy in the twentieth century /
  edited by Clive Bloom.
     p. cm.
   Includes index.
     ISBN 0-7453-0664-0. – ISBN 0-7453-0665-9 (pbk.)
     1. Horror tales. English–History and criticism. 2. Fantastic
fiction, English–History and criticism. 3. English fiction–20th
century–History and criticism. I. Bloom, Clive.
   PR888. T3C74 1993
   823'.0873809–dc20   92-36706
                                                              CIP

Designed and produced for Pluto Press by
Chase Production Services, Chipping Norton
Typeset in Stone by Stanford DTP Services, Milton Keynes
Printed in Finland by WSOY

For Yasmin and Tony

Contents

Contributors

Clive Bloom (editor) is author and editor of numerous books and articles on cultural history, literary theory and popular fiction. He currently teaches at Middlesex University and has recently completed *Dark Knights: the New Comics in Context* (Pluto, 1993) with co-author Greg McCue.

Victor Sage is the author of books and articles on supernatural fiction and is currently co-editing a collection of essays on gothic fiction with Allan Lloyd Smith. Dr Sage teaches at the University of East Anglia.

Gina Wisker writes on popular and romantic fiction and is the editor of *Black Women's Writing*. Dr Wisker teaches at Anglia University Polytechnic.

John Simons is Head of English at Edgehill College of Higher Education. He is a regular contributor to works on popular culture as well as being an acknowledged expert on medieval and tudor literature. He is Editor of *From Medieval to Medievalism*.

Alasdair Spark teaches at King Alfred's College. His work includes articles on science fiction, popular culture and Vietnam.

Dennis Butts is an acknowledged authority on books for children and has recently edited *Stories and Society: Children's Literature in its Context*. He teaches at Reading University and is Chairman of the Children's Books History Society.

Nicholas Rance teaches English at Middlesex University. He is a contributor to many collections on popular and nineteenth-century fiction and author of *Wilkie Collins and other Sensation Novelists*.

John Nicholson is one of the founder members of the Small Press Group of Great Britain. He is the author of political and satiric pamphlets and an expert in popular and small press publications.

Amanda Boulter is a research student at Southampton University. Her research work has centred upon William Hope Hodgson and imperial fiction.

Allan Lloyd Smith is currently chair of the International Gothic Society. Convenor of a recent major conference on Gothic fiction he is co-editor of a collection of essays on the gothic with Victor Sage. Dr Lloyd Smith teaches at the University of East Anglia.

Andrew Smith has written numerous articles on popular fiction and culture. He is now preparing a collection of essays on the politics of reading at Southampton University.

Preface

The horror tale in Britain has a venerable history and its gothic origins are still visible among the carnage that is the subject matter of contemporary horror authors. Yet the variety of incarnations the genre has undergone presents the reader with a rich and neglected vein of popular literary taste and popular cultural history. While most volumes about horror and supernatural fiction take a broad and international approach, this collection of critical essays makes a detailed enquiry into the fiction which has come out of Britain since the beginning of the twentieth century. By any standards the variety and remarkable diversity of the productions of this century would suggest the thriving nature of popular fiction which concentrates on horror and a continuing readership that enjoys 'things that go bump in the night'.

As with most popular fiction, it has been horror fiction's translation into other media that has guaranteed its survival. Many people remember with a nostalgic affection those Hammer horror movies, filmed with low budgets and uncannily reoccurring sets upon whose sound stages moved the fledgling stars of television's soap operas. Others will remember the Pan and Fontana anthologies which accompanied the flower-power years of the early 1960s and which now turn up in rather unhappy condition at jumbles and trunk sales. It has always been the critical mass of the genre that has been important rather than individual authors although some, like M.R. James have a prestige accorded only to 'serious' authors and some, like Clive Barker or Shaun Hutson have had a 'cult' following. Others like E.F. Benson wrote horror stories only on an occasional basis and are not remembered as especially associated with the genre and still others, like the once popular Dennis Wheatley, seem to have gone into a terminal decline despite writing one of the great novels of the genre: *The Devil Rides Out.*

The writers included in this volume span this century and reflect its concerns and obsessions. Alongside M.R. James, Arthur Machen and Dennis Wheatley are Clive Barker, James Herbert and Daphne du Maurier as well as many others both well known and less well known, classic writers and schlock authors, some of the great tales of the genre and some that are destined for oblivion.

The world of supernatural and horror fiction is no less diverse in the themes and images it uses than any other field of writing. The chapters included in this volume acknowledge the diversity and range of the subject matter and offer not merely a clear and lucid account of the development of the genre, but also give insight into the individual authors and books discussed. Using a variety of critical methods to interrogate the subject of British horror fiction in the twentieth century this volume is guaranteed to appeal both to the serious enthusiast as well as the professional academic or student of popular fiction. The chapters that follow are a piquant introduction and analysis of the aesthetics of the horrible in the modern British imagination and a reminder that the genre, however minor or discounted, has refused to lay down and, like the living dead it is so fond of, it is still capable of haunting our literary tastes after almost a century.

Acknowledgements

The Editor would like to thank Brian Docherty and Gary Day for their support and encouragement, Anne Beech of Pluto Press for her faith in the project and for her willingness to listen to ideas however eccentric, Pauline Foley, Monique Polins and Lesley Bloom for their help in preparing parts of the typescript.

In fact, I may tell you our ghost department is not what it used to be. People are indifferent to apparitions nowadays, in this country, at any rate, and ghosts are so sensitive that they don't go where they are not wanted.

Henry A. Hering
'The Telepather'

He was, beyond question, experiencing all the mental variations of – *someone else*! It was un-moral. It was awful. It was – well, after all, at the same time, it was uncommonly interesting.

Algernon Blackwood
'The Occupant of the Room'

Death.
This is death – Silence. Trapped in a dark void. Forever. The void.

Peter James
Dreamer

Do what thou wilt shall be the whole of the Law

Aleister Crowley
The Book of the Law

Part I: Into the Crypt

1 Empire Gothic: Explanation and Epiphany in Conan Doyle, Kipling and Chesterton

Victor Sage

The history of the gothic is the history of a set of cultural responses, not a genre. Nowhere is this more evident than in what I shall call, for want of a better word, Empire gothic; that flowering of popular magazine stories in the early twentieth century whose subject matter is often the borderline between English culture and the (perceived) culture of the Empire, the apotheosis of which is probably Conrad's *Heart of Darkness*. The real form of all these stories, irrespective of whether they are classifiable as horror stories, detective stories, creepy stories or spy stories (these are all the names of famous later anthologies) is a dynamic of foregrounded testimony, a reported witnessing of the uncanny and the marvellous, if not the miraculous. The miracles of the devil are included; horror plays across all these evolving sub-genres irrespective of their particular formal shapes and demands. And it is in this act of dramatised witnessing – itself a mixture of theology and law – that certain forms of cultural unease are expressed with differing degrees of fictional self-consciousness.

The gothic tradition involves a specific kind of fragmentation of the reader's response. The narrative method, from the earliest gothic novels on, has foregrounded multiple subjective testimony and in the traditional gothic it is used to throw into question the cultural guarantees of belief in a dividing line between superstition (the past, the other) and rationality (the present, the reader). This tradition goes back to eighteenth-century discussions about the authority of biblical testimony for miracles. Pressure falls upon the epistemological guarantees for truth in the eighteenth century, due largely to Hume and his attack on the validity of testimony to the miraculous. In the nineteenth century this pressure diversified and increased with the advent of positivism and the work of continental scholars on the origins of the biblical narratives.[1] The notion of 'superstition' became even more fascinating and threatening to a readership whose certainties were in the process of being eroded, as people became aware

3

of ideas like sympathetic magic and ritual pollution – the materials of Frazer's *The Golden Bough*.

In the later popular fiction of the Empire period, the anthologies thrive on boundary experiences. But whereas in the early gothic, there was an obsession with setting action back in time (to the feudal past, for example, or whatever pictures of a remote and barbarous age the author could conjure up), the 'other' is now also a contemporaneous and geographical phenomenon. It is a question of cultural space.[2]

Boundaries in this fiction manifest themselves in a counterpoint between two rhetorical modes: the Epiphany (reported through an eye-witness, and usually horrible), and the Explanation (often piquantly unsatisfying, raising more questions than it solves). Explanation is fore-grounded as a necessity, yet often forbidden to be singular. It is put into relationship with other frameworks of explanation. And with this process the genre signals are disrupted. Todorov with his law of hesitation might seem to help, but these narratives thrive on deliber-ately provoked conflict between explanations of the horrid epiphanies, the casual yet compelling violations of the laws of nature, which they offer to the reader. In fact, they really exist in the gaps between the explanations.

I will begin with something which appears the very counter-example to this argument, what I think of as closed testimony; a story with a thirst for closure. The nicest example of this I can find is a horror story – a kind of vampire story, in fact, which masquerades as a detective story: Arthur Conan Doyle's 'The Speckled Band'.

'The Speckled Band' is the story of a medical doctor who invents a particularly ingenious perfect crime. Relying on ignorance of poisonous snakebites among English country coroners and the incapacity of English country doctors to analyse rare poisons even if the bite were discovered, he imports a swamp adder, the deadliest snake in all India, and introduces it into the bedroom – on to the bed, to be precise – of his two stepdaughters while they are asleep. The first daughter is bitten, and dies. The second, who does not understand how her sister died but suspects some kind of foul play, approaches Sherlock Holmes in desperation.

The 'Speckled Band' is a 'case', set back in the year 1883, and kept secret by Watson until the death of the last surviving witness, the second of the stepdaughters, Miss Helen Stoner.[3] It concerns 'the well-known Surrey family of the Roylotts of Stoke Moran'. Watson comments immediately in the first paragraph,

It is perhaps as well that the facts should now come to light, for I have reasons to know there are widespread rumours as to the death of Dr Grimesby Roylott which tend to make the matter even more terrible than the truth.[4]

This is exactly the same justification for telling the story as the one given by the narrator in Poe's famous 'The Facts in The Case of M. Valdemar', the model for all 'strange cases'. Rumour needs to be scotched by first-hand evidence. Truth is at a premium even though Watson has already observed that Holmes, since he was working for his art not for money, 'refused to associate himself with any investigation which did not tend toward the unusual, and even the fantastic'. There is thus, in the outer fictional frame of Watson's recording of the 'case', a possibility of testimony to both the true and the marvellous.

It is with these ambiguous expectations that we are confronted with out first-hand witness, Miss Stoner, herself the very emblem of fear and a living sign of the secrecy and unease at the heart of the story.

A lady, dressed in black and heavily veiled, who had been sitting in the window, rose as we entered.

'Good morning, madam', said Holmes cheerily. 'My name is Sherlock Holmes. This is my intimate friend and associate, Dr Watson, before whom you can speak as freely as before myself. Ha, I am glad to see that Mrs Hudson has had the sense to light the fire. Pray draw up to it, and I shall order you a cup of hot coffee, for I observe that you are shivering'.

'It is not cold which makes me shiver', said the woman in a low voice, changing her seat as requested.

'What then?'

'It is fear, Mr Holmes. It is terror'. She raised her veil as she spoke, and we could see that she was indeed in a pitiable state of agitation, her face all drawn and grey, with restless, frightened eyes, like those of some hunted animal. Her features and figure were those of a woman of thirty, but her hair was shot with premature grey, and her expression was weary and haggard.

Miss Stoner's story begins by making a firm connection between the dissolution of aristocratic Saxon cultural roots and the emigration of the last remaining scion of the stock, her stepfather Dr Grimsby Roylott, out to India to avoid debt and dishonour.

The family was at one time among the richest in England, and the estate extended over the borders into Berkshire in the north, and Hampshire in the west. In the last century, however, four successive heirs were of a dissolute and wasteful disposition, and the family ruin was eventually completed by a gambler, in the days of the Regency. Nothing was left save a few acres of ground and the two-hundred-year-old house, which is itself crushed under a heavy mortgage, the last squire dragged out his existence there, living the horrible life of an aristocratic pauper; but his only son, my stepfather, seeing that

he must adapt himself to the new conditions, obtained an advance
from a relative, which enabled him to take a medical degree, and went
out to Calcutta, where, by his professional skill and his force of
character, he established a large practice.

So far so good, but Roylott murders a native and ruins everything.

In a fit of anger, however, caused by some robberies which had been
perpetrated in the house, he beat his native Butler to death, and
narrowly escaped a capital sentence. As it was he suffered a long term
of imprisonment and afterwards returned to England, a morose
and disappointed man.

He turns inward and becomes a recluse in the decaying old family
home, Stoke Moran. The implication is that he has become criminalised,
but Miss Stoner's language suggests only a psychological dimension at
this stage – that he has inherited a strain of mania. The gothic stereotype
of the mysterious, ruined, Uncle Silas figure – in this case a wicked
stepfather, is updated, embedded and disguised in the social story of
a scandal in the Empire.
The conscious level of motivation in the case is closely worked out
in parallel, and embedded in Miss Stoner's evidence. Financially, this
reclusive existence is made possible by his marriage.

When Dr Roylott was in India he married my mother, Mrs Stoner,
the young widow of Major-General Stoner, of the Bengal Artillery.
My sister Julia and I were twins, and we were only two years old at
the time of my mother's remarriage. She had a considerable sum of
money, not less than a thousand a year, and this she bequeathed to
Dr Roylott entirely whilst we resided with him, with a provision that
a certain sum should be allowed to each of us in the event of our
marriage. Shortly after our return to England my mother died – she
was killed eight years ago in a railway accident near Crewe. Dr
Roylott then abandoned his attempts to establish himself in practice
in London, and took us to live with him in the ancestral house at
Stoke Moran, the money which my mother left was enough for all
our wants, and there seemed no obstacle to our happiness.

This financial independence leads Roylott, however, contrary to
these expectations, to become the outsider that he is. His mania can
now show itself. The neighbours, 'who had at first been overjoyed to
see a Roylott of Stoke Moran back in the old family seat' are shunned.
There are brawls and episodes of violence and he becomes the terror
of the village.

It is at this point that the idea of an encroachment from the Empire is first raised and this quite different idea is woven in, apparently seamlessly, with his attraction to the gypsies, who confirm his status as an outsider by his choice of companions:

> He had no friends at all save the wandering gypsies, and he would give these vagabonds leave to encamp upon the few acres of bramble-covered land which represent the family estate, and would accept in return the hospitality of their tents, wandering away with them sometimes for weeks on end. He has a passion also for Indian animals, which are sent over to him by a correspondent, and he has at this moment a cheetah and a baboon, which wander freely over his grounds, and are feared by the villagers almost as much as their master.

The gypsies are, of course, a red-herring; but the text, through the headlong rush of Miss Stoner's first-hand testimony, plays upon the reader's willingness to suspect a conspiracy of outsiders; that Roylott, fallen, and infected by a criminal past, has 'gone native' in his own country and become a social threat rather than a mere eccentric; while the 'Indian animals', on the other hand, which look at this stage merely like a decorative trapping of 'eccentricity', are crucial to the outcome of the case. The Empire will strike back, literally.

———

We can see here that there are different threads of explanation intertwined, even in the framework of the case. As the narrative proceeds, both at the level of plot, the thing to which Miss Stoner is testifying, and of discourse, the present time in which she is testifying, the reader, locked into the first-person narratives of the witnesses and not allowed an overview, is constantly teased and offered wrong explanations of what has actually transpired.

We are even challenged by an incidence of what Poe calls 'intolerable yet objectless horror', the sublime, inexplicable epiphany of sister Julia's death.

> 'I could not sleep that night, a vague feeling of impending misfortune impressed me. My sister and I, you will recollect, were twins, and you know how subtle are the links which bind two souls which are so closely allied. It was a wild night. The wind was howling outside, and rain was beating and splashing against the windows. Suddenly, amidst all the hubbub of the gale, there burst forth the wild scream of a terrified woman. I knew that it was my sister's voice. ... As I ran down the passage my sister's door was unlocked, and revolved slowly upon its hinges. I stared at it horror-stricken, not knowing what

was about to issue from it. By the light of the corridor lamp I saw
my sister appear at the opening, her face blanched with terror, her
hands groping for help, her whole figure swaying to and fro like that
of a drunkard. I ran to her and threw my arms round her, but at that
moment her knees seemed to give way and she fell to the ground,
she writhed as one who is in terrible pain, and her limbs were
dreadfully convulsed. At first I thought that she had not recognized
me, but as I bent over her she suddenly shrieked out in a voice I shall
never forget, 'O, my God! Helen! It was the band! The speckled
band!' There was something else she would fain have said, and she
stabbed with her finger into the air in the direction of the Doctor's
room, but a fresh convulsion seized her and choked her words.'

There is something about stories based on reconstruction that recon-
structs to excess. Some information is deliberately present in order not
to be in the final explanatory frame – for example, the reader's already
carefully cultivated prejudice against the gypsies is played off against
the common belief that twins are telepathic, the two beliefs combining
to produce an interpretation of this horror-epiphany which is quite
wrong. In fact the only 'knowledge' which Julia Stoner transmits to her
sister, Helen, is the metaphor of 'the speckled band' which the latter
interprets literally and associates with the headgear of the gypsies,
producing the distracting image of a spotted handkerchief. In fact, it
is Holmes, as he later admits, who elicits the testimony from Helen
which misleads us. Then immediately come the ambiguous signals of
dissatisfaction which suggest that this is not the final explanation – or,
if it is along these lines, then it is much more horrible ('Holmes shook
his head like a man who is far from being satisfied. "These are very deep
waters," said he.')
Julia also makes a clear, but non-verbal indication that she believes
the horror comes from her father's room, but this is very difficult for
the reader to respond to as evidence. It enhances our frustration,
because it places the reader on the same level as the characters. We in
a sense still know no more than the coroner who was convinced that
Roylott was guilty but was quite unable to find the evidence.
This continuous generation of alternative, but false explanations
applies also to Roylott's motivation for the murder of his daughters.
Retrospectively, we can see there is minimal sexual motivation in
Roylott – but his menacing invasion into Holmes's chambers on the
trail of his daughter technically leaves the case open.

A large face, seared with a thousand wrinkles, burned yellow with
the sun, and marked with every evil passion, was turned from one
to the other of us, while his deep-set, bile-shot eyes, and the high

thin fleshless nose, gave him somewhat the resemblance to a fierce old bird of prey.

Here he is firmly presented, under the old Galenic scheme, as choleric, full of yellow bile; and a person infected (the description of the face sounds more stereotypically Chinese than Indian in some ways) by the East. 'Every evil passion' couldn't be more inclusive, however, and the reader is obliged to entertain the idea of the sexual jealousy of the patriarch, because we already know that every time one of the daughters meets someone eligible at the aunt's in Harrow, he attacks. It is entirely possible this is for money, but it is not insisted on until Holmes takes the precaution of inspecting the terms of Mrs Roylott's will at Doctor's Commons and it becomes clear to the reader that Roylott stands to lose more than Helen Stoner had suspected. At that time, the potentiality of a conscious sexual motivation in the stepfather is carefully closed off.

At this point in the narrative all the reader knows is that the murder is 'Eastern' and peculiarly devilish – it seems to defy physical causes – and it is about to occur again. When Holmes and Watson (illegally) enter the grounds of Stoke Moran at night for the purpose of replacing Helen Stoner in her bedroom in order to conduct first-hand observations, they are greeted by another unpleasant and startling, and apparently irrelevant, epiphany.

> Making our way among the trees, we reached the lawn, crossed it, and were about to enter through the window, when out from a clump of laurel bushes there darted what seemed to be a hideous and distorted child, who threw itself on the grass with writhing limbs, and then ran swiftly across the lawn into the darkness.
>
> 'My God!' I whispered, 'did you see it?'
>
> Holmes was for a moment as startled as I. His hand closed like a vice on my wrist in his agitation.

In this Eastern parody of a domestic world, baboons are children. The reader is presented with the full puzzle before Holmes suddenly realises what the creature is, and laughs with relief. Again the epiphany presents the full horror of the incomprehensible, and then immediately dissipates it into an explanatory frame, which demonstrates the fallibility of the senses.

In fact this frame is the one which will 'solve' the whole crime and the major epiphany of the story, but the reader can't know this the first time round. When it happens, we see what Holmes sees and strikes at only through Watson's view of his friend's face:

For half an hour I sat with straining ears. Then suddenly another sound became audible – a very gentle, soothing sound, like that of a small jet of steam escaping from a kettle. The instant that we heard it, Holmes sprang from the bed, struck a match, and lashed furiously with his cane at the bell-pull.

'You see it, Watson?' he yelled, 'You see it?'

But I saw nothing. At the moment when Holmes struck the light I heard a low clear whistle, but the sudden glare flashing into my weary eyes made it impossible for me to tell what it was at which my friend lashed so savagely. I could, however, see that his face was deadly pale, and filled with horror and loathing.

Roylott, in the bedroom next door, suddenly gives out a terrible shriek, and when they go in to see him, the final epiphany is in the mode of the full grotesque – curiously it teases the reader by putting into visual form the mistaken interpretation of the testimony of the first sister, Julia Stoner, which gives to the story its title. Roylott is actually wearing the Speckled Band – just as the reader earlier had been invited, quite erroneously, to imagine him doing.

It was a singular sight which met our eyes. On the table stood a dark lantern with the shutter half open, throwing a brilliant beam of light upon the iron safe, the door of which was ajar. Beside this table, on the wooden chair, sat Dr Grimesby Roylott, clad in a long grey dressing-gown, his bare ankles protruding beneath, and his feet thrust into red heelless Turkish slippers. Across his lap lay the short stock with the long lash which we had noticed during the day, his chin was cocked upwards, and his eyes were fixed in a dreadful rigid stare at the corner of the ceiling. Round his brow he had a peculiar yellow band with brownish speckles, which seemed to be bound tightly round his head. As we entered he made neither sound nor motion.

'The band! the speckled band!' whispered Holmes.

I took a step forward. In an instant his strange headgear began to move, and there reared itself from among his hair the squat diamond-shaped head and puffed neck of a loathsome serpent.

Roylott sits like a cross between a Gypsy King, a Turkish Pasha and a Male Medusa, a snake God, who threatens to turn the reader to stone with the drama of the snake's complete possession of the man. The snake provides the image of a living corpse which has all the horror of an object that cannot be touched – the image defamiliarised completely until its component parts are known.

When this happens, the conventional providential scheme, which has been waiting in the wings all along, also enters the story:

'It is a swamp adder!' cried Holmes – 'the deadliest snake in India. He has died within ten seconds of being bitten. Violence does, in truth, recoil upon the violent, and the schemer falls into the pit which he digs for another.'

Despite the story's drive towards a closure, the explanation and the epiphany here are not compatible. The epiphanic structures contain an excess of the grotesque and the bizarre. Roylott is a magician ('a clever and ruthless man with an Eastern training') who lives in a world of inverted (Eastern) values; he keeps a snake in his safe, creates dummy bell-ropes that don't ring, ventilators that don't ventilate, repairs that aren't repairs, children that are baboons, dog-leashes which are not for dogs and so on. The explanatory drive is meant to reduce all this to one, or rather two , simple logics – money and hereditary manic violence. But what does Roylott need the money for – so that he can neglect himself even further and become a gypsy? It is the invasion by the East, the sense of the culture of Empire coming home to roost in the English countryside, that lingers in the reader's mind beyond the explanatory framework of 'criminalisation'.

As, indeed it should be said, does the sexual connotation of the central epiphany itself. The wicked stepfather usually codifies the incest taboo. The violence of the sexual image offered to the reader is enhanced by the almost sadistic pleasure the text takes in tormenting the reader, while it insists on evacuating all explicit references to sexuality and, as I have said, converting all conscious motivation of this type strictly into bile and money. There is only one explicit sexual joke in the story. That is when Holmes proposes to Helen Stoner that he and Watson spend the night in her bedroom.

'It is very essential, Miss Stoner', said he, 'that you should follow my advice in every respect.'
'I shall most certainly do so.'
'The matter is too serious for any hesitation. Your life may depend on your compliance.'
'I assure you that I am in your hands.'
'In the first place, both my friend and I must spend the night in your room.'
Both Miss Stoner and I gazed at him in astonishment.

That Holmes could behave in any way less than a gentleman is, of course, unthinkable, but we are meant to perceive that his thought processes being so dramatic and deep he is, rather amusingly, here not in control of the ambiguity of his phrasing. In a moment, he will restore all propriety by explaining that Miss Stoner will, of course, not be in the room. However, the dialogue is almost a music hall gag, especially with Miss Stoner's rather unfortunate, 'I assure you that I am in your hands.' Why is the joke there? Its effect for the reader is unmistakably to raise and dismiss the idea of a violation of sexual propriety. After all, the fantasy is of an illegal but connived-at entry into private property and of permitted entry into a woman's bedroom.

Yet compare this delicate safety-valve with the central fantasy of the story, in which a wicked stepfather bolts his stepdaughters' bed to the floor and bores a hole in the wall above it and puts a snake through that hole every night. Then the snake slithers down its own double, the wicked stepfather's thick dummy bell-pull, and lands always in the same place on the bed. The fantasy of violation comes not from any sexual innuendo, but from the horror which lies in the innocent details as the reader follows Holmes's penetrating but as yet ignorant gaze around the room.

> Holmes drew one of the chairs into a corner and sat silent, while his eyes travelled round and round and up and down, taking in every detail of the apartment.
>
> 'Where does that bell communicate with?' he asked at last, pointing to a thick bell-rope which hung down beside the bed, *the tassel actually lying upon the pillow*. (My italics)

Here the text talks to the reader without Holmes's mediation, though in fact we need the explanation of the crime to re-read this italicised phrase as an epiphany, unless we have guessed the whole thing. This fantasy, though dramatically obvious in the story, had to be approached by inference and is, apparently, sanitised totally by plot and social setting.

―――――

Open testimony is quite different, because it seeks no such closure and the detective format. Kipling's early 'The Mark of the Beast' is a displaced werewolf story.[5] It is the tale of how a drunken Englishman in the province of Dharmsala who pollutes a temple effigy of the Monkey God, Hanuman, by stubbing out his cigar on the statue's forehead, is immediately touched by The Silver Man, a faceless leper and an informal priest of the temple, whose sinister laying on of hands leaves Fleete with a curious mark on his chest. After this, Fleete's character appears to his old friends to change and regress to that of a beast – symptoms which the local doctor interprets as those of hydrophobia.

Kipling's tale ironically foregrounds the boundaries between explanations of a phenomenon, and in doing so it questions the relations between religion and culture in cases of East and West. The openness of the story is partly due to the 'club' tale as opposed to the detective story which is much more inclined to leave a tale open. But not entirely; it seems to be Kipling's intention also to satirise the comfortable beliefs of Protestant English readers about Empire, by setting his tale in a world in which values have become radically distorted. We are left with an uncomfortable gap, as the opening of the story stresses.

East of Suez, some hold, the direct control of Providence ceases; man is there handed over to the power of the Gods and devils of Asia, and the Church of England providence only exercising an occasional and modified supervision in the case of Englishmen.

This theory accounts for some of the more unnecessary horrors of life in India; it may be stretched to explain my story.

But this stretching process, needless to say, will not 'explain the story' to the point where the reader feels comfortable or satisfied about the fate of the two main characters at all, even within the framework of alternative religions and the mysteries of the East. The official explanation – that Fleete has contracted hydrophobia from an old dog bite – is left in place but cannot be believed by either of the two witnesses present.

The explanation that Strickland, the narrator, and we, are forced to entertain, and which challenges our automatic but unconscious conversion of chance coincidence into providence, is that Fleete – a curiously apt name for one who is to turn into a large cat or wolf – polluted the temple idol and is polluted in return. This is what the ominous words of the priest immediately after the incident imply;

Then, without any warning, a Silver man came out of a recess behind the image of the god. He was perfectly naked in that bitter, bitter cold, and his body shone like frosted silver, for he was what the Bible calls 'a leper as white as snow'. Also, he had no face, because he was a leper of some years' standing, and his disease was heavy upon him. We two stooped to haul Fleete up, and the temple was filling and filling with folk who seemed to spring from the earth, when the Silver Man ran in under our arms, making a noise exactly like the mewing of an otter, caught Fleete round the body and dropped his head on Fleete's breast before we could wrench him away. Then he retired to a corner and sat mewing while the crowd blocked all the doors.

The priests were very angry until the Silver Man touched Fleete. That nuzzling seemed to sober them.

At the end of a few minutes' silence one of the priests came to Strickland, and said, in perfect English, 'Take your friend away. He has done with Hanuman but Hanuman has not done with him.'

The method of the story is again one of opposing a horrid epiphany – the moment of undeniable eye-witness perception of an uncanny event – to a series of explanations. The narrator's reference to the Bible (2 Kings 5: 27) is far from comforting for the Christian reader because it seems to confirm the possibility of such possession and uncleanliness. Different fears seem to jostle together in the description; taboo and possession and pollution and infection by disease are all present within the moment as well as retributive punishment and in this disturbing complex all of these secretly cross the boundaries between the cultures which the rhetoric of the story has established. There is an opportunity for us to recognise retribution, for example, and bow to it. Does the Old Testament not say 'an eye for an eye?'

But this 'open' structure of witnessing in the story, which leaves the reader in a state of conflict between religious and social values, is deeply ironic in a quite different way. It is a distraction from the real level of commentary, which is social and political. Strickland of the Police, like George Orwell in Burma, is said to have 'a weakness for going among the natives' and Kipling's irony about English policy in India is at its clearest in describing this character's attitudes.

> While we were drinking he talked of the trouble in the temple, and admitted that it baffled him completely. Strickland hates being mystified by natives, because his business in life is to overmatch them with their own weapons. He has not yet succeeded in doing this, but in fifteen or twenty years he will have made some small progress.

It is the nature of this 'progress' which forms the most disturbing level of the story. Strickland is hoping (and, ironically, praying) that the managing committee of the temple will bring a criminal action against Fleete for insulting their religion and the narrator reassures him that 'there was a section of the Indian Penal Code which exactly met Fleete's offence', but this is not to be. Instead, the mark where Fleete has been touched comes up like a blister in the shape of the spots on a leopard, Fleete's horses suddenly become terrified of him, he is overtaken by a craving for raw chops, and the next day they find him crawling around in the flower beds and wanting to eat outside in the bitter cold of December in Northern India.

> 'Come in', said Strickland sternly, 'Come in at once.'
>
> Fleete came, and when the lamps were brought, we saw that he was literally plastered with dirt from head to foot. He must have been rolling in the garden. He shrank from the light and went to his room, his eyes were horrible to look at, there was a green light behind them, not in them, if you understand, and the man's lower lip hung down.

Strickland said, 'There's going to be trouble – big trouble – to-night. Don't you change your riding-things.'

We waited and waited for Fleete's reappearance, and ordered dinner in the meantime. We could hear him moving about his own room, but there was no light there. Presently from the room came the long-drawn howl of a wolf.

People write and talk lightly of blood running cold and hair standing up, and things of that kind. Both sensations are too horrible to be trifled with. My heart stopped as though a knife had been driven through it, and Strickland turned as white as the tablecloth.

The howl was repeated, and was answered by another howl far across the fields.

This gothic epiphany – corroborated by the testimony of Strickland and the narrator – drives Strickland to action. He decides that they must rescue their friend. The doctor Dumoise diagnoses acute hydrophobia and certain death. But Strickland decides that they must reverse the spell by compelling the Silver Man to take it back. It is at this point that the witnessing ends and the text becomes extremely coy and reticent about their methods, clearly torture of some kind:

'I think I was right', said Strickland. 'Now we will ask him to cure this case.'

But the leper only mewed. Strickland wrapped a towel round his hand and took the gun-barrels out of the fire. I put the half of the broken walking stick through the loop of fishing-line and buckled the leper comfortably to Strickland's bedstead. I understood then how men and women and little children can endure to see a witch burnt alive; for the beast was moaning on the floor, and though the Silver Man had no face, you could see horrible feelings passing through the slab that took its place, exactly as waves of heat play across red-hot iron – gun-barrels for instance.

Strickland shaded his eyes with his hands for a moment and we got to work. This part is not to be printed.

The paradox is that the witnesses have to betray themselves as Englishmen in order to rescue their friend. They have to deny their own Protestant rationalism and belief in providence. They have to believe in the Gods of the Other, and the references to witchcraft clearly reveal that putting the Silver Man to the question, far from one of progress, is actually one of shameful cultural regress into superstition which has long been surpassed in English culture.

However, it works, and Fleete recovers. The astonished and insulted doctor Dumoise is told that there must have been something wrong with his diagnosis. The priests of the temple deny smoothly that any white man ever touched their idol, and we are left at the end of the story with the mystery of whether it really was as it appeared. The final paragraph of the story returns us to the dilemma of belief which is the pretext of the story:

> Some years later, when Strickland had married and was a church-going member of society for his wife's sake, we reviewed the incident dispassionately, and Strickland suggested that I should put it before the public.
>
> I cannot myself see that this step is likely to clear up the mystery; because, in the first place, no one will believe a rather unpleasant story, and, in the second, it is well-known to every right-minded man that the gods of the heathen are stone and brass, and any attempt to deal with them otherwise is justly condemned.

It is clear from the narrator's last attempt to reassert the boundary that he hasn't really quite understood the significance of what has gone on in the story he has just told – our witnesses are neither Christian Englishmen nor rationalists – they have passed 'beyond' this condition. The paradox of having to believe in something in order to defeat it is set against the social explanation of their cruelty, cynicism and self-deception about all religion; either way the story's unresolved horror, existing in the gaps between explanations, presents a challenge to the imperial comforts of Protestantism and providence.

―――――

G.K. Chesterton's Father Brown stories are obviously a form of meta-physical detective fiction and Brown and Flambeau are built at least in part on the model of Holmes and Watson. But Chesterton, who was a Catholic convert and who dissents from the Protestant confidence in the British Empire, was very concerned with some of the questions we have already been discussing. One example, the story 'The Wrong Shape', shows him foregrounding the question of the nature of evil as opposed to mere human wickedness; Eastern religions and the relation between cultural decadence as expressed in the doctrines of aestheticism, and Empire.[6]

Chesterton deals with testimony to the miraculous and the distinction between that and the marvellous by adopting a third-person narrator of limited omniscience, so to speak, who is capable of withholding information from the reader, in a manner reminiscent of Mrs Radcliffe's narrative ambiguities. Chesterton's 'case' is a murder which is committed while the narrative is still under way, and Brown and Flambeau are on the spot, visiting Quinton, the aesthete poet, and an old acquaintance of Flambeau's student days, at his house in a North London Suburb. The story begins with a rather sub-Dickensian piece of urban picturesque which quickly begins to hint at the presence of Empire and the Eastern theme.

Certain of the great roads going north out of London continue far into the country a sort of attenuated and interrupted spectre of a street, with great gaps in the building, but preserving the line. ... If anyone walks along these roads he will pass a house which will probably catch his eye, though he may not be able to explain its attraction. It is a long, low house, running parallel with the road, painted mostly white and pale green, with a veranda and sunblinds, and porches capped with those quaint sort of cupolas like wooden umbrellas that one sees in some old-fashioned house. In fact, it is an old-fashioned house, very English and very suburban in the good old wealthy Clapham sense. And yet the house has a look of having been built chiefly for the hot weather. Looking at its white paint and sun-blinds one thinks vaguely of pugarees and then of palm trees. I cannot trace the feeling to its root; perhaps the place was built by an Anglo-Indian.

Although the story is not set in Clapham, Martin Gardner reminds us that Chesterton wrote eloquently about Clapham in his autobiography, a passage of which is worth quoting here:

What was called my medievalism was simply that I was very much interested in the historic meaning of Clapham Common. What was called my dislike of Imperialism was a dislike of making England an Empire, in the sense of something more like Clapham Junction. For my own visionary Clapham consisted of houses standing still, and not of trucks and trains rattling by.

Present at the house is a mysterious Hindoo, who is acting as consultant for Quinton, the owner of the house, over an epic the latter is writing; the Indian is acting the role of, as the narrator puts it sarcastically, 'a Virgil to guide his spirit through the heavens and hells of the East'. But the Indian, in terms of the plot, is a complete red-herring: Quinton the poet turns out to have been murdered by his hearty, energetic, atheistic Social Darwinist doctor, Harris, who desires to possess his wife.

The crime is thus staggeringly quotidian and unexotic – Clapham rather than Delhi – and, from the point of view of the plot, the elaborately introduced Eastern theme appears to have no function other than a false clue in the process of detection.

But the story conceals an allegory in its domestic setting: it brings together the aestheticism of the late nineteenth century, and the threatening presence of the Empire. The East is shapeless, and aestheticism in art is a flirtation with that shapelessness, the shapelessness of colour at the expense of form. Thus, of the aesthete Quinton, the narrator tells us that he,

> was a man who drank and bathed in colours, who indulged his lust for colour somewhat to the neglect of form – even of good form. This it was that had turned his genius so wholly to eastern art and imagery; to those bewildering carpets or blinding embroideries in which all the colours seem fallen into a fortunate chaos, having nothing to typify or to teach.

This is an explanatory line which Father Brown, who senses the presence of real evil at the house throughout the story, also echoes. When by sheer chance, they find the oriental dagger with which Quinton is to be killed by the doctor, the priest shares this same prejudice with the narrator:

Father Brown had stopped for a moment, and picked up out of the long grass where it had almost been wholly hidden, a queer, crooked, Oriental knife, inlaid exquisitely in coloured stones and metals.

'What is this?' asked Father Brown, regarding it with some disfavour.

'Oh, Quinton's, I suppose,' said Dr Harris carelessly, 'he has all sorts of Chinese knick-knacks about the place, or perhaps it belongs to that mild Hindoo of his whom he keeps on a string.'

'What Hindoo?' asked Father Brown, still staring at the dagger in his hand.

'Oh, some Indian conjuror,' said the doctor lightly, 'a fraud, of course.'

'You don't believe in magic?' asked Father Brown, without looking up.

'O crikey! magic!' said the doctor.

'It's very beautiful,' said the priest in a low, dreaming voice, 'the colours are very beautiful. But it's the wrong shape.'

'What for?' asked Flambeau, staring.

'For anything. It's the wrong shape in the abstract. Don't you ever feel that about Eastern art? The colours are intoxicatingly lovely, but the shapes are mean and bad – deliberately mean and bad. I have seen wicked things in a Turkey carpet.'

The stage is set for a defence of *form* here, not only in art, but in religion and culture as well. The Indian, who is perfectly blameless of this particular crime and of all others for all we know, keeps staring in through the window of the house at Quinton, who is, we learn later, writing a weird tale, 'The Curse of a Saint' which is about how an Indian hermit makes an English colonel kill himself by thinking about him. Presumably Quinton needs his Indian to pose as thinking about him so that he can get the right psychology. The atmosphere builds in the gathering darkness of the garden to what is presented as a menacing epiphany. Flambeau, unconsciously echoing Horatio, but behaving like Dogberry, seeks to confront the Indian and treat him like a common trespasser, even though he is no less a legitimate house guest than Flambeau himself. The big man is suddenly dwarfed by the presence of another reality:

> 'Well, we will speak to it, at any rate,' said Flambeau, who was always for action. One long stride took him to the place where the Indian stood. Bowing from his great height, which overtopped even the Oriental's, he said with placid impudence:
> 'Good evening, sir. Do you want anything?'
> Quite slowly, like a great ship turning into a harbour, the great yellow face turned, and looked at last over its white shoulder. They were startled to see that its yellow eyelids were quite sealed, as in sleep. 'Thank you,' said the face in excellent English. 'I want nothing.' Then, half opening the lids, so as to show a slit of opalescent eyeball, he repeated, 'I want nothing.' Then he opened his eyes wide with a startling stare, said, 'I want nothing', and went rustling away into the rapidly darkening garden.

This rather disturbing epiphany of the Other leads us into the distinction between two types of mystery, the miraculous and the marvellous, the simple and the complicated.

The modern mind always mixes up two different ideas: mystery in the sense of what is marvellous, and mystery in the sense of what is complicated. That is half its difficulty about miracles. A miracle is startling; but it is simple. It is simple because it *is* a miracle, it is power coming directly from God (or the devil) instead of indirectly through nature or from human wills. Now, you mean this business is marvellous, because it is witchcraft worked by a wicked Indian. Understand, I do not say it was not spiritual or diabolic. Heaven and Hell only know by what surrounding influences strange sins come into our lives [as] men. But for the present my point is: If it is pure magic, as you think, then it is marvellous; but it is not mysterious, but its manner is simple. Now, the manner of this business is the reverse of simple.

We have four basic positions in the story, which might be schematised thus:

(a) Eastern: evil doesn't exist for Hinduism, only nothingness, shapelessness. It is therefore a menacing source of magic and evil.

(b) Western atheistic positivism: real evil doesn't exist, because evil doesn't exist *per se*. Shapelessness.
(c) Aestheticism: flirts with (a) to its cost, seeking to liberate itself from form and exist only in colour. Probably the other side of (b).
(d) Western (Catholic) Christianity: recognises a distinction between the mystery of natural wickedness (complicated) and the mystery of metaphysical evil (simple), though both are 'dark'. It is itself therefore the essence of form, the right shape.

Unexpectedly, it is attitude (b) which is the cause of the murder in the story, but it tries to masquerade as (a).

But the story is not reducible to its plot. Hence the title, 'The Wrong Shape', has more than one application. Ironically, Quinton's house is built in the shape of a cross, so it is about the only thing in the story that is the right shape. The murder weapon is Eastern, so is the wrong shape, (snaky) and is good for no honest function (only torture). The suicide note has the corner snipped off by the doctor in an effort to disguise its origin in Quinton's manuscript (MS) and pretend that it is a suicide note, when it is actually part of a fictional story; this is the wrong shape in the sense of being an artificial construct of human reason. Because it is inconsistent, it gives the doctor away to Father Brown.

Finally, a word about the plot in this story. Unlike Doyle's plots in Sherlock Holmes, it is based entirely on confession. Chesterton's use of 'deduction' is not concerned with a simple and continuous parody of empiricism in favour of providence. This is perhaps because the drive for closure is not persistently maintained.

When Father Brown comes back from telling Mrs Quinton about her husband's death, which the doctor has asked him to do, the narrator presents us with a lacuna in the evidence: 'When he came out again he looked a little pale and tragic, but what passed between them at the interview was never known, even when all was known.' He then immediately asks Dr Harris for a written confession in his coolest tone of certainty and understatement.

'Will you do me a favour?' said the priest quietly. 'The truth is, I make a collection of these curious stories, which often contain, as in the case of our Hindoo friend, elements which can hardly be put into a police report. Now, I want you to write out a report of this case for my private use. Yours is a clever trade', he said, looking the doctor gravely and steadily in the face. 'I sometimes think that you know some details of this matter which you have not thought fit to mention. Mine is a confidential trade like yours, and I will treat anything you write for me in the strictest confidence. But write the whole.'

The reader is shut out completely at this point and can only make inferences, of which there are a startling number possible. This an authorial joke: the confessional is sacred and cannot be divulged, even, it seems, to the reader. The implication is, however, that Mrs Quinton has wittingly or unwittingly said enough to reveal that Dr Harris has killed her husband. And this is why he immediately accepts Father Brown's challenge, because he senses that this has happened, as the priest means him to.

The doctor, we learn, has discovered remorse immediately after the deed, much to his own surprise, as if he were a character in one of Byron's poems. He is so much the crude positivist and atheist, so pre-ethical, we infer, that he has no idea of such emotions and associates them with fiction. He seems to have no intention of confessing at that stage. Now he specifically asks Father Brown to convey the news of Quinton's death to Mrs Quinton. Why doesn't he do this himself? Perhaps the answer is that he wants to distract Father Brown whom he sees has understood his ploy of cutting the corners of a whole quire of Quinton's MS in order to disguise the fact that he has cut off one corner of a specific sheet which forms the suicide note. Ironically, he thus provides her with the opportunity to confess or make some remark or articulate some suspicion to the priest. But it may be that he thinks that Father Brown understands all along that he is having a relationship with Quinton's wife. Consider the following snippet of dialogue, which seems to be in code, at least for Father Brown. Intuitively, he guesses something about her from her manner.

They found themselves abruptly pulled up and forced to banish their bewilderment by the appearance of Mrs Quinton, with her heavy golden hair and square pale face, advancing on them out of the twilight. She looked a little stern, but was entirely courteous.

'Good evening, Dr Harris', was all she said.

'Good evening, Mrs Quinton', said the little Doctor heartily. 'I am just going to give your husband his sleeping draught.'

'Yes', she said in a clear voice. 'I think it is quite time.' And she smiled at them and went sweeping into the house.

'That woman's over-driven', said Father Brown, 'that's the kind of woman that does her duty for twenty years, and then something dreadful.'

The little doctor looked at him for the first time with an eye of interest. 'Did you ever study medicine?' he asked.

If Mrs Quinton is so transparent to him, then Father Brown has almost guessed the whole set-up at this point, and this is what Dr Harris is registering in his final comment – that the observation is purely objective, like science. Harris, however, tells us in his confession that he hadn't yet made up his mind at that point that he would kill her husband on that day. But the reader has reached his limits. We can't quite tell for sure whether the doctor has declared his plans to Mrs Quinton or not. Is she saying: 'Get it over with!' to Harris. Is this the meaning of her 'clear voice'?

The doctor's confession to Father Brown reveals that positivism rushed into the gap left by aestheticism.

> I put his own hand on the knife and drove it into his body. The knife was of so queer a shape that no one but an operator [i.e. one who performs operations] could have calculated the angle that would reach his heart. I wonder if you noticed this.

This is the knife that was the wrong shape to have an honest function. Positivism is the wrong shape, too, in finding a function for it.

Although there is a structure of witnessing and a format of detection, there is an almost complete frustration of the drive towards closure which we find in Conan Doyle. This is because Chesterton's text is an allegory about different religious and cultural values in a period of decadence, which seeks to leave them all in place and which the plot does not seek to close – 'detection' is an allegory about the difference between simple and complicated forms of evil.

———

The fragmentation of the reader's response is a powerful common factor in all of these pieces, split as they are between epiphany and explanation. The moments of darkness are moments where a boundary or a set of boundaries are invoked and the reader is left helpless for a moment, facing a cultural blank in which some encroachment has occurred, some line has been crossed, some orientation been lost. A nasty epiphany in other words, which defamiliarises the reader's experience without explanation. 'Explanation' I have been arguing comes before or after, but never quite matches this experience, and often raises problems; it may even contain, unwittingly, the conditions of another epiphany. The fiction thrives on these gaps.

In each example, this is demonstrably a question of foregrounded testimony, corroborated in some instances and withheld (from the reader) in others. My point is that this particular readerly experience plays across the obvious sub-genre markings – detective or clubhouse – that each piece displays, and that this tendency is a cultural, not a merely formal or literary, factor. We do not need to invent a genre of genres to account for this 'form' – the problems of the guarantees for knowledge which these stories allude to are not merely literary. In historical terms, by the end of the nineteenth century, the Empire is a source of excitement and an extensive vocabulary of unease which has passed into the bones – the very narrative methods – of many different kinds of popular magazine fiction. Horror stories are traditionally obsessed with superstition, and the conditions under which it does and does not operate: the Empire gives them a whole new set of conditions under which to scrutinise these boundaries.

Notes

1. I'm thinking here of the impact of Renan's *Vie de Jésus*. The uncertainties of the testimonies of the Gospels, interestingly, are referred to in the famous passage of dialogue in Beckett's *Waiting for Godot* in which Vladimir seeks to convey the twentieth-century dilemma of an absence of guarantees for knowledge to his friend, Estragon – without success. The two refer to themselves as having been young in the 1890s. For an interesting discussion of this topic and its relation to fictional narrative, see Frank Kermode, *The Genesis of Secrecy*, for discussion of the impact of Hume, see Sir Leslie Stephen, *A History of Thought in the Eighteenth Century*.
2. See, for example, the series of retrospective anthologies published by Hutchinson; *A Century of Creepy Stories*, ed., Dennis Wheatley; *A Century of Horror*, ed., Dennis Wheatley; *A Century of Detective Stories*, ed., G.K. Chesterton; and *A Century of Spy Stories*, ed., Dennis Wheatley (all of these undated).
3. This story first appeared in *The Strand* (1892).
4. All quotations from *Sherlock Holmes: the Complete Short Stories*, London (1929, repr. 1977), pp. 173–201.
5. 'The Mark of the Beast' first appeared in various magazines in July 1890 (e.g. *Pioneer; Pioneer Mail; Weeks News;* and *New York Journal*) and was collected in *Life's Handicap*, July 1891. All quotations from *Life's Handicap* (1891) ed., and with an introduction by A.O.J. Cockshuft (Oxford: 1989).
6. The story was first published in *The Storyteller* (1911).

2 *The House on the Borderland*: the Sexual Politics of Fear

Amanda Boulter

> It is turning, slowly, in my direction. ... It sees me. Two huge, inhumanly human, eyes are looking through the dimness at me. ... A fresh horror has come to me. I am rising from my chair, without the least intention ... something is impelling me towards the door that leads out into the gardens.[1]

The motifs of fear that Hope Hodgson exploits in this passage are instantly recognisable to the modern reader. As the writer of this journal is forced toward letting the alien creature into the private spaces of the house, we experience the fear of invasion and loss of control that comes from such a forced collusion with the enemy. The possibility of coming face to face with the creature of our nightmares, of being objectified by the alien's gaze is one that structures a politics of terror. These images have become common currency in the modern horror genre, particularly in films such as *Nightmare on Elm Street* and *Friday the 13th*.

In Hope Hodgson's text these themes permeate the narrative, as the central character, known only as the Recluse, struggles desperately both psychologically and physically to secure his house against the hordes of creatures from the pit. These creatures are represented in his writing as chimera; hybrids existing on the borderlands of life and death, humanity and bestiality, fantasy and reality. They betray a 'human intelligence', but it is an intelligence made 'horrible' by its co-existence with intense desire. This hybrid identity is represented by the creatures' appearance which combines human and animal features. The Recluse represents them as 'swine-things' – their perceived humanity only making them more abhorrent.

This hybridity, and ultimately doubt even as to the creatures' existence, marks from the outset the importance of the image of the borderland in this text. The alien-ness of the creatures is that they are neither human nor non-human: they exist on the borderlands of the definitions, and their existence is terrifying.

24

In her book *The Powers of Horror*, Julia Kristeva outlines the place of abjection, 'We may call it a border. ... On the edge of non-existence and hallucination, of a reality that, if [we] acknowledge it, annihilates [us].'[2] Hope Hodgson constructs the border as the key image in his text: both thematically within the narrative and structurally in the organisation of the text as a whole. This essay will explore the pervasiveness of this metaphor and exploit it to produce a psychoanalytical reading of the sexual politics of fear.

A manuscript, written by the Recluse, forms the core of the text which the reader comes to via a series of ostensibly self-contained discourses that are placed around it. First we read a dedication, 'To my Father'. We are then introduced to the figure of the editor, Hope Hodgson, who possesses the ancient MS we are about to read. After the introduction the text is prefixed by a poem entitled 'Grief', reportedly found gummed to the inside of the MS. There then follows the seemingly incongruous first-person narrative by a young English man telling how he and his friend found the MS on a fishing trip. This story actually frames the MS both physically and by interpretation as it is introduced by the young men's anticipation and epilogued by their reactions.

This framing of the primary text does initially seem both confusing and irrelevant: a heavy-handed attempt to distance the author from the text and therefore heighten the authenticity of the MS. But this textual framing is in fact integral to the story. These tales exist *within* and *as* the borderlands of the manuscript text. In this way the images of the borderland within the narrative are realised in the structure of the text. This process of assimilation means that for any reading of the politics of fear, our gaze must be diverted to the edges of the text.

The final confrontation between the creature and the man is a confrontation in which, we already fear and suspect, the Recluse will die. The inevitability of this defeat has already been determined by the events of the previous night, when the Recluse's dog was attacked by the luminous green creature from the 'Arena'. In tending the dog the next day the Recluse allowed him to lick his hand. Now he has 'a slight greenish discoloration' around a scratch on his hand. His body has been penetrated, infected by the creature. Soon the 'dread growth' that it has become will consume him utterly.

I am swathed in terror. I feel ever the burning of this dread growth. It has covered all my right arm and side, and is beginning to creep up my neck. Tomorrow, it will eat into my face. I shall become a terrible mass of living corruption. There is no escape.

After an arduous struggle to prevent the invasion of his house, it is, ironically, the more personal spaces of the Recluse's body that are first invaded. The man has been infected by his dog, his trusted companion, and now the house may be entered freely by the creature: 'Hush! I hear something, down – down in the cellars. It is a creaking sound. My God, it is the opening of the great, oak trap.'

Ultimately it is the transgression of boundaries, particularly the boundaries of the body, that comprises the ultimate fear and the ultimate loss. And yet throughout the MS the anxieties and fears evolved in the Recluse's account in fact disguise a stream of desire that flows submerged throughout the text, but can find neither satisfaction nor expression within the terms of the narrative. Like the stream that disappears beneath the house, reappearing around the edges of the garden, it is to the edges, the borders of the text, that we must look for the reappearance of desire. The stream, which eventually consumes the ruins of the ancient house, runs through a ravine in the garden, which, described as 'the pit', is the place from which the creatures are supposed to appear.

The MS tells the bizarre and often chilling story of the events in the house that precede its collapse into the gulf and stream below. Found on an outcrop of rock jutting across the cavernous mouth, the MS is the only object salvaged from the house: a solitary status that reinforces the instability and insubstantiality of the fantasy. In this journal the Recluse tells how he began writing to record a vision he experienced, in which he travelled through space to a barren and hellish planet where he saw a huge replica of his house. The structure stood within an arena of mountains which themselves housed figures of the immortal gods of death. Here, for the first time, the Recluse saw a creature desperately trying to break into the house, a creature that both, 'attracted him and frightened him'. The man is 'compelled forward' towards the monster who sees him and begins to run at him with, 'an expression of desire upon his face such as [he had] never seen in this world'. The Recluse's initial 'thrill of apprehension' becomes, 'a feeling of unmitigated horror' as the brute nears him. But it is only 'in the very moment of [his] extremity and despair' that he is suddenly borne aloft, 'I was rising, rising'. This imagery of escape through an ecstatic rising, suggestive of erection and orgasm, introduces for the first time the sexualisation of the narrative expression of fear. The reaction of the Recluse to the creature is one of fascination as well as fear, desire as well as abhorrence. The monster, excluded and distinguished from him *because* of his desire, also represents this desiring man. Julia Kristeva describes this complex relationship thus,

There looms, within abjection one of those violent, dark revolts of being, directed against a threat that seems to emanate from an exorbitant outside or inside, ejected beyond the scope of the possible, the tolerable, the thinkable. It lies there, quite close, but it cannot be assimilated. It beseeches worries, and fascinates desire, which, nevertheless, does not let itself be seduced.[3]

The Recluse will not let himself be seduced by this creature – he will fight against it with words and weapons. He will valorise his fear and reject his desire, projecting what is repressed on to that which is outside: the monsters from the 'pit'. These creatures, smaller than the one in the Arena and deathly white, stalk and attack the house at night. He must protect the house, his sister and himself from their advances.

The narrative action then alternates between the earth battles and hallucinogenic adventures in space. This conflagration of horror and science fiction motifs enables a cosmic, pseudo-scientific journey to Heaven and Hell. In Heaven the Recluse rediscovers his long lost love, claiming that it is her presence that binds him to the house: 'Strangely, she warned me; warned me passionately against this house; begged me to leave it. ... I just asked her, again, whether she would come to me elsewhere, and she could only stand, silent.'

Within the terms of the narrative she is the stated object of his desire, and we are to assume, the subject of the poem 'Grief', found pasted into the MS:

An hungered to the shore I creep,
Perchance some comfort waits on me
From the old Sea's eternal heart;
But lo! from all the solemn deep,
Far voices out of mystery
Seem questioning why we are apart!

But upon the Sea of Sleep the Recluse finds no respite from his 'hunger'. When he reaches out to her he is rejected, his lover pushes him away with 'tenderly stern hands'. It is precisely at this point in the narrative that the MS is damaged and illegible: 'NOTE – Here the writing becomes undecipherable, owing to the damaged condition of this part of the MS.' The editor thus presents to us, 'the legible portions of the mutilated leaves. ... through tears ... noise of eternity in my ears, we parted. ... She whom I love. O, my God!'

The 'mutilation' of the MS at this point in the narrative suggests the way in which a negotiation between desire and fear is always on the edge of a socialised and structured language. The sexual anxiety engendered by the Recluse and his lover's relationship is displaced so that the woman's anticipated sexual violence is transferred from the body to the text. Although it is the creatures that are represented as being ultimately threatening, it is the woman who slips away from the narrative, obscured in the fragments of this representation. The desire focused on the woman can never be freed from abjection, freed from the fear of self-defilement. Although she is in Heaven, bodiless and purified by death, her corporeal unreality does not alleviate the fear of her sexuality. The presence of such anxiety is reinforced much later in the text when for the first time we hear of a 'formless thing' that 'haunts' the shores of the Sea of Sleep, its presence implying the danger of the Recluse's meeting with his lover. Is this thing, externalised and formless, a representation of the narrator's hungered self, or is it more sinisterly a physical enactment of the anxiety inherent in his sexual encounter with his lover?

'A troubled memory came to me – of the Formless Thing that had haunted the shores of the Sea of Sleep. The guardian of that silent, echoless place.'

This inconsistency in the text, this reference to an unrelated experience, whether it be the Recluse's or Hodgson's oversight, implies that the encounter evokes a fear that remains subconscious and unresolved. The security of Heaven is as ambivalent as the repulsiveness of Hell. The representation cannot be sustained as an opposition because both places are inhabited by creatures that exist on the borderlands of *man*kind: the male alien and the female human.

The editor's interruption into this scene both mediates and obscures the desiring voice, and demonstrates the way in which the Recluse's projection of desire on to the alien creatures is echoed in the textual strategies which project desire away from the central narrative and on to the texts and characters that surround it.

Moreover, it is not only for psychological and sexual desire that we must turn to the framing discourses of the text. We must also look towards these edges to understand the social and political implications of the narrative. These texts, by placing the MS within their own fictional contexts, also (re)place it, changing the terms in which it must be read, making perhaps even more ironic the editor's invitation to 'each reader' to 'uncover the inner story according to ability and desire'.

Taken by itself the MS is unplaceable: there are no temporal or geographical references to establish its historical context. It must be read as archetypal, the tale of one man's struggle against the alien forces of an unknown evil; a struggle for the conquest of rationality over savagery, humanity over bestiality. The story of the MS's recovery from the ruins of the ancient house however places these horrors within a remote part of Ireland, around the middle of the nineteenth century. Located in this way the text becomes shadowed with the images of Irish colonialism. Is it possible that these swine creatures that attack the house are in fact representations of Irish peasants, living and starving around the house of the English landlord? Placed in the context of the bestialised, racist depictions of the Irish in the late nineteenth century the image of the swine things, and the Recluse's desperate attempt to kill them becomes more sinister. An article from *Punch* magazine (1862) makes this relation explicit,

> The Irish Yahoo generally confines itself within the limits of its own colony, except when it goes out of them to get its living. Sometimes, however, it sallies forth in states of excitement, and attacks civilised human beings that have provoked its fury.[4]

Is one of the stories we are meant to 'uncover' the story of an insane and deranged man murdering in his attempt to defend his property against the rights and needs of the native people?

This reading is reinforced by the reaction of the Recluse's sister, Mary, the only other person living in the house. From the outset it is clear that she doesn't 'see' the terrible creatures in the eyes of her brother. She runs from them because he runs from them, and the fear in her eyes is a fear of him: 'I think it must have been the terror in my voice that spurred Mary to run so; for I feel convinced that she had not, as yet, seen those hell-creatures that pursued.' But Mary never does 'see' the creatures.

> Noticing that she seemed giddy, I put my hand out to steady her. At that she gave a loud scream, and, scrambling to her feet, ran from the room. ... Could she be afraid of me? But no! Why should she? I could only conclude that ... she was temporarily unhinged.

Mary's reaction inevitably colours our reactions as readers to the text. Within the text she is silenced, marginalised and literally locked up on the borders of the battle as a 'mad woman'. But it is this silence that shouts so insistently to the reader that there is another horror story to be told: the story of a woman locked away by a frenzied and violent brother, frightened for her life using silence to survive. Her imprisonment follows her attempt to escape from the house, an attempt the Recluse sees only in terms of letting in the outside evil and not as letting herself out. But this imprisonment doesn't remove her from the text, instead she becomes a shadowy reminder of an alternative discourse. The character of the sister becomes increasingly important because, as the only other voice we can trust, however disguised and mediated, it is her reaction that questions the Recluse's sanity. This woman's silence ultimately subverts her brother's discourse.

However, the sister's shadowy presence is extraordinarily centred when the Recluse describes his sister's violent reaction to his efforts to restrain her: 'She trembled, violently, gasping and sobbing, as though in the last extremity of fear.'

This animation of the woman through her fear is quite shocking. It is a vivid expression of her terror, or her madness, as seen through her brother's eyes and represented and mediated by his pen. This moment of fear is thus caught between the brother and sister as both a reality and a fantasy, a representation and a displacement of his fear on to her.

The way in which the horror is focused in this text makes this relation clearer. The house has always at some level been a symbol of the body. The threat of invasion by alien creatures corresponds to the threat of bodily infection: infection with the unholy desire that motivates the creatures in the first place. Consequently, the study is initially the room most vulnerable to attack, and thus has to be protected most vigorously. The study represents, in this schema, the Recluse's conscious mind, his rational intellectual self that must be protected from the ever increasing danger of irrational desire – his own irrational desire. In terms of this structural logic then the cellars are the most foreboding place, for it is they that represent the dark sub-regions of the Recluse's unconscious: 'Of all the great awe-inspiring rooms in this house, the cellars are the hugest and weirdest. Great, gloomy caverns of places, unlit by any ray of daylight.'

Although the Recluse keeps the key on his person, and therefore is the only one who can enter, he is terrified of what he might find in these dark under regions. However, the image of the unconscious, already theorised by Freud as harbouring secret and inexpressible desires, is shadowed by an alternative reading. When entering the cellar the Recluse throws, 'the barrel of [his] weapon forward', and descends, 'into the darkness of the underground regions'. The phallic connotations of this description of his weapon, and his entry into the dripping, dark cellars are clear as the imagery becomes increasingly sexualised. When crossing the cellar the Recluse falls upon a trap door. When he opens it, as of course he must, he hears the noise of the stream in the pit below. But he does not recognise the sound – instead he mistakes it for laughter.

> I seemed to hear, far down, as though from untold depths, a faint whisper of sound ... I could have sworn to hearing a soft titter, that grew into a hideous chuckling, faint and distant. ... Even then [after the trapdoor is shut] I seemed to hear that mocking, suggestive laughter; but this I knew must be my imagination.

This imagined laughter is suggestive of a paranoid self-humiliation; a humiliation that is perhaps rooted in sexual failure and fear. The borders between anxiety and appetite however are never stable and fear gives way to fascination in a continuum of displaced desire.

> Sometimes I have an inexplicable desire to go down to the great cellar, open the trap, and gaze into the impenetrable, spray-damp darkness.

At times this desire becomes almost overpowering in its intensity. It is not mere curiosity that prompts me; but more as though some unexplained influence were at work. Still, I never go, and intend to fight down the strange longing, and crush it; even as I would the unholy thought of self-destruction.

The sexualisation of his investigation into the cellars prefixes his later desire to look into those 'impenetrable' underground regions. Throwing his weapon forward, he penetrates the darkness, responding to an 'overpowering' desire to return to the 'hellpit'. The journey is allegorised as a journey of sexual discovery and obsession; and yet he will resist this temptation, 'not let [him]self be seduced' by its intensity. The analogy to thoughts of self-destruction contains traces of a Victorian moralism that deemed masturbation self-abuse. The power of the horror is rooted equally in the repressiveness of the culture as it is in the psychology of repression.

This divulgent denial of desire is characteristic of the MS as a whole. (Sexual) desire finds neither expression nor satisfaction in the MS but is instead eased out of the text and into the surrounding discourses. The only explicit moment of arousal, when the Recluse meets his lover, has been mutilated by time and can only be mediated to the reader by the intervention of the editor, interrupting the text, reminding us of his presence before allowing the tale to continue.

This intervention by the editor, which draws our attention to the introduction, is completely consistent with the strategies of the text. As readers we can engage with the writer's fears but our access to the underlying desire is blocked. Desire is pushed away from the centre and into the borderlands. In other words, away from the writer and into the arena of the reader both fictional and actual: first the two Englishmen; then Hope Hodgson as the editor and finally us, the contemporary reader of the texts.

In his introduction Hope Hodgson insists upon being recognised as a reader and not as a writer. This retreat from authority, while implicitly claiming greater authenticity for the MS, also forces Hope Hodgson into the edges of his own text. He is placed in a position where, like the swine-creatures, he must invade the MS to find a way into the text. The notes he continually fixes on to the narrative often jar, coming from an entirely contrary position from that of the Recluse, insisting on scientific accuracy; interrupting the text with details that have no place in the hallucinogenic fantasy of horror and fascination.

Hope Hodgson's insistence on being seen as reader demands that the reader must literally visualise him in this role.

You must picture me when first it [the MS] was given into my care, turning it over curiously, and making a swift, jerky examination [and again] conceive of me comfortably a-seat for the evening, and the little, squat book and I, companions for some close, solitary hours ... I read. ... Amid stiff sentences I wandered [in] the mutilated story.

As a reader he is not our equal, he is first in a hierarchy of power and interpretation. He is able to change the text, invade the text, write upon the text. Hodgson as editor does not just possess the narrative, he possesses the MS as an object and it is this possession that comes to be so blatantly sexualised. He goes on to describe the 'queer, faint pit-water smell of it' and has 'subconscious memories of the soft "cloggy" feel of the long damp pages'. No mention is made of fear or terror, the impression is one of a sexualised pleasure, a pleasure experienced by the reader through the act of reading. This act, and this pleasure, was one that was becoming increasingly available to a mass audience when Hope Hodgson was writing. This text, and the eight or so others that he produced, were part of the expanding market of pulp fiction that both popularised reading and responded to the changing nature of the reading public. Hope Hodgson caters for all, promising his readers 'certain thrills just taking the story as a story'. As readers we can experience the full pleasure of the text without the need to engage in the interpretive scope allowed for by his contextualising of the horror.

Hope Hodgson's pleasure as editor and as reader is rooted in the physicality of the reading experience. The smell of the pit, the fear of which dominates the MS, is here described nostalgically as increasing that sensory pleasure. The desire for the pit, unspeakable in the MS, slips away from the centre of the texts and is expressed at the margin. The last words of the entire text are those from the young Englishman who originally discovered the MS beside the gaping pit.

Sometimes, in my dreams, I see that enormous pit, surrounded, as it is, on all sides by wild trees and bushes. And the noise of the water rises upwards, and blends – in my sleep – with other lower noises; while, over all, hangs the eternal shroud of spray.

The emotions related to this image are ambivalent – the metaphorical associations are not. Published the year after Freud's *Interpretation of Dreams* this final image seems clearly related to fantasies of female sexuality and women's sexual power. Through a psychoanalytical reading of this text we can see how the fear in this novel is co-existent with, and indeed motivated by, a desire that is repressed and dispersed to the edges of the narrative. However, the textual strategies that facilitate such an artificial splitting also betray the way in which that separation is motivated by a sexual denial.

The borderland narratives (re)place the archetypal impetus of the text by framing it within a specific historical and political moment. Hope

Hodgson's thematic insistence on the image of the borderland cannot be isolated from the cultural context in which he was writing. Late nineteenth-century psychiatric texts, such as Andrew Wynter's *The Borderlands of Insanity* (1875), had already marked the image as one implying madness. Elaine Showalter however, demonstrates the way in which 'the borderland', as a metaphor of madness in these medico-legal discourses, implied more about the outside than the inside of asylums.

> The imagery of the borderland reflected the anxieties of late Victorian psychiatrists, who felt that they were in a temporal and sexual limbo where the traditional boundaries of gender, labour and behaviour were being challenged by New Women and decadent men.[5]

Hope Hodgson was writing in an atmosphere of terrific social upheaval. By 1908, when *The House on the Borderland* was published, many of the technologies we think of as characterising the modern age were known (cars, telephones, radio, planes, cinema) and the modern era promised immense change both culturally and scientifically. H.G. Wells captured the optimism in the mood of this turn-of-the-century modernity when he wrote of Queen Victoria's death, 'Queen Victoria was like a great paper-weight that for half a century sat on men's minds, and when she was removed their ideas began to blow about all over the place haphazardly.[6]

However, this releasing of the imagination threatened confusion as well as promising liberation. Modernity threatened to 'destroy everything we have, everything we know, everything we are.'[7] The image of the borderland reflects an experience of modernity that suggests instability; progress as well as degeneration. It also locates a fantastical story within the political and social debates of its time.

It is both impossible and unnecessary for us to 'decide' upon the Recluse's insanity. Although his sister's actions imply his madness, many of the bizarre things he claims to have seen are reinforced by textual evidence. Within the narrative there is no way to reconcile such contradictory elements of the text, as fantasy and reality are inextricably blurred in his self-representation. His borderland abjection is both personal and social; both a psychological enactment of sexual anxiety and a fantastic, fatalistic response to the massive changes harboured by the twentieth century.

Notes

1. William Hope Hodgson, *The House on the Borderland*. (London: (1908) 1990) p. 166.
2. Julia Kristeva, *Powers of Horror*, trans., Leon S. Roudiez (New York: 1982) pp. 2 and 9.

3. Kristeva, p. 1.
4. Quoted from Lewis P. Curtis Jr, *Apes and Angels: The Irishman in Victorian Caricature* (Newton Abbot: 1971) p. 100.
5. Elaine Showalter, *The Female Malady* (London: 1987) pp. 105–6.
6. Quoted from Frank McConnell, *The Science Fiction of H.G. Wells* (New York: 1981) p. 34.
7. Marshall Berman, *All That Is Solid Melts Into Air* (London: 1983) p. 15.

3 Horror in the 1890s: the Case of Arthur Machen

John Simons

Occasionally, however, a 'real' writer emerges from the fog to write pornography for bread and butter, and one of these was Arthur Machen, who enjoyed a reputation in the nineties and Edwardian era as a writer of horror stories by using the simple device of piling up adjectives like 'unnameable' and 'unutterable' and then not qualifying them.[1]

Ronald Pearsall's concise debunking of the styles of Arthur Machen's fiction is, like many attempts to write aphoristic criticism, more telling in its potential to amuse than in its power to enlighten. Machen was, it is true, a writer for whom the drive towards clarity was frequently blocked or diverted by the desire to decorate but his fiction deserves more than cursory dismissal. The type of horror which Machen develops in his short stories and novellas is, as Pearsall suggests very often couched in the vaguest terms and his style sometimes borders on the incoherent; but this quality is not the result of technical ineptitude or imaginative failure. Rather the difficulties of Machen's horror fictions derive from the two very different and, arguably, contradictory streams of influence that are their source.

It is very easy to dismiss Machen as just another of the throng of literati of the 1890s who have narrowly failed to achieve canonical status. Even worse it is easy to see him as someone who hung on to the style of the 1890s and did not have the decency to die young of TB, syphilis or suicide or to fade away covered by a tartan blanket in a genteelly shabby Eastbourne hotel. Certainly, we find throughout Machen's work all of those things which became the clichés of the 1890s. His work is lushly embroidered with the aureate diction of *The Yellow Book*, it breathes the heavy atmosphere of the study in which a collection of rare erotica is displayed to only the closest friends, it is bathed in the pallid gleam of the Celtic Twilight. There is an almost ecstatic relish in the discovery of the horror which lurks beneath the surface, the unimaginable frenzies of the sublimated abyss. Yet even where we find all these voguish decorations we also find a novelist who is no mere follower of trends. All the while Machen is developing the form of his narratives. He refuses the conventional strategies of structural irony and teases his readers with the tales of multiple or unreliable narrators.[2]

If Machen appears to be rooted in the aesthetic of *The Yellow Book* as far as some aspects of his style go, the deeper levels of his narrative, the sublimated sex and violence which are manifested in the vision of horror and the authentic *frisson* of terror, derive from other sources, Stephen Prickett has provided some clues as to the nature of those sources:

> Arthur Machen, himself a confessed Coleridgean, tried to create a fiction that would adequately convey his own 'over-powering impression of "strangeness", or remoteness, of withdrawal from the common ways of life' that accompanied the most ordinary events of lower middle-class London.[3]

But Machen's vision encompassed not only the lower middle class. It concerned a London which, since the middle of the nineteenth century, had been a source of fascination to the comfortably off whether they were Pooters or Palmerstones. This was the London of Doré and Mayhew, the London of Jacks of both the Ripping and the Spring-heeled varieties, the London which the middle class saw from cabs, in their newspapers and in the writings of journalistic reformers. It is this combination of the decadent and the socially aware which gives Machen's horror writing its distinctive flavour and which roots it firmly not only into the specific world of the 1890s but also into a far deeper tradition of Victorian writing.

Machen's earliest published writing shows how at the age of 17 his obsessions were beginning to centre on the hidden potentials of the ordinary and the close relationship between landscape and time. The most innocent of country walks could culminate in a confrontation with the forces of a primeval nature which is always horrific and malevolent even in its most refined anthropomorphic guises:

> Hark the trumpet sounds!
> Upon the steps the holy herald stands
> And bids the worshippers prepare to see
> The glory of the goddess.
> How awful darkness broods, and one by one,
> They pass within; but what is seen by them
> Within the temple; who of men shall tell.
> Only dim legends handed down and told
> From age to age; but no man knows the truth,
> Only they tell that sudden light was seen,
> And then the darkness covered all again.[4]

This passage conveys Machen's characteristic sense of the hidden but also his preparedness to concentrate not on the revelation itself but on the contexts and processes of the revelation. Thus, the horror is rarely explicit; rather the reader is led to a climax which is never fully manifested. Fifty years on Machen commented on his juvenilia and on the incidents which led up to the creation of his poem.

> I believe it was in Autumn of 1880 that I set out one morning to walk to Newport; for no particular reason that I can remember. ... I had climbed up the long hill from Llantarnam, and was on my way towards Malpas when I saw the mountain, from Twyn Barlwm to the heights above Pontypool, all a pure, radiant blue under a paler blue sky. ... I experienced an indescribable emotion; and I always attribute to that moment and to that emotion my impulse towards literature. For literature, as I see it, is the art of describing the indescribable; the art of exhibiting symbols which may hint at the ineffable mysteries behind them; the art of the veil, which reveals what it conceals. ... I chose the mysteries first and I chose them last: seeking always that secret which is hidden beneath the barley ... the one secret which is concealed beneath the various assemblage of sensible appearances.[5]

It is notable how consistently Machen carried out the mission of displaying the horror which is to be found in the relationships of the natural and the supernatural, the mundane and the marvellous. In *Eleusinia*, Machen began the programme which would subsequently occupy him for almost all of his writing life.

Machen learned at least some of his techniques, perhaps especially that of multiple narration from one of his earliest professional commissions as the translator of Marguerite of Navarre's *Heptameron*. Pearsall reminds us that in spite of the erotic content of some tales 'no writer who has been dead for four hundred years could be less than respectable'.[6] But Michael timidly admits that 'the tales ... are often improper'.[7] What is important is that in his work on *Heptameron* and on Casanova's *Memoirs* to which he subsequently turned, he found the diction which would mark his style as consciously archaic for the rest of his life and also the gorgeous decadence which had already been explored by Wilde and Beardsley and which gave him his entry to the world of the 1890s. Indeed, his novel, *The Hill of Dreams*, is best read in the context of *The Yellow Book* and is strongly redolent of Beardsley's fictional fragment *Under the Hill* which appeared in *The Savoy* at much the same time that Machen was working on his own text.[8]

In *The Hill of Dreams*, Machen is working a strongly autobiographical vein and charts the life of Lucian Taylor, the odd and intellectual son of an impoverished Welsh clergyman. Lucian goes to London to become a writer but dies, drug-crazed, in a boarding house. If the fabulous Abbé Fanfreluche in *Under the Hill* is a mannered self-portrait by Beardsley (Abbé = A.B.) then Lucian Taylor is surely the bearer of many of the young Machen's experiences. However, the baroque and decadent landscapes of Beardsley's work are not to be found in Machen whose vision remains obstinately fixed on the glowering hills of Wales and the smoggy alleys of the East End. If anything, Taylor is a poor version of Joris-Karl Huysmans's aristocratic hero Des Esseintes. Certainly Des Esseintes and Taylor share the same transgressive taste in literature. Here is Huysmans:

> One section of the bookshelves lining the walls of Des Esseintes' blue and orange study was filled with nothing but Latin works – works which minds drilled into conformity by repetitious university lectures lump together under the generic name of 'the Decadence'.[9]

Here is Machen:

> Lucian went slowly, but not discreditably, up the school, gaining prizes now and again, and falling in love more and more with useless reading and unlikely knowledge. He did his elegiacs and iambics well enough, but he preferred exercising himself in the rhymed Latin of the middle ages.[10]

This preference for the non-canonical, for the barbarian horde over the civilising legion, leads easily into the development of Lucian as an outsider to whom the hidden powers will become all too fleetingly visible.

Before he leaves Wales Lucian wanders in the landscape to which Machen will return time and again. It is the landscape of a vanished kingdom but one in which the previous histories have not been completely erased but can be read dimly as if written on a palimpsest. The innocent surface bears the traces, for those who can read, of a race driven underground to the elemental forces pulsing beneath the fields. Lucian has a disastrous encounter with such forces in a Roman fort.

> Green mosses were hair, and tresses were stark in grey lichen; a twisted root swelled into a limb; in the hollows of the rotted bark he saw the masks of men. His eyes were fixed and fascinated by the simulacra of the wood, and could not see his hands, and so at last, and suddenly, it seemed, he lay in the sunlight, beautiful with his olive skin, dark haired, dark eyed, the gleaming bodily vision of a strayed faun. ... He fell asleep, and lay still on the grass, in the midst of the thicket. ... As he awoke, a brief and slight breeze had stirred in a nook of the matted boughs, and there was a glinting that might have been

the flash of sudden sunlight across shadow, and the branches rustled and murmured for a moment, perhaps at the wind's passage. He stretched out his hands, and cried to his visitant to return; he entreated the dark eyes that had shone over him, and the scarlet lips that had kissed him. And then panic fear rushed into his heart, and he ran blindly, dashing through the wood.[11]

This encounter leaves him forever marked. The use of the adjective 'panic' is not accidental and is demonstrative of Machen's close attention to the detail of his disclosures. The horror is glimpsed from the corner of the eye and the landscape remains ultimately inscrutable to the uninitiated.

If the countryside offers an enlightenment which takes both sanity and health, the town is more obviously cruel. Lucian's progressive disgust with the provincial society which denies him his education and torments him with its propriety is manifested in a linked series of descriptions of cruelty to animals. Lucian comes upon a 'healthy boy' kicking a sick cat and then hanging a puppy and these incidents are contrasted with the 'harmless amusement' of children who 'gradually deprive a fly of its wings and legs' with 'mamma's nail scissors'. The move to London is thus a move to a cruelty more explicit than that of the country but less dangerous except that the symbols and hiero-glyphics of the horror which Lucian has glimpsed have somehow become inscribed on his body. He has taken with him the contami-nation and elemental sickness of the old fort and, in homage to de Quincey, wanders the London streets in what we learn to be drug-induced trances. A woman runs from him in the road but a prostitute offers to go with him after refusing other clients.

He muttered something about being very sorry, and fled down the hill out of the orgy, from the noise of the roaring voices and the glitter of the great lamps very slowly swinging in the blast of wind. He knew that he had touched the brink of utter destruction; there was death in the woman's face, and she had indeed summoned him to the Sabbath.

This reminds us of 'the horrible Sabbath he had imagined as he lay sleeping on the hot soft turf' and of the strange encounter which has destroyed Lucian's humanity. All along the nature of Lucian's vision is never made explicit and we will see how important this technique is for Machen's claims for the horror of the every day. *The Hill of Dreams* illustrates many of Machen's characteristic themes. Most importantly it illustrates how his obsession with the world of the Romano-Celts and the sinister world of fairy dovetails neatly with his sense of the strangeness of London.

In one of his best-known stories, 'Green Tea', an important fore-runner of Machen, Sheridan Le Fanu, demonstrated that it was possible to derive the vision of horror entirely from the internalised obsessions of a deranged personality. He also showed how the fiction of improbability could be validated by the accumulation of documents from 'reliable' medical narrators. These lessons were learned by Machen. By the 1920s, when he came to write *The Shining Pyramid*, the techniques of *The Hill of Dreams* had come to full maturity. The hieroglyphs which Lucian Taylor had merely *read* are now *interpreted* by the expert Dyson who balances scientific reason with a healthy respect for the powers of the occult. Dyson goes into the countryside to clear up an occult mystery but he leaves behind him a London described somewhat mechanistically, in the terms of the 1890s.

> London in September is hard to leave. Doré could not have designed anything more wonderful and mystic than Oxford Street as I saw it the other evening; the sunset flaming, the blue haze transmuting the plain street into a road 'far into the spiritual city'.

The story concerns the abduction, abuse (sexual it is implied) and sacrifice of a young woman by a band of supernatural beings. Dyson is able to track the band down by his interpretation of the strange signs which begin to appear around his friend Vaughan's house. But Dyson is no Holmes: his semiotic expertise cannot prevent horror. He can show his friend the truth about a fairy world far removed from the *politesse* of Perrault but he can do nothing to intervene.

> He looked aghast, choking back sobs of horror, and at length the loathsome forms gathered thickest about some vague object in the middle of the hollow, and the hissing of their speech grew more venomous, and he saw in the uncertain light the abominable limbs, vague and yet too plainly seen, writhe and intertwine, and he thought he heard, very faint, a low human moan striking through the noise of speech that was not of man.

Again we see a horror which is only indistinctly visual. It is the signs of the occult on the landscape which take up the narrative, not the occult itself. Again, the old spirits are seen as implacably malevolent and dangerous and their existence is made all the more credible by Dyson's rational approach.

If Machen learned his narrative art and his style from the 1890s and found strangeness there at the limits of sensation, he learned from the reforming journalists the trick of seeing the unknown in the metropolis. In the second half of the nineteenth century and up to the Great War writers had plunged into the East End in search of the materials which would fuel their political indignation at the gross effects of the material inequalities which characterised British society. This reformist zeal and social indignation seems sometimes modified by an almost anthropological fascination with the condition of the working class. Writers, scholars, philanthropists all donned boots and cloth cap and disappeared into the slums of London just as explorers like Sir Richard Burton had donned burnous and sandals and vanished into the souks of Cairo. Each returned with traveller's tales of the most fantastic wildness and the most distressing nature. The social explorers did not find in the urban working class the refreshing innocence which, a century earlier, Wordsworth claimed to have found among the rural poor. Instead, they found a culture which had been hopelessly corrupted and degraded, both physically and morally, by an extreme and unrelenting deprivation.

If you were not able to enter the slums yourself or serious minded enough to read the works of the social reformers you could nevertheless learn of this terrible situation through the frequent and detailed newspaper reports of the more titillating sex and violence cases which came before the courts. Indeed, one Victorian gentleman, William Bell MacDonald, Laird of Rammerscales, spent the years between 1832 and 1869 happily in his study (where his family apparently thought he was translating classical Greek literature) compiling a massive and carefully organised archive of just such reports.[12] In these cases the world of the social reformers and the Penny Dreadfuls collided head on and it is out of this strange blend that Machen derived some of his vision of the city.

When *The Great God Pan* was published in 1894, Oscar Wilde exclaimed that it was 'Un succès fou! Un succès fou!'[13] However, the novel is more than a sustained exercise in delicate grotesquerie. It is a text in which the full range of Machen's imagination is brought into play, one which orders his themes into a clear hierarchy and distributes the elements of his vision neatly into an almost formulaic plan. The plot moves from the laboratory (site of reason), to the countryside (site of mystery) to the city (site of horror) and its multiple narrative enables these basic blocks to be easily manipulated. If, in 1913, Holbrook Jackson was able to say that 'Arthur Machen, in *The Great God Pan* (1894), took romance once more into the abode of terror in a manner as startling as it was elementally true', by 1989 John Stokes could identify the prison and the mortuary as locations which are just as important for our understanding of 1890's culture as the music hall or the *salon*. The truth of this insight is surely demonstrated by Machen's fiction.[14]

At the beginning of the novel Clarke witnesses an experimental operation at the laboratory of his friend Dr Raymond. The procedure is carried out on the brain of his ward Mary and is designed to enable her to enter the spirit world and to see the great god Pan. There is the usual suppressed hint of eroticism in the air:

> 'But you remember what you wrote to me? I thought it would be requisite that she – '
> He whispered the rest into the doctor's ear.
> 'Not at all, not at all. That is nonsense, I assure you. Indeed, it is better as it is; I am quite certain of that.'[15]

As Clarke waits to witness the operation he experiences the disorientation which is usual in Machen's fiction. The English landscape drops away and through it he glimpses the Mediterraneanised Romano-Celtic landscape it has replaced. In a half-dream half-hallucination he dimly encounters the pagan god:

> the beech alley was transformed to a path beneath ilex trees, and here and there a vine climbed from bough to bough, and sent up waving tendrils and drooped with purple grapes, and the sparse grey-green leaves of a wild olive tree stood out against the dark shadows of the ilex ... he was wondering at the strangeness of it all, when suddenly, in place of the hum and murmur of the summer, an infinite silence seemed to fall on all things, and the wood was hushed, and for a moment of time he stood face to face there with a presence that was neither man nor beast, neither the living nor the dead, but all things mingled, the form of all things but devoid of all form.

Mary sees the god but is transformed into 'a hopeless idiot' unable to communicate her vision.

The scene shifts and we learn of more mysterious encounters between two children, one of whom is called Helen V., and a satyr. The incidents are never described, only hinted at in fragmentary narrative and unreported conversation:

> Rachel told her wild story. She said –
> Clarke closed the book with a snap, and turned his chair towards the fire. When his friend sat one evening in that very chair, and told his story, Clarke had interrupted him at a point a little subsequent to this, had cut short his words in a paroxysm of horror. 'My God!' he had exclaimed, 'think, think what you are saying.'

We are then moved to London where Villiers, a friend of Clarke, meets Herbert an old college friend who has become a beggar. Herbert tells the tale of how he has lost his fortune because of his evil but fascinating wife. Clarke hears the story and is disturbed to learn that Herbert's wife was called Helen Vaughan and that the strange house in which the

Herberts live is somehow connected with a wave of suicides and mysterious deaths. The suicides are brought painfully to the attention of the protagonists through the medium of the very sensationalising journalism from which the vision of London as a place of bizarre danger is so easily drawn: 'as Villiers spoke, an answer rang up from the pavement: "THE WEST END HORRORS: ANOTHER AWFUL SUICIDE; FULL DETAILS!".' Helen Vaughan is tracked down and kills herself and it is disclosed that when Mary saw the god she conceived the baby Helen. Dr Rowlands knew of Helen's paternity because we learn that he has several times discovered her with supernatural playmates. Helen's last moments are disclosed through a series of documentary fragments. First there is (written in Latin in best style of Victorian sexology), the account of a Dr Matheson who witnessed Helen's death.

I watched, and at last I saw nothing but a substance as jelly. Then the ladder was ascended again ... [here the MS is illegible] ... for one instant I saw a Form, shaped in dimness before me, which I will not further describe.

Then we have the inscription on an old stone found in the vicinity of the childrens' encounter.

DEVOMNODENTi
FLAvIVSSENILISPOSSVit
PROPTERNVPtias
quasVIDITSVBVMra
'To the great god Nodens (the god of the Great Deep or Abyss) Flavius Senilis has erected this pillar on account of the marriage which he saw beneath the shade.'

The novel ends in a more or less epistolary form where all narrative, all attempts to make explicit the truth of the horrific events, are deferred and represented in ever more ingenious documentary forms. The encounter with Pan which, for Machen, is paradigmatic of the encounter with horror – as we saw in the case of *The Hill of Dreams* – is thus described not only through the highly oblique narrative but also through a seemingly endless chain of fragments. The process by which the indescribable is described thus becomes a game of circulation, and the moment when the horror is fully explicit is endlessly put off.

Although *The Great God Pan* was written early in Machen's career it is in some ways the most developed of his fictions. The abyss of the landscape is matched by the abyss of the streets. Indeed, the reforming journalists usually chose metaphors of the underground, the pit or the abyss to describe their descent into the slums. The working class were seen as living in an underworld. A selection of titles will make the point:

James Greenwood, *Low-Life Deeps*, Jack London, *The People of the Abyss*, Charles Masterman, *From the Abyss*, Mary Higgs, *Glimpses into the Abyss*.[16] Machen's use of these metaphors and his presentation of a city which could have come straight out of more sensationalised journalism leads me to wonder as to the extent to which the dangers of the potentially violent and sexually abandoned working class are, in his fiction, neatly covered by the supernatural dangers which lurk in the streets, much as in modern American movies the rural poor are often imaged as subnormal monsters ready to rob and rape the unwary tourist from the city.[17] The literally unspeakable nature of this dreadful parallel may go some way towards explaining Machen's consistent reluctance to face the actual site of horror in his stories but instead to hedge it about with circumlocution, opacity of style and mountains of fabricated documents. It is perhaps significant that in *The Shining Pyramid* the abduction and the strange signs are blamed on foreign sailors, gypsies and children (all potentially subversive groups outside polite society) before the truth is disclosed.

Machen's technique of multiple narration finds its most extreme expression in *The Three Imposters* (1895).[18] Here a complex and evil conspiracy is played out entirely through a series of tales told by unreliable narrators. The opening section however includes an enlightening debate on the nature of fiction between two reliable characters, Dyson and Phillipps:

> 'My dear sir,' said Dyson, 'I will give you the task of the literary man in a phrase. He has got to do simply this – to invent a wonderful story, and to tell it in a wonderful manner.'
> 'I will grant you that,' said Mr Phillipps, 'but you will allow me to insist that in the hands of the true artist in words all stories are marvellous and every circumstance has its peculiar wonder.'

A synthesis of these views, Dyson's insistence on 'pure imagination' and Phillipps's that 'all literature ought to have a scientific basis' does, of course, lead somewhere near the common manner of Machen's own fiction where, as I have consistently shown, the marvellous and the everyday jar together and are often reconciled through the scientific imagination. The novel is set in an unreal city where 'a veil seems drawn aside, and the very fume of the pit steams up through the flagstones'. Through the medium of multiple narratives Machen is able to visit the landscapes which form such an important aspect of his vision. The possibility of the marvellous is, however, exposed from the very start and as the tales are told we are consistently confronted with the curious connections between the occult and the scientific. Nowhere is this connection made more clear than in the 'Adventure of the Missing Brother'. Here an awful transformation much like that of

Helen in *The Great God Pan* is described largely through a document entitled 'The Statement of William Gregg, F.R.S., etc.' While in *The Novel of the White Powder* the history of a young man who is turned into a puddle of malevolent slime by the inadvertent administration of an inappropriate drug is resolved by the report of a Dr Chambers.

The narratives which comprise *The Three Imposters* are eventually linked when the potential of the landscape is finally re-located in the city. Dyson and Phillipps find themselves in the sort of mansion which would have delighted the 1890s devotees of the rococo. Perhaps, uncharacteristically, Machen shows a house beginning to develop the menacing anthropomorphic decay which he usually reserves for the Welsh countryside.

The floor was thick with the dust of decay, and the painted ceiling fading from all gay colours and light fancies of cupids in a career, and disfigured with sores of dampness, seemed transmuted into other work. No longer the amorini chased one another pleasantly, with limbs that sought not to advance, and hands that merely simulated the act of grasping at the wreathed flowers; but it appeared some savage burlesque of the old careless world and of its cherished conventions, and the dance of the Loves had become a Dance of Death; black pustules and festering sores swelled and clustered on fair limbs and smiling faces showed corruption, and the fairy blood had boiled with the germs of foul disease.

This could almost be Beardsley and it demonstrates how closely connected for Machen was the style of the decadence and the vision of horror. The house, just as the landscape elsewhere in his writing, has witnessed scenes of evil and is displaying its history in its very fabric.

Kurtz died crying out at 'The Horror' and it may be said that for the original Edwardian audience the blend of insanity and savagery which Conrad manipulates into *Heart of Darkness* was more shocking than for the modern reader. However, is this true? I have suggested that Victorian journalism and popular culture provided ample material for the imagination to be well stocked with terror and with representations of the supposed savagery of the Empire. What Conrad did was to merge the techniques of the serious novelist (though did he do much more than the immensely popular but now largely forgotten W.W. Jacobs?) with popular images of imperialism. Machen, I believe, did the same thing but he grafted popular culture, popular sociology and science together with an eclectic and learned history and decadent style. In his vision of horror Machen may well, as I have suggested above, use this blend in order to carry out a deeply sublimated commentary on the class relationships of his age. He also, it could be claimed, challenges the divide between the high and popular which gesture is currently seen as a feature of the post-modern world view. Yet Machen was not unambiguously popular; he wrote and published within a highly specialised literary milieu. It is obviously the case that in the 1890s popular and high art did, to some extent, have a shared, if privileged, audience. When we turn to see this same phenomenon today perhaps we should not be so confident that it is the harbinger of a new post-industrial culture.

Notes

1. Ronald Pearsall, *The Worm in the Bud* (Harmondsworth: 1971) p. 466.
2. This point is made by Peter Keating in *The Haunted Study* (London: 1989) p. 351.
3. Stephen Prickett, *Victorian Fantasy* (Brighton: 1979) p. xiv.
4. Arthur Machen, *Eleusinia* and *Beneath the Barley* (West Warwick: 1988).
5. Ibid.
6. Pearsall, p. 466.
7. D.P.M. Michael, *Arthur Machen* (Cardiff: 1971) p. 6.
8. See R. Langenfeld, *Reconsidering Aubrey Beardsley* (Ann Arbor: 1989).
9. Joris-Karl Huysmans, *A Rebours* (1884).
10. Arthur Machen, *The Hill of Dreams* (London: 1954).
11. Machen, *The Shining Pyramid* (undated).
12. See T. Boyle, *Black Swine in the Sewers* (London: 1990).
13. Michael, p. 11.
14. Holbrook Jackson, *The 1890s* (London: 1913); John Stokes, *In the Nineties* (Brighton: 1989).
15. Machen, *The Great God Pan*.
16. A selection from these works may be found in Peter Keating, *Into Unknown England* (London: 1976).
17. For example: *Straw Dogs; Deliverance; Southern Comfort*.
18. In Martin Secker ed., *The Eighteen-Nineties* (London: 1949).

4 A Word kept back in *The Turn of the Screw*

Allan Lloyd Smith

As successive critics have discovered to their cost, *The Turn of the Screw* challenges and even defies interpretation. Shoshana Felman has observed that the naive will see ghosts, but the sophisticated will be suspicious of the governess and so repeat her mistake: 'the invitation to undertake a reading of the text is perforce an invitation to repeat the text, to enter into its labyrinth of meanings'.[1] In that labyrinth, it is indeed uncanny how critics have been led into hallucinatory readings, on occasion even inventing their own ghosts, as if those provided by the text were not enough, demonstrating the way in which the unreadability of the text provokes extreme positions in the reader.[2] Something is being very decisively not said, and our apprehension of it causes peculiar tricks of vision. Even the most skilful interpreters seem to trip up, even at the points where their eyes are most open. Felman, for example, while correcting Edmund Wilson's reductive Freudianism in the episode involving Flora's play with pieces of wood, nevertheless manages to leave out of her account, that is, to not see, some important material that gives substance to Miss Hessel's apparition:

> [Flora] had picked up a small flat piece of wood, which happened to have in it a little hole that had evidently suggested to her the idea of sticking in another fragment that might figure as a mast and make the thing a boat. This second morsel, as I watched her, she was very markedly and intently attempting to tighten in its place.
>
> [Felman omits the next part] 'My apprehension of what she was doing sustained me so that after some seconds I felt I was ready for more. Then I again shifted my eyes – I faced what I had to face.' [Then comes the chapter break – again omitted by Felman and Chapter Seven begins:]
>
> I got hold of Mrs Grose as soon after this as I could ... (and I can give no intelligible account of how I fought out the interval. Yet) I still hear myself cry as I fairly threw myself into her arms: They know – it's too monstrous: they know, they know!'
>
> 'And what on earth – ?' (I felt her incredulity as she held me.)
>
> 'Why all that we know – and heaven knows what else besides!'

The implication of the omitted parts is on the whole 'apparitionist', it gives more weight to the notion 'Flora saw'. But because Felman wants to pursue the question of phallicism, the mast[er] as a 'key to meaning, or master-signifier'; the question of the ghost of Miss Jessel is subordinated, exorcised.

Felman says, 'In its efforts to master literature, psychoanalysis – like Oedipus and like the Master – can thus but blind itself: blind itself in order not to see, and not to read, literature's subversion of the very possibility of psychoanalytic mastery.' To take up the position of mastery is to take up the place of the uncle, the place 'precisely, of the textual blind spot ... to occupy a spot within the very blindness one seeks to demystify, that one is in the madness, that is always, necessarily, in literature'.[3] Flora's innocent game, becoming a topos for psychoanalytical mastery, becomes enmeshed in a never ending series of registrations of phallicism, so that (as John Carlos Rowe observes) any effort to interpretatively master *The Turn of the Screw* is only a displacement of the uncle's power, producing displaced images of his repressive authority, his authority as repression and censorship. Allegorical readings of the hidden sexual or moral drama that governs the narrative serve to hide his mastery from view, to ascribe responsibility to another agent, who is always in the uncle's secret service.[4]

But equally, we may argue, such Freudian, Lacanian or even simply political and legal abstractions encourage us not to look closely enough at what has all too evidently been happening at Bly.

At the very centre of the narrative we have the figure of a little girl inserting and tightening a piece of wood into a hole in another piece of wood. I discussed this in an earlier study of the uncanny, but now retrace this crucial material in order to correct my own misreading or negative hallucination; I similarly failed to see what the episode – linked so deeply even to the title of the story – is actually about.[5] My previous reading argued that our attention is wrongly directed by critics like Felman to phallicism, to the boat and the mast[er], to the effect that the female ghost is erased, the 'woman in black, pale and dreadful – with such an air also, and such a face! – on the other side of the lake', who 'only fixed' the child, with 'such awful eyes'. This I read as the dreaded return of female sexuality, as the Medusa, who 'fixes' what she looks upon, a mirror-image of the governess, who later sobs, 'I don't save or shield them.' But now I think it has to be read not as allegory, nor as the sexually frustrated neurotic vision of the governess (whatever remains the truth of that understanding), but rather as symptom; we must ask what it is that Flora is telling through her actions. What her gesture allusively represents is the act of sexual penetration. It may be correct, ultimately, to refer this to a patriarchal structure informed by phallicism, a series of relays of authority from the 'Master' through Quint or the hysteria of the governess. But surely it is appropriate first to recognise the enactment for what it immediately is: something done *by* Flora, representing something done *to* Flora.

In redirecting our attention as readers to the meaning of Flora's game I do not of course assume that Flora (or Miles, or the governess) is anything but a literary representation, a figure without life outside the realm of the text. But, on the other hand, literary characters are coded to point to a continuing existence, a past of their own, and the codifications may be complex and even contradictory in certain respects. Where the character's hidden past is the focus of the text's hermeneutic drive, it is reasonable to explore all the various signals that reveal what that experience might be.

Miles is expelled from school (the 'little horrid unclean school-world'), for reasons too improper to be spelled out by the headmaster ('stupid sordid headmasters'). The governess's reaction is that he must have been 'an injury to the others', a risk of corrupting, she sarcastically adds, 'his poor little innocent mates'. On hearing the news, Mrs Grose gives a look of comprehension, but then 'visibly, with a quick blankness, seemed to try to take it back'.

Miles himself says, eventually, that it was because he 'said things'. What 'things' then, we may ask, would cause a child's dismissal from an English school? Only those 'things' which other children should not (could not) know. One of the more ingenious interpretations of this problem is Jane Nardin's: she argues that Miles has revealed intimate knowledge of an illicit love affair between a 'base menial' and a 'lady', Quint and Jessel (who she opines were in love but prevented from marrying for class reasons). 'If Miles loved Quint and Miss Jessel and sympathised with their love for each other, then perhaps what he did at school was simply to discuss their relationship and his feelings about it with his closest friends.'[6] It is not impossible that Miles was expelled for talking about an affair between his governess and a valet; it is merely unlikely. Gossip like that would be conventional in an upper-class English school. Talk which indicated graphic personal knowledge of homosexual practices between a child and an adult, however, would certainly have been seen as corrupting, particularly so since this was the great area of difficulty in the English public schools.

According to Nardin, in 'secretly voicing egalitarian sentiments about Quint and Miss Jessel, Miles would have been striking at his school's *raison d'être*: the preparation of status-conscious gentlemen to fit their places in a stratified society'.[7] Thus the cause of Miles's expulsion was really his innocence in speaking indiscreetly of rank and sex. The dichotomy between his 'seeming sweetness and his disgrace at school can thus be resolved without having recourse to theories of deep deceit or demonic possession'.[8]

But of course the alternative is not between deep deceit and demonic possession. If Miles speaks of what he knows, to those he 'liked', he isn't practising 'deep deceit' or being wicked, any more than any abused child who becomes complicit in the activities practised upon him or her by the adult. This seems to me the fatal mistake of critics of *The Turn of the Screw*: to believe that the complicit child is guilty, or wicked, instead of perceiving the affair from the child's point of view. For that matter, 'demonic possession' is really a very apt description of the situation of such a child, whose behaviour may cause others to see 'ghosts', *the ghosts of the actions of the abuser*. Jane Nardin comes nearer to this point of view when she says that 'the ghosts are the logical offspring of the governess's attempt to understand a complex human situation in terms of a cultural tradition incapable of yielding real insight', that is, her religious moral training, which cannot comprehend that Miles may have committed a serious offence and yet not be a complete reprobate.[9] She does not, however, have a satisfactory explanation of the processes whereby this seeing of ghosts comes about. It is my contention that the hallucinations are provoked by the symptomatic behaviour of the children and Mrs Grose. This is made more comprehensible by Nicholas Abraham and Maria Torok's psychoanalytic work on 'the phantom', which 'offers a new way to interpret the behaviour of fictional characters and some insight into how texts made enigmatic, if not illegible, by the mute presence of secrets may be explained'.[10] 'What haunts are not the dead, but the gaps left within us by the secrets of others', suggests Nicholas Abraham in 'Notes on the Phantom: a Complement to Freud's Metapsychology'.[11]

———

Nicholas Abraham and Maria Torok's theory of 'The Phantom' proposes a radical departure from the universalising tendency of psychoanalysis, with powerful implications for the study of the uncanny in literature. Abraham and Torok argue that it is not axiomatic that childhood development proceeds in predetermined ways, nor that any particular event is traumatic for all individuals. Instead they stress that the process of individuation is 'potentially nonlinear, and that in certain cases it is constituted by specific influences outside the individual's immediate or lived experience'.[12] The process begins with the child's differentiation from the mother (a process which is never completed), within which the infant 'with no conscious or unconscious of its own other than the mother's ... perceives the mother's words, gestures, and physical attributes without distinguishing between the mother's conscious or unconscious intent or charge'.[13] The maternal unconscious, communicated without having been spoken, 'resides as a silent presence within the newly formed unconscious of the child. As the child matures, it will add its own repressions – produced by its own lived experiences – to this central core.'[14] There is no preprogrammed sequence of drives and repressions as in Freud's formulation of developmental stages, nor any single and privileged drive and repression, such as is represented by the phallus in Lacan's formulation. But since every mother is herself the child of another mother there is a genealogical inheritance of the unconscious. 'We are all the products of our infinitely regressive family histories.'[15] Abraham and Torok as practising psychoanalysts inevitably focused most closely on family dynamics, but at this point we may stress the openness of their model to *cultural* determinants as well as more strictly personal ones: the child is absorbing a cultural inheritance incorporating certain secrets, absences or silences. 'The Phantom' is Abraham and Torok's designation of the unknowing awareness of another's secret which 'introduces, via the concept of "transgenerational haunting", a novel perspective on the potential configurations of psychic history and on their role in pathogenic processes and symptom formation'.[16] According to Abraham,

The phantom is a formation of the unconscious that has never been conscious – for good reason. It passes – in a way yet to be determined – from the parent's unconscious into the child's. Clearly, the phantom has a function different from dynamic repression. The phantom's periodic and compulsive return lies beyond the scope of symptom-formation in the sense of a return of the repressed; it works like a ventriloquist, like a stranger within the subject's own mental topography.[17]

Abraham and Torok assert that characters in literary texts 'may be construed as cryptic poetic entities whose words and actions can be heard to tell the secret history generating their existence'.[18] The implications of this for literary study of the uncanny are of course considerable. Esther Rashkin argues that,

this means that the linguistic elements of the text are considered to be incomplete and need to be joined with their missing complements, whose traces are hidden in the text. The reading of these traces and the union of missing complements enables the interpreter to perceive or conjecture a drama or dramas concealed within a character's history. ... This does not mean that a character's past is conceived to be real, or that it is afforded a status different from the character's 'present'. [This means] understanding that the text calls upon the reader to expand its apparent parameters to include invisible scenarios whose traces are symbolically and perhaps cryptonymically inscribed within it. Although predating the events of the text, these unelaborated dramas have no reality outside the limits of the text. ... Approaching these texts with conceptual and interpretive tools such as anasemic analysis, symbol, cryptonymy, and the phantom, can offer new insights into the problems of textual production, the genesis and motivation of narrative, and the connections between structures of repetition and concealment, inscription and significa-tion.[19]

Some of these terms require further explanation. Anasemic analysis is the name given by Abraham and Torok to the process of discover-ing why a particular event has been experienced as traumatic and concealed as a secret. It consists of a constant movement 'back up toward' (Greek, ana) earlier sources of signification (semia) that lie beyond perception.

Anasemia allows [us] to construe an individual's experience as con-stituted by the constant creation of symbols in response to traumas. It enables [us] to read these symbols – and thus the individual's life – as a series of telltale symptoms that tacitly speak of their founding silence beyond perception.[20]

The symbols in question are not understood precisely as literary symbols would be but are instead fragments or broken halves of a missing whole which need to be reconnected to their absent comple-ments. The symbol plays the role of a relay in a functional circuit: it is not a question of a one-to-one correspondence but something that functions dynamically in relation to objects. But it is not a question of asking what the symbols of the text mean, but rather: 'how and with what does something symbolize? What constitutes the text's symbolic operation?'[21]

Cryptonymy is another of Abraham and Torok's terms for establishing a signifying process, a theory of readability. In 'Towards a Cryptonymy of Literature' Nicholas Rand explains:

A theory of readability does not define the act of reading but rather attempts to create avenues for reading where previously there were none. More radically, it demonstrates that interpretation is possible even in the face of obvious obstruction. Such a theory is primarily concerned with converting obstructions into guides to under-standing.[22]

Words, as carriers of veiled lexical relationships, can be cryptonyms, words that *hide*. Through synonyms, for example, reference may be made to an unstated term which is concealed within the sequence, a word which should appear but does not. This is not far from Freud's reading techniques, and has resemblance to the Lacanian process of interpretation. Where this process differs is that Abraham and Torok avoid any standardised decoding. 'In a cryptonymic reading', Rashkin explains, 'we can stop at a signifier if we can determine what it hides, how it hides it, and what drama might be linked to its process of hiding.'[23] In contradiction to the idea of a signifying chain as composed of a potentially infinite sequence of empty signifiers, 'the signified is not secondary'.[24] Rashkin sees the difference here primarily in the notion that the bar or sign of repression can itself be made into an object of investigation.

In relation to the uncanny, the most obviously promising of these terms and procedures is the notion of the phantom. Abraham argues that 'what haunts [is] not the dead, but the gaps left within us by the secrets of others', and that, 'what comes back to haunt are the tombs of others'.[25] This concept of the phantom enables Abraham and Torok to postulate how influences outside an individual's lived experience can determine psychic development. It does this by linking certain states of mental disarray to the concealment of a secret rather than to that individual's unconscious understood as a repository of repressed wishes. The phantom is a formation outside any developmental view of human behaviour. 'It holds the individual within a group dynamic constituted by a specific familial (*and sometimes extrafamilial*) topology that prevents the individual from living life as her or his own.'[26] A possibility suggested by the italicised phrase above is to consider the unspeakable, or at any rate unspoken, secret or secrets in a larger cultural sense; everything that is denied within the culture, and yet remains the truth; as in Schelling's definition of the uncanny, as 'everything that ought to have remained ... secret and hidden but has come to light'.[27] In this model, the author, like contemporary readers, could be unaware of the secret that nevertheless shaped character's actions or their fictional destinies. We could then usefully speak of 'the phantom' at points where the character's actions, the narrator's comments, or the structures of plot are contradictory in terms of authorially postulated conditions, but *are* consistent with other unspoken determinants.

Right from the beginning, when she is so unmistakably relieved to welcome the governess, Mrs Grose's discourse and reactions are often expressive of something else,

> she has told me, bit by bit, under pressure, a great deal; but a small shifty spot on the wrong side of it all still sometimes brushed my brow like the wing of a bat; and ... I felt the importance of giving a last jerk to the curtain.

The governess believes that she is bolder, more imaginative and more willing to face it – whatever it may prove to be – than Mrs Grose, her ignorant and unlettered assistant. But Mrs Grose, nearer to the grosser aspects of life, as her name implies (nearer perhaps even to a sense of 'gross indecency'?) is likely to know *some* things that the governess, the Austenish youngest daughter of a Hampshire vicar, whose reading did not even extend to eighteenth-century novels and whose sexual experience can be reasonably assumed to be negligible, would not. So a macabre comedy ensues when the two are at cross purposes over Miss Jessel, who has obviously been abused by Quint: Mrs Grose says, 'And afterwards I imagined – and I still imagine. And what I imagine is dreadful.' 'Not so dreadful as what I do', replies the governess, thinking of her own supernatural horrors. Or again, in talking of Flora's relation to Miss Jessel, Mrs Grose tries a grim joke, 'Perhaps [Flora] likes it!', which links with the governess's following remark regarding Miss Jessel, 'It must have been also what she wished!' Most suggestively of all, in terms of Abraham and Torok's theories of the cryptonym, 'There was a word Mrs Grose had kept back.' Indeed there was, although arguably Mrs Grose knows what it is little more than does the governess. These suggestive absences in Mrs Grose's discourse open the door for the governess's hallucinations to begin when she misunderstands the latter's comment, 'He seems to like us young and pretty!'

> 'Oh he did', Mrs Grose assented: 'it was the way he liked everyone!' She had no sooner spoken than she caught herself up. 'I mean, that's his way – the master's.' I was struck. 'But of whom did you speak first?' She looked blank, but she coloured. 'Why of him.' 'Of the master?' 'Of who else?' There was so obviously no one else that the next moment I had lost my impression of her having accidentally said more than she meant.

It would be impossible to list all of the misconstructions entailed by the governess's comparative ignorance of what was, after all, not talked of in her society (or even, I shall argue later, James's). I will simply instance the exchange: 'But now that you've guessed.' (Mrs Grose): 'Ah, I haven't guessed. How can I if you don't imagine?', or the episode in which the governess sees in Mrs Grose's face 'the delayed dawn of an idea I myself had not given her and that was as yet quite obscure to me'. These enigmatic traces of 'something else', the brush of the bat's wing, become the fabric that sustains the apparitions seen by the governess, even to the extent that 'It was as if in my friend's own eyes Miss Jessel had again appeared.'

Mrs Grose tells the governess that Quint and Miss Jessel were infamous, and that he 'did what he wished ... with them all'. In the following passage we see how the implications of child sexual abuse can become subtly apparent in Mrs Grose's discourse, but are missed by the governess. The two are talking about the period when Miles and Quint had been perpetually together:

'He [Miles] denied certain occasions'.

'What occasions?'

'When they had been about together quite as if Quint were his tutor – and a very grand one – and Miss Jessel only for the little lady. When he had gone off with the fellow, I mean, and spent hours with him.'

There is a discrepancy here between the notion of Quint behaving as a 'grand tutor' and Miles 'going off with the fellow' which implies less respectable activities. The governess however misses this nuance:

'I see. He lied'.

'Oh!' Mrs Grose mumbled. This was a suggestion that it didn't matter.

Mrs Grose sees her companion going in the wrong direction, and adds to it by saying that Miss Jessel didn't mind, and didn't forbid him, thus reinforcing the theme of collusion between Quint and Jessel in exploiting the children.

I considered. 'Did he put that to you as a justification?'

At this she dropped again. 'No, he never spoke of it.'

'Never mentioned her in connection with Quint?'

She saw, visibly flushing, where I was coming out.

'Well, he didn't show anything. He denied', she repeated; 'he denied.'

Lord, how I pressed her now! 'So that you could see he knew what was between the two wretches?'

'I don't know – I don't know!' the poor woman wailed.

Unable to articulate what she did know – or suspect

'You do know, you dear thing', I replied; 'only you haven't my dreadful boldness of mind, and you keep back, out of timidity and modesty and delicacy, even the impression that in the past, when you had, without my aid, to flounder about in silence, most of all made you miserable. But I shall get it out of you yet! There was something in the boy that suggested to you', I continued, 'his covering and concealing their relation.'

Which Mrs Grose could take to imply the relation between Miles and Quint.

'Oh he couldn't prevent – '

'Your learning the truth? I dare say. But heavens', I fell, with vehemence, a-thinking, 'what it shows that they must, to that extent, have succeeded in making of him!'

'Ah nothing that's not nice now!' Mrs Grose lugubriously pleaded.

Among the tests for child abuse the display of unexpected knowledge, as well as compulsive re-enactment of sexual scenarios in symbolic terms, is now – and although it was not so then, a writer as perceptive as James could have understood this intuitively – commonplace. Flora's 'appalling' language points to the same conclusion, as does Miles's sexual precocity in his 'saying things' at the school; his unexpected maturity in his dealings with the governess in the areas of implicitly sexual behaviour is a further clear marker of the experience of abuse. The behaviour of the children contains certain systemic lacunae: the fact, for example, that 'Never, by a slip of the tongue, have they so much as alluded to either of their old friends' (Quint and Jessel); their angelicism versus sexual precocity; Miles's excellent behaviour contrasted with his expulsion. This causes the governess to imaginatively 'fill in' the vacant spaces. A nice example of the process comes when the governess expresses through prurient innuendo her intuition of the children's potential for abuse: 'They were like those cherubs of the anecdote who had – morally at any rate – nothing to whack!' She goes on to discuss Miles's baffling lack of a past in terms that show how her cognition is vexed and thwarted.

I remember feeling with Miles in especial as if he had, as it were, nothing to call even an infinitesimal history. ... He had never for a second suffered. I took this as a direct disproof of his having really been chastised. If he had been wicked he would have 'caught' it, and I should have found the trace, should have felt the wound and the dishonour. I could reconstitute nothing at all, and he was, therefore an angel. He never spoke of his school.

'Nothing to whack', 'nothing at all' to 'reconstitute': we are reminded of the governess's decision in response to the letter from school to say 'Nothing at all'. But this nothing is a something, to have caused Miles's dismissal, and there is clearly *something* that causes the children's unnatural behaviour, leaving such marks as make the governess see 'a queerness in the traceable increase of their own demonstrations' (of beguilement), or believe Miles to be 'under some influence operating in his small intellectual life as a tremendous incitement'. Abraham and Torok propose that 'symptoms can occur when a shameful and therefore unspeakable experience must be barred from consciousness and "kept secret"'.[28]

When Flora plays with her bits of wood her behaviour is symbolic. The mistake made by critics has been to read this symbol as a hieroglyph standing for the structures of phallicism. But as Abraham understands it,

> a first distinction must be made between, on the one hand, the symbol-thing considered as a hieroglyph or symbolic text – the symbol dead as a symbol – and, on the other hand, the symbol included within a process, that is, the operating symbol, animated by meaning and implying concrete subjects, all together considered as a functioning unit. To interpret a symbol consists in converting the symbol-thing into an operating symbol. A thing must never be taken as the symbol of another thing.[29]

Flora's symbolic play constitutes this kind of functioning unit, representing her unsayable drama. Another example of the operation of 'the phantom' in the effect of Flora's behaviour on the governess is also apparent in the toy boat episode. When the governess sees the apparition she notices that Flora's voluble chattering has abruptly ceased and she has turned her back to the water. This convinces the governess that Flora 'knows'. But isn't it rather the case that Flora's spontaneous sounds cease when she is compulsively re-enacting a sexual experience with the two pieces of wood, producing a silence that the governess interprets as uncanny in relation to such an 'innocent' activity as boatmaking, and this 'causes' the ghost to appear? Flora didn't tell; the governess's comment, 'Not a word – that's the horror. She kept it to herself! The child of eight, that child!' is then, true in another sense as well. Shoshana Felman registers the implication of Flora's action when she comments of the governess's 'They know – its too monstrous: they know, they know!' that, 'to know, indeed, is both "to possess reliable information" and "to have sexual intercourse with"'; yet instead of following up the clear implication of this aperçu, Felman moves instead – like all other critics of the story – to the problem of the governess, and even in her section titled 'A child is being killed', manages to avoid the implication of her own perception.[30]

If the symptomatic behaviour of the children and Mrs Grose, circling around the 'secret' of their having been sexually abused, creates an enigma that can only be resolved for the governess by her 'filling in' the absent figures of Quint and Miss Jessel, the same can eventually be said of her own behaviour towards the children, her own keeping of the 'secret' that she doesn't 'know'. In Abraham and Torok's theory, the originator of the traumatic secret has to be simply

> an identifiable member of a particular family whose secret, and whose reason for keeping a secret, are determined by a specific

psychic constellation. By the same token, the effect on those to whom the individual transmits the secret – as well as their identity (whether child, grandchild, nephew, niece or non-relative) – cannot be pre-determined or predicted.[31]

The consequence of incomprehension is an increasing sense of interrelated suspicion and performance, on both sides, so that the governess works on her small charges as they work on her.

the element of the unnamed and untouched became, between us, greater than any other, and ... so much avoidance couldn't have been made successful without a great deal of tacit arrangement. It was as if, at moments, we were perpetually coming into sight of subjects before which we must stop short, turning suddenly out of alleys that we perceived to be blind, closing with a little bang that made us look at each other – for like all bangs, it was something louder than we had intended – the doors we had inadvertently opened.

The governess is in the role of mother to the orphaned children, handing on her unconsciousness to them through her unwillingness – and indeed inability – to articulate their situation. As she puts it, 'I flung myself about, but I always broke down in the monstrous utterance of names.' What the governess thinks she means is the names of Quint and Jessel, but what she really fails to articulate – because she cannot think it – is the 'word' that Mrs Grose (similarly inarticulate, if better aware of the world), 'kept back'. The subtle awareness of all four of what is not to be said undercuts the apparent harmony of their 'cloud of music and affection and success and private theatricals'.

What it was least possible to get rid of was the cruel idea that, whatever I had seen, Miles and Flora saw more – things terrible and unguessable and that sprang from *dreadful passages of intercourse*, [my italics] in the past. Such things necessarily left on the surface, for the time, a chill that we vociferously denied we felt.

In the end, this chill becomes so extreme as to cause Miles's death when he is finally forced to articulate the forbidden name: replying to the governess's interrogation 'Whom do you mean by "he"?' with 'Peter Quint – you devil!'. Here a comment of Abraham and Torok's is particularly apposite. In 'The Wolf Man's Magic Word' they claim:

It is not a situation including words that becomes repressed; the words are not dragged into repression by a situation. Rather, the words themselves, expressing desire, are deemed to be generators of a situation that must be avoided and voided retroactively. ... For this to occur, a catastrophic situation has to have been created precisely by words.[32]

The words Quint and Jessel fulfil these criteria, when with catastrophic results, Flora becomes suddenly aged, 'she was literally, she was hideously hard, she had turned common and almost ugly', by having to re-encounter the traumatic word Jessel; and Miles is actually killed by the stress of articulating the name of Peter Quint. A further argument of Abraham's may be brought into the discussion on this point of Miles's death in naming Quint.

A surprising fact gradually emerges: the work of the phantom coincides in every respect with Freud's description of the death instinct. First of all, it has no energy of its own; it cannot be 'abreacted', merely designated. Second, it pursues in silence its work of disarray. Let us add that the phantom is sustained by secreted words, invisible gnomes whose aim is to wreak havoc, from within the unconscious, in the coherence of logical progression. Finally, it gives rise to endless repetition and, more often than not, eludes rationalization.[33]

That the governess 'always broke down in the monstrous utterance of names' is an anticipation of the far more stressful effect of this naming on Flora and Miles. To name Quint, in the context of the governess's intervention, her insertion of Miles's unnamed experience into the frame of social opinion (or the symbolic order) is to strip away the child's defence (his 'innocence'), in naming as disgusting or evil the activities he has been shaped by. This is what kills him: not simply his 'fright' at the vehemence of her (or for that matter perhaps even his own) belief in the occult. In his article on the phantom, Abraham discusses the 'special difficulty' in such analyses (as the one that the governess is in effect undertaking), which

lies in the patient's horror at violating a parent's or a family's guarded secrets, even though the secret's text and content are inscribed in the unconscious. The horror of transgressing, in the strict sense of the term, is compounded by the risk of undermining the fictitious yet necessary integrity of the parental figure in question.[34]

We are not simply in literature here (*pace* Felman); or if we choose to be so we are merely re-enacting the systematic not knowing of the culture which produces the text itself as symptom. In the period immediately preceding James's writing of *The Turn of the Screw* there *had* been an increase in public apprehension and concern about child sexual exploitation, but this focused chiefly not on the abuse of small children by parents or other carers but on the scandal of under-age prostitution, into which such concern was rapidly diverted. In 1885, W.T. Stead's articles entitled 'Maidens of the Modern Babylon' in the July *Pall Mall Gazette* drew attention to the use of under-age girl prostitutes. A brief alliance of Anglican bishops, free thinkers and reformers succeeded in a campaign to raise the age of consent from 13 to 16 years.[35] On this issue of child prostitution Gorman notes a division of attitudes to girl children who were conceived as either 'the female child redeemer' or, on the other hand, 'the little girl as evil incarnate'. The result of illicit sexual intercourse was seen as producing permanent corruption, and 'the earlier the "corruption" took place the more ingrained was the evil'.[36] Stead's colourful version was that 'the foul passion of the man seemed to enter into the helpless victim of his lust'.[37] These attitudes are obviously relevant to *The Turn of the Screw*'s dualisms. It is, however, striking that studies of the history of sexuality do not deal with child sexual abuse. Although documentary evidence from the period is often quite remarkably outspoken about homosexuality, masturbation or 'extreme' sexual practices; we find in the documentary evidence no more than such innuendoes as this: 'if only the parents are not completely demoralised and actually teach the children evil ways'.[38] G.J. Barker-Benfield's study of nineteenth-century American sexuality similarly does not acknowledge the existence of child abuse; his chapter on children is focused on contemporary concerns about onanism. Another and more famous example of the suppressions operating in society about this issue is the shift in Freud's reading of the meaning of his patients' accounts of sexual experience in childhood away from their truth as testimony and towards instead the symbolic registration of infantile desire.[39]

What this perspective on *The Turn of the Screw* produces is a reorientation of our position so severe as to amount almost to a reversal. Instead of seeing the children as simply the occasion of adult interpretation and fantasy, we come to see implied pretextual but determining experience as the cause of that whole problematic. Their actions and attitudes sketch for the inexperienced governess a history, a situation, that she cannot understand but equally cannot ignore, causing her to fill in the spaces of their communications with appropriate figures.[40]

No critic can resist another turn: there is additionally in the governess herself an element that can perhaps be recognised as a species of sadism: for her own reasons she keeps the children incommunicado, retaining the letters they write to their uncle, and making them the victims – it is her own word – of her remorseless observation and lucidity. 'My lucidity must have seemed awful, but the charming creatures who were the victims of it', provides a typical example. Her imagination of them has frequently a sinister note, she sees them as

vulnerable in their beauty, as 'blameless and foredoomed', and muses
on how the rough future would 'handle them and might bruise them.
In this connection we may wish to put another gloss on the way that
the governess finds herself repeating the actions of the ghosts; staring
in at the window, sitting at the foot of the stairs, or at the writing desk.
At least potentially, she too is drawn into a repetition of the servants'
sadistic use of the children, their desire – when alive, and now in the
childrens' memory – to get closer to them, to engage with them
sexually.

And yet another turn: the governess thereby repeats the action of
the text as a whole, a sadistic mechanism in which the children, and
the young ingenue herself, are on display, exposed to 'the very worst
action small victims so conditioned might be conceived as subject to',
for the delectation, amusement and even sexual *frisson* of those who,
in James's words, are 'not easily caught ... the jaded, the disillusioned,
the fastidious'. As Allon White remarks, 'the fascinating thing in James
is the complex interpenetration of social and sexual censorship against
a felt desire to "know" things which he could not reveal without
indicting himself by his own standards'.[41] James's disclaimer

> Only make the reader's general vision of evil intense enough, I said
> to myself – and that is already a charming job – and his own
> experience, his own imagination, his own sympathy (with the
> children) and horror (of their false friends) will supply him quite suf-
> ficiently with the particulars. Make him think the evil, make him
> think it for himself, and you are released from weak specifications.

This acknowledges the unsayable as nearly as possible. His success in
making readers 'think the evil' is apparent in contemporary reviews:

> The feeling after perusal of the horrible story is that one has been
> assisting in an outrage upon the holiest and sweetest fountain of
> human innocence, and helping to debauch – at least by helplessly
> standing by – the pure and trusting nature of children. Human
> imagination can go no further into infamy, literary art could not be
> used with more refined subtlety of spiritual defilement.[42]

That he did not himself, however, consciously register the unacceptable fact of child abuse in his society is suggested by his reaction to such
reviews.

> How can I feel my calculation to have failed, my wrought suggestion
> not to have worked, that is, on my being assailed, as has befallen me,
> with the charge of a monstrous emphasis, the charge of all indecently
> expatiating? There is not only from beginning to end of the matter

not an inch of expiation, but my values are positively all blanks save so far as an excited horror, a promoted pity, a created expertness – on which punctual effects of strong causes no writer can ever fail to plume himself – proceed to read into them more or less fantastic figures.

That the story is constructed of 'blanks' does not therefore preclude its having a strong current of suggestiveness as to their probable content. As John Carlos Rowe says when discussing class issues in *The Turn of the Screw* 'there is no "proper" undecidability; it is always the effect or product of a certain forgetting of motives and drives that have awakened interest'.[43] To evade the censor in this manner is paradoxically to reinforce the sense of censorable (censurable) material. In a letter to Louis Waldstein in October 1898, on 'That Wanton Little Tale', James expressed in somewhat sentimental terms the complex that I have been attempting to elucidate.

My bogy-tale dealt with things so hideous that I felt to save it at all it needed some infusion of beauty or prettiness, and the beauty of the pathetic was the only attainable – was indeed inevitable. But ah, the exposure indeed, the helpless plasticity of childhood that isn't dear or sacred to somebody! That was my little tragedy.[44]

James's description of his intended readers as 'the jaded, disillusioned and fastidious', could, however, now also be seen as *fin de siècle* code for the knowing, or even corrupted, who relish the poignancy of the victims exposure to the 'very worst'; that is, the worst that the culture contains but does not admit into its discourse.

Notes

1. Shoshana Felman, 'Turning the Screw of Interpretation' in Shoshana Felman ed., *Literature and Psychoanalysis: the Question of Reading: Otherwise* (Baltimore: 1982) p. 190.
2. I have referred extensively here to Esther Rashkin's very useful summary of Abraham and Torok's thought in 'Tools for a New Psychoanalytical Literary Criticism' in *Diacritics* (1988) pp. 31–52.
3. Felman, p. 199.
4. John Carlos Rowe, *The Theoretical Dimensions of Henry James* (London: 1985) p. 143.
5. See Allan Lloyd Smith, *Uncanny American Fiction* (London: 1989).
6. Jane Nardin, '*The Turn of the Screw*: the Victorian Background' in *Mosaic*, vol. 12 (1978) pp. 131–42.
7. See Stanley Renner, 'Sexual Hysteria, Physiognomical Bogeyman and the "Ghosts" in *The Turn of the Screw* in *Nineteenth-Century Literature*, vol. 43 (1988) pp. 175–94.

8. Nardin, p. 135.
9. Ibid.
10. Rashkin, p. 37.
11. Nicholas Abraham, 'Notes on the Phantom: a Complement to Freud's Metapsychology', in *Critical Inquiry*, vol. 13 (1987) pp. 287–92.
12. Rashkin, p. 32.
13. Ibid., p. 34.
14. Ibid.
15. Ibid., p. 35.
16. Ibid., p. 37.
17. Abraham, ibid.
18. Rashkin, p. 50.
19. Ibid., p. 51.
20. Ibid., p. 50.
21. Ibid., p. 48.
22. Nicholas Rand, 'Towards a Cryptonomy of Literature' in Nicholas Abraham and Maria Torok, *The Wolf Man's Magic Word: a Cryptonomy*, trans. Nicholas Rand (Minneapolis: 1986) pp. i–ii.
23. Rashkin, p. 45.
24. Ibid.
25. Abraham, pp. 287–8.
26. Rashkin, p. 40 (italics added).
27. See Freud's definition of the uncanny.
28. Rashkin, p. 37.
29. Ibid., p. 47.
30. Felman, ibid.
31. Rashkin, p. 41.
32. Abraham and Torok, p. 20.
33. Abraham, p. 291.
34. Ibid., p. 290.
35. See Jeffrey Weeks, *Sex, Politics and Society* (London: 1981) p. 87. See also Deborah Gorman 'Maidens of the Modern Babylon re-examined: Child Prostitution and the Idea of Childhood in late Victoria England' in *Victorian Studies*, vol. 21 (1978) pp. 353–87.
36. Gorman, ibid.
37. *Pall Mall Gazette* (8 July 1885) quoted in Gorman, p. 372.
38. Robert H. Bremner, *Children and Youth in America: a Documentary History* (Cambridge, Mass.: 1971) p. 592.
39. H.G. Beigel, *Advances in Sex Research* (New York: 1963) pp. 248–55.
40. Renner, ibid.
41. Allon White, *The Uses of Obscurity* (London: 1981) p. 135.
42. *The Independent* (5 January 1899) quoted in Robert Kimbrough ed., *The Turn of the Screw* (New York: 1966) p. 175.
43. Rowe, p. 44.
44. Kimbrough, p. 110.

5 M.R. James and his Fiction

Clive Bloom

M.R. James was and remains one of the greatest *minor* writers of this century. To place such a contradictory judgement upon his work, to see it as both 'great' and yet in a minor league, is in the very nature of any attempt to classify those stories that saw the first light of day as Christmas tales for Cambridge colleagues and Eton students. In an age of experiment his style was doggedly conservative, in an age of epic he was a miniaturist and in an age of modernity his writing refers to a world both slower and more stable. His output, apart from scholarly work was restricted to the slim collection of 'ghost' tales for which he is famous and which began appearing separately and in collections from 1904. On reading these short excursions into the supernatural one is less inclined to place James among his contemporaries (although he admired Arthur Conan Doyle) than with Isaak Walton and John Bunyan. Furthermore, of the writers of ghost stories, James most admired Sheridan Le Fanu who may have inspired him but seems to have done little else. Of his contemporary and namesake Henry James and his work in the genre, M.R. James had only this to say, 'I have read *The Turn of the Screw*'.[1] This silence may have been related to his father, another Henry James but it is hardly helpful.

In this essay I want to explore some of the reasons for James's longevity as a writer still avidly read and to consider two points especially. The first concerns James as an 'artist' and his relationship with modern literary taste. The second is a wider cultural question aimed at the thematic (rather than stylistic) concerns displayed by James.

Montague Rhodes James was born into an ecclesiastical family in 1862. Brought up in the rural surroundings of a Suffolk village and with a precocious childhood interest in antiquities and medieval manuscripts he seems to have enjoyed a life of relative security and continuity: the life of the country parsonage, a life which had its origins in the eighteenth-century squirearchy and which was dramatised in novel after novel from Jane Austen onwards. Thus James's background was essentially eighteenth century in style with the antiquarian interests of the eighteenth century established early on. The various accommodations and compromises of village life which accompanied the development of a squirearchical cadre were themselves little changed since the previous century. Indeed, it is rarely remembered that alongside high Victorian gothicism there was a remarkable revival of Queen Anne-style architecture and the raffishness of the mashers and stage door Johnnies was a conscious imitation of the dandyish of the previous century. In the sophisticated comedies of Wilde the urbanity of Sheridan can be glimpsed. Whereas most commentators emphasise the medieval interests of James, I am asserting, the equal, if not greater, importance of a cultural continuity with the previous century and its growing emphasis on respectability and middle-class decorum: the life of the gentleman. It is ironic that across the Atlantic James's great horror writing contemporary and Anglophile H.P. Lovecraft longed for the life, education and freedom of an eighteenth-century gentleman brought up through the public school and university system of England. Lovecraft, the son of a failed salesman, was an autodidact.

The relative stability of village social relations occurred against a background of massive rural depopulation in James's youth, yet when James began to publish there was a distinct drift back towards the country through suburbanism, the garden movement led by Gertrude Jekyll, the garden cities of Edward Lutgens and the beginning of a tourist industry. The tones of the publications that publicised this now hidden and unknown parochial landscape were conveyed in the affected tones of eighteenth-century antiquarianism. Here is P.H. Ditchfield waxing lyrical in *The Charm of the English Village*.

> No country in the world can boast of possessing rural homes and villages which have half the charm and picturesqueness of our English cottages and hamlets. Wander where you will ... in no foreign land have you seen a village which for beauty and interest can compare with ... our English land.
>
> Sometimes we, whose lot it is to live in an English village, sigh for a larger outlook ... but life in the country is wondrously attractive to those who love nature, and we are thankful that we have been called to work amidst the fields and lanes of rural England, and are able to appreciate the charm of an English village.[2]

The book itself was illustrated by Sydney Jones who picked out the picturesque and the quaint, occasionally portraying a character in eighteenth-century dress. Thus the countryside awaited its 'rediscovery' and prepared itself with tea shoppes and cream teas to participate in a new rural pursuit: catering for tourists. The countryside's authenticity was now revitalised in a myth of tradition, a myth of Hereward the Wake, Robin Hood, Maid Marion and Morris Dancing. The Englishness of England, its continuity and stability found resonance in the byways and hedgerows, hamlets and estates of an exhausted and depleted rurality.

James's own upbringing belonged firmly within the acknowledged pathways of the ruling élite and the governing class except that he excelled as a scholar and found a spiritual home in the semi-ecclesiastical surroundings through which he rose. Beginning as a student at Eton he ended as Provost of Eton, having been to King's, Cambridge and having been Provost of King's and Vice-Chancellor of Cambridge University. The highly privileged education he received (restricted to less than 2 per cent of the population) and the highly distinguished career he pursued as a educationalist and as a very great medievalist and antiquarian bibliophile crowned a life, that, like John Buchan's led to the very top. And, yet, beyond all this James's reputation remains rooted in his short tales of ghostly goings on, with their antiquarian atmospheres, topographical piquancies and belles-lettres style so reminiscent (and this is where the trick of style works so well) of an eighteenth-century gentleman amateur whiling away a few hours with a story written merely for a moment's *diversion*. Even the frequent appearances of cars, trains and games of golf fail to lift this totality of ambience provided by reading all the tales in quick succession. James's photographic portraits reveal an authoritative, sophisticated and urbane intelligence and it is these qualities that give to the highly parochial settings of his tales their special atmosphere and quality.

The very particularity of his Englishness (as it reveals itself in his fiction) was the result of his wider intellectual and touristic pursuits. The characteristic outcome of this mixture was a literature at once urbane *and* determinedly middlebrow: a blend of careful attention to plot and narrative structure and an avoidance of extra literary 'meaning' – a meaning related to concerns outside the necessities of the tale itself. Julie Briggs tells us that,

> his avowed motive in writing was to tell a good story, and having discovered from his wide reading certain well-established structural patterns, he adopted them ... and the resulting pieces exhibit ... an exceptional grasp of the force of traditional elements. Without being in any sense experimental or exploratory, his stories demonstrate the power that the classically well-made tale may still exert over a modern reader.[3]

In such a way, and because of this century's own obsession with meaning, James's 'art' (never more than sophisticated entertainment?) has been considered beneath the attention of most serious academic gothicists. Here the two questions I posed at the opening of this chapter come together, the one about James's style and place as a great minor writer and the other about James's cultural (thematic) norms as found within his work. The two questions cannot be easily disentangled, nor should they.

Critics of the genre tell us little about M.R. James and his concerns as a writer. Stephen King simply ignores his work in *Danse Macabre*.[4] Rosemary Jackson offers these elusive comments, 'Ghost stories are a special category of the fantastic, evolving from folklore and developing through Gothic horror fiction to become widely popularized in the Victorian period, through the works of Sheridan Le Fanu and M.R. James.'[5] This will get us only a very little way indeed, but she continues, 'the effect of ghost tales ... imply [sic] the return of the dead as the undead. ... By attempting to make visible that which is culturally invisible and which is written out as negation and as death, the fantastic introduces absences.[6] Her comments here are the insights gained from a schooling more in linguistic theory than a close attention to either historical context or artistic content. Read James and you will find few genuine ghosts and only a suggested number of returns from the dead. James's presences, those poised to break the veil are much more hobgoblins than the returned undead. The term 'dead' hardly applies to these creatures beyond life or death. Equally, the tales make no attempt to make the 'invisible' *culturally* 'visible'. In other words the tales refuse a *political* reading indicated by either 'absences' or lacunae in a text which the bourgeois author is unable to paper over in his attempt to naturalise the legitimacy of his class (as represented in his fiction). For James's work, as for most popular fiction, the *overt* message is *written clearly* and displayed almost naively.

Popular fiction always *displays* its ideology: in James's case that of an aesthetic based on the pleasure of avoidance of deeper symbolic meaning. There are no absences in James, no covering over problematic areas. James's oeuvre *as a whole* demands, perhaps, to be interrogated for its knowing and ironic innocence of purpose – the pleasure of frivolous entertainment. You cannot undermine the literary nature of James's work with a 'political' reading for the *subversive* and politically sophisticated reading of the modern critic is met by the ironic, bland and sophisticated refusal of any of the stories to yield to such a subversion: the tales do not open to reveal the contradictions of the bourgeois age. Consequently, political subversion is defeated by the complacency of the literary aesthetic James supported: that of a gentleman scholar, amateur stylist and belle-lettrist. If the aesthetic is a political issue and aesthetics an ideological battlefield then James's work displays a professionalism unassailable by either F.R. Leavis (a young don at the time of James's vice-chancellorship) or the numerous sub-Marxist critics whose politics diverted from Leavis's only in as much as they disagreed over the method of disturbing the complacency of the governing class and the literature that appeared to support it.

Jackson's comments imply something more. That the story without *suitable* material for the critic to work on (in order to *disrupt* the text and denaturalise the message) is less important as literature than a text which is rich with openings for sociological rather than formal comment.

David Punter in his classic account of supernatural literature takes this latter argument further. He begins, however, with the type of general observation we have already found in Jackson.

And 'Gothic' is also used in a less tendentious sense to refer to horror fiction itself, in the common form of the ghost story. Here there is a clear historical element in the usage: many of the best-known masters of recent supernatural fiction – Algernon Blackwood, M.R. James, H.P. Lovecraft – derive their techniques of suspense and their sense of the archaic directly from the original Gothic fiction, and many of their crucial symbols of the supernatural were previously the property of these older writers. This is not, of course, to say that all twentieth-century horror fiction has its roots in the Gothic: but it is remarkable how much of it does, how much it relies on themes and styles which, by rights, would seem to be more than a century out of date.[7]

Like Julie Briggs, Punter stresses the longevity of traditional elements, but again he fails to locate the specificity of the ghost tale. Hardly surprising, for neither Lovecraft nor James (if we ignore Blackwood) wrote traditional ghost stories. As I have already pointed out, James's creatures are demonic hobglobins and distinctly non-temporal. Punter continues,

Gothic has become a habit, and displays the repetitive power which habits possess. The kinds of basic fear which he exploits – fear of the archaic, the irruption of chaos into an ordered world – are precisely those of the Gothic writers, but his stories are perfected forms drained of content. They *work* well, but they *mean* almost nothing, because they are not independent: they are extended footnotes, further examples of a kind which, it is assumed, we already know. In this sense James represents a final decay of the Gothic into formalism.[8]

These acute comments by Punter are in his eyes matters for denigration with James taking the traditional gothic tale into a type of decadence or feeble dotage. However, it is these very qualities, the ones Punter so dislikes, that allow James to escape his grasp. It is these that I would argue are the important ingredients of James's success and longevity. Against James, Punter resurrects the forgotten writer David

Lindsay and his novel *The Haunted Women*. For Punter, Lindsay is a more interesting and, indeed, more important writer (even though unread) because 'one can still sense the pressure exerted on the form by the material with which it is trying to cope – issues about the relations between sexes, about the power of social convention'.[9] As with Jackson so too Punter cannot find enough contradictory material in James; there is an embarrassment of literary form over sociological content. Somehow, at the point of politicisation James's texts force an aesthetic (that is, *literary* aesthetic) response.

James's literariness was born of many influences, especially, perhaps, those most associated with the last third of the nineteenth century during which he spent his formative years in the depopulating rural world of Suffolk. The mixture of stability and crisis which characterised the Edwardian period, is hardly apparent. To an *urban* mind, it is the importance of the nostalgically *rural*, conditioned by a nascent tourism that is the central message of these tales. The destructiveness that occurs within the stories is not a manifestation of deep social crises: a fear of the countryside as alien playground of the 'other'. Not at all. These tales are all told knowing the reader *already knows* the rules of the game. The denouements, when they arrive, lift a veil on to nothing at all and are effective acts of psychic disturbance *because* they speak to an *open* and acknowledged desire. This writing is already nostalgic, for its own age, let alone a past one, the tales speak of a passing moment. But they auger nothing. P.H. Ditchfield in his *Charm of the English Village* talked of the 'charm' lent to manor houses by the residence of a friendly ghost! Indeed, such a convivial house guest guaranteed a worthwhile destination for any tourist. Ghosts added to the correct 'atmosphere': English, eccentric, rural and harmless. Essentially the appearance of apparitions and haunted houses was rapidly becoming part of the 'charm' of 'Olde England'.

> Ghosts often frequent the old houses of England, and our artist's sketch [by Sydney R. Jones] of the haunted house, Harvington Hall, Worcestershire, which looks delightfully picturesque in the moonlight, certainly suggests the appearance of a ghostly resident. ... ghosts and legends, add greatly to the charm of our old houses.[10]

James follows this 'tradition', the haunted house as 'location' and as viewpoint: the eighteenth-century concept of the picturesque and the local. James's middle-brow belles-lettres vision is itself a last ditch attempt (albeit unconscious) to avoid extra structural meaning: the sociological and psychological dimensions of modernistic professional writing. In James, the text moves towards a final irrevocable 'act', but this act, a final curtain, is an elaborate and ritualised moment, played out in haunted bedrooms, studies, libraries, mazes and ruins.

What lingers in these stories is the atmosphere of the Faustian contract, between the scholar and the demonic. Yet when hell opens it is contentless and vacuous; Count Magnus might linger at the crossroads with his familiar, but the image carries no political message. James's stories belong to modernity and the age of the tourist. Their nostalgia is urban and whimsical and complacently upper middle class in which literature is something worn lightly and passed over quickly during an idle moment. The demons of this literature are the guides to picturesque 'unspoiled' tourist *haunts*. The railway excursion, the baby Austin, the motorbike and sidecar and the hiker accompany James's prose, nostalgic for rural retreats.

Much went into the creation of these tales, but they refuse to be read as sexual, psychological or social allegories. Indeed, James once said,

Reticence may be an elderly doctrine to preach, yet from the artistic point of view I am sure it is a sound one. Reticence conduces to effect, blatancy ruins it, and there is much blatancy in a lot of recent stories. They drag in sex too, which is a fatal mistake.[11]

What these tales do is convert such areas into a literary structure: the ghost tale or tale of the supernatural. In such a conversion the terms are no longer reversible into any meaningful extra-linguistic dimension.[12] While James's tales obfuscate their endings they *display* their nature. The point of the literary structures of the tales is that nothing is hidden and there is nothing *behind* the horrors beyond hints and local gossip. There is nothing hidden except the horror in M.R. James. And the horror is doubly effective because of its unspoken origin (the horrors rarely have 'explanations'). What is left is a series of *images*, stark eldritch *displays* of the beyond which remain with the atmosphere of haunted places.

By the time James was completing his oeuvre the day of the magazine short tale was over and the ghost genre had had its day also. The mythic haunted Britain of these tales is essentially an aesthetic place – its ghosts the comfortable fiction of modernity; his 'ghosts' and goblins speak not of rapture and absence, but of what all ghosts tell us. Ghosts tell us of stability and permanence. In a world of rapid change they speak of the unchanging and the traditional: the ghost is innately conservative. The modern critic is confronted in James with a content that will not speak of its sociological beyond and a form which refuses to be handled except as literature (as formal structure): the belles-lettres essayist who writes of the paranormal: M.R. James psychic entertainer.

Notes

1. M.R. James quoted in Peter Haining ed., *M.R. James: Book of the Supernatural* (London: 1979) p. 30.
2. P.H. Ditchfield, *The Charm of the English Village* (London: (1910?) 1985) p. 1 and p. 161 facing.
3. Julie Briggs quoted in Haining, p. 19.
4. Stephen King, *Danse Macabre* (London: 1981).
5. Rosemary Jackson, *Fantasy: the Literature of Subversion* (London: 1981) p. 68.
6. Ibid., pp. 68–9.
7. David Punter, *The Literature of Terror* (London: 1980) p. 3.
8. Ibid., p. 340.
9. Ibid.
10. P.H. Ditchfield, p. 38.
11. M.R. James quoted in Haining, p. 27.
12. Rosemary Jackson's discussion of 'absences' and 'desire' is here both inaccurate and inappropriate. See Jackson, p. 3.

Part II: Fiends in the Cellar

6 Harry Price and the Haunted Rectory

Clive Bloom

I do *not* like careless talk about what you call ghosts.

Oh, Whistle, and I'll Come to You My Lad.
M.R. James

Anyone interested in haunted houses will certainly be aware of the ghost hunter Harry Price. Since his death in 1948 however his reputation as a trustworthy authority has been severely dented, most notably by Trevor H. Hall in *The Haunting of Borley Rectory* (1956) and the later biography *Search for Harry Price* (1978) in which he established Price as both a fraud and an egotist.[1] And yet, Price's name has a minor cult following and his two works about the Essex rectory in the hamlet of Borley, although sometimes out of print, are firmly established in the lists of books regularly borrowed from local public libraries. Indeed, first editions of both, '*The Most Haunted House in England*' and *The End of Borley Rectory* command high prices when they appear on the second-hand market.[2]

For those unfamiliar with the story of Borley I shall offer an outline, but let it suffice for the moment to say that the old Victorian rectory in Borley, Essex was supposed to be haunted by headless coachmen, a ghostly nun, good and evil poltergeists and many other bizarre psychic phenomena all of which finally ended in the fire that destroyed the place in 1939. My own fascination with the story began when as an adolescent I borrowed Price's two books from my local library. My sister read them too and we agreed that these were the most terrifying books we'd ever read – why? Because they were meant to be true accounts. Although we read them avidly they were never read too late at night in case they might give us nightmares. The memory and fascination remained and many years later I visited the site of the rectory with my wife when we lived not far away in the town of Colchester in Essex.

Approaching Borley is rather bleak even in good weather, the lanes have deep ditches on either side, the land is dead flat and uniform and the area depopulated. As you approach the 'village' you are reminded of the atmosphere of an M.R. James short story or of the threatening isolation of Fenchurch St Paul in Dorothy L. Sayer's *The Nine Tailors*. This is the classic landscape of East Anglia.[3]

Borley itself consists of a church, and a small number of old houses and farm buildings. It neither threatens nor welcomes and when we arrived children were playing happily in a back garden unmindful of the ghosts and supernatural occurrences that the place had become known for. Nowadays it is the church that is believed to be haunted and a group in 1979 (if my memory of an old television programme is correct) recorded spirit footsteps and whisperings near the old Waldegrave Monument. When we came on the scene there was a note pinned to the graveyard gate. It read, 'No ghost hunters after dark'. (The note, alas, no longer exists and modern bungalows cover the site of the original rectory.) In its heyday this sleepy hamlet was a stop for curious tourists and charabanc parties. On the 17 June 1929, the *Daily Mirror* reported,

> The Rectory continues to receive the unwelcome attention of hundreds of curious people, and at night the headlights of their cars may be seen for miles around. One 'enterprising' firm even ran a motor coach to the Rectory, inviting the public 'to come and see the Borley Ghost', while cases of rowdyism were frequent. (Hall)

We left after visiting the church and having failed to be accosted by a madly careering horror coach driven by headless coachmen we went home.

The unwanted visits of noisy tourists must irritate those who have to live in Borley, but for those who do visit the place it takes on the strange, isolated atmosphere of Price's books, for even though Trevor H. Hall and others have 'proved' that Price indulged in a massive hoax there is still enough of the weird left to leave the visitor with that especially enjoyable *frisson* of doubt. The place and its stories have regularly appeared in the media, on radio, on television and in the press. Paul Tabori followed Price's own autobiography with his biographical account *Harry Price: The Biography of a Ghost-Hunter* (1950) and Price's books were reprinted.[4]

By 1975 (when Price's reputation was under investigation and when the memory of Borley was fading into a cosy nostalgia for the 1920s and 1930s), *Business Travel World* could still advertise 'Psychic Research Tours', a holiday package, including Borley, organised by Enjoy Britain and the World Ltd. The cost of the eight-day holiday was £145.

The questions raised by this minor and yet controversial figure and his quest for 'life beyond the grave' are what were the motivational forces which established Price's dubious reputation and what it is in the nature of his work on Borley that makes these works classics of their kind, despite of or maybe because of their disputed status as factual documents?

Harry Price was born in 1881. The 1880s and 1890s were crucial in establishing a thriving popular and sensationalist press which was consumed by a voracious and half-educated populace. Mass readership was now catered for by a large and well-organised press machine which 'homed in' on lower-middle-class and working-class readers. The thriving newspaper industry reached its zenith when reinforced by the appearance of radio and film, stories from one medium feeding the other two. Both George Orwell and Richard Hoggart record this process. By the late 1920s Price was established as a 'psychic journalist'. For a poor boy with big ambitions and with no prospect of higher education or 'preferment', the popular press offered a direct route to 'easy' money, fame and a recognised knowledge gained through the 'university of life'. Price, like his better known journalist/author contemporaries, chose this route to fame.[5] The life he chose spanned hack journalism and an acknowledged thirst for the thrill of showmanship. The life work of Harry Price was, perhaps, the promotion of 'self' based upon increasingly unusual means.

Price claimed throughout his life that his origins were rural and his stock a decayed middle-class respectable Shropshire family. This was not so. Hall has shown that Price's origins were humble, urban and hardly respectable. Rather than coming into the world, the son of a 'well-known paper manufacturer' of Shrewsbury he was, in fact the son of Edward Ditcher Price, a commercial traveller for a London pen and ink manufacturer and one-time failed grocer. His mother, who came from Newington in South London, met his father at 14 and married him at 16 – Edward Price was 40. When his father died, he left virtually nothing. To cover these inadequacies Price began his career of deceit. In all of it, even and especially through his work on psychical research, he craved *respectability*. Ironically, the more sensational and unlikely Price behaved the more this was done to gain that respect never accorded to Price's family and never accorded by the middle classes to that invisible 'underclass' of tradespeople from whom his family hailed. Far from being the 'solicitor' he pretended to be on the marriage certificate (professional, middle-class and having a position in society) Price's maternal grandfather was, in fact, a newspaper reporter (feckless, rootless and without respectability). Hall bluntly declared 'I was dealing with a family of liars', but in this drive toward respectability there may be more to consider.

Until his marriage Price scratched a living as a 'numismatic' journalist on a Kent newspaper, a photographer of grocery shops, a manufacturer of glues and a creator of patent medicine (alongside other quacks, such as Dr Crippen: the arch example of the type of lower-middle-class rootless male we are studying). In 1908, however, Price finally found a degree of respectability in his marriage to Constance Knight, the daughter of a wealthy 'perfumer' from middle-class Brockley, a suburb of South London. His wife brought middle-class respectability and the comforts of money. After this date Price could live out his 'fantasy' version of the respectable life of a middle-class gentleman and use his fantasy to promote his own idea of becoming a household name. In this, Price combined a peripheral knowledge of advertising knowhow and commercial sense with an inbred distaste for the very money that had eluded his own family. Price's business knowledge was founded not on the 'solid' principles of engineering or paper manu-facture (as he claimed) but rather upon the fairground principles of the shyster or the wartime 'spiv'. He combined this knowledge with a deep-seated desire (I suggest) to live the life of an amateur gentleman collector – an eccentric and rather cautious investigator and collector of curiosities: a very special kind of English gentlemanly type. After his marriage, Price could indulge a spurious knowledge of archaeology (for which he was exposed), display a deceitful knowledge of numismat-ics (which he plagiarised) and gain expertise in the history of magic and legerdemain (about which he was an expert but about which he still felt the need to lie). These eccentric gentlemanly pursuits failed to bring any real reward (Price craved respectable, that is, institutional recognition). What nearly brought him what he wanted was psychical research.

One important factor in Price's story is his constant need to 'rewrite' his own history or to write in episodes at points that elsewhere he had included as occurring at another time or place. Hall points out at least two of these incidents. Without a strong sense of his own 'reality' or perhaps oppressed by too much of this reality, Price created the history of his life as it suited him. In this he became, not a commercial failure and an impossibly ill-educated drifter, but a lively, creative, middle-class boy with leanings towards engineering and the knowledge that he would inherit his father's business in Shrewsbury.

One incident recorded as true in his autobiography (and investigated by Hall and proved totally false!) was the visit Price 'witnessed' as an eight-year-old boy in the market place in Shrewsbury. Here 'the Great Sequah' put on his medicine show. The show may or may not have occurred and Price probably did not witness it (although a 'Sequah' was actually an American called Hartley who came to Britain, Price may have seen the show in London). It is of great interest to us to find out why Price felt an especial need to record the effect of the incident in his life. It appears to have had a direct effect on Price's psychological growth – yet as a 'fictional' memory in his autobiography it also seems to serve to *justify* the darker side of Price's psychic makeup: the master showman, flamboyant, American, magical and charismatic. We are told,

One cold January morning the 'Great Sequah', with his brass bands, gilded chariots, and troop of 'boosters' in the garb of Mohawk Indians, pitched his tent – so to speak – in Shrewsbury's principal square. ... During the whole of this eventful morning I stood, cold but happy, open-mouthed at this display of credulity, self-deception, auto-suggestion, faith-healing, beautiful showmanship, super-charlatanism, and 'magic'. The miracles of the market-place left me spellbound.

What is important here is the recording of 'miracles' and the knowledge of 'credulity' and 'self-deception'. The ambivalence is important – Price both 'knew' and did *not* know about his deceptive schizoid nature: a nature well placed to create two of the 'greatest' books on psychical investigation, themselves a mixture of miracles and self-deception. Here, Price became both 'Sequah' (to whom he added the revealing epithet 'Great') and the sceptical, aloof investigator. The description of the 'Great Sequah' which mixes, in the same paragraph, real astonishment at the 'truly' magical and a knowledge that this is all the product of a 'cheat' describes and reveals the Harry Price that Price himself would not have recognised. That which left him 'spellbound' happened in 'the market-place' (the proper place of a tradesman's son?) is, perhaps, also revealing of the important relationship that the modern supernatural has with capitalism and consumerism. In the 'projected' figure of the 'Great Sequah', Price accomplished the fantasy of the gentleman collector (this was the moment Price became interested in magic) and the fantasy of the charismatic showman.

And this *dual* fantasy was worked upon all Price's life, not least in his gentleman's library with its 'fake' bookplates and its air of antiquarianism, but also in his association with psychic extravaganzas. The first instance was Price's opening (accompanied by national publicity) of the sealed 'box' of the religious fanatic Joanna Southcott (who had died in 1814). Needless to say, the box, which was meant to contain items useful during a national emergency, contained nothing of interest. The second incident, which was played out to an international audience was the attempt to raise the devil in 1932 in the Hartz Mountains. The devil failed to materialise. In both these instances, and through the creation of the National Laboratory of Psychical Research, Price hoped to establish his credentials as a 'scientific' investigator: one worthy of respect among academics. On the Brocken Mountain, Price had had Dr C.E.M. Joad with him, and in the investigation into the haunting of Borley a group of undergraduates from Cambridge had conducted experiments into the phenomena there. Price always hoped for a university chair, honorary doctorate and university department. He donated his collection of work on magic to the University of

London, but he was deprived of what he considered his right: a department of psychical research. What emerges through these exploits, is the curious way Price's life becomes a lived fiction and the overriding *social* (that is *socialised*) unconscious of the man and his need, at almost any cost, to project a *public* persona.

In turning to Price's best-known works, it is necessary to fill in the story of Borley as it is narrated in '*The Most Haunted House in England*' and *The End of Borley Rectory*. The narrative covers a series of bizarre supernatural occurrences that had persisted from the late nineteenth century until the Second World War. The 'plot' consists of Price's investigation into these occurrences from his initial acquaintance with the case in 1929 to the early 1940s. Through ghostly visitations, poltergeist activity, spontaneous 'spirit' writing and planchette sessions, a story emerges of kidnap, murder and secrecy: a story either of a love affair between a nun and a monk which ended in tragedy or (more plausibly, at least in terms of the 'evidence') a love affair between the lord of the manor and a French 'nun' during the seventeenth century which ended, somewhat obscurely, with a 'rape' and 'murder' and three centuries of secrecy. Included within this double narrative (which forms the detective thriller part of the two books) is another tale of the eccentric clerics and their families who occupied the rectory since the time of Henry Bull in the late nineteenth century. Both books consist of collected reports and anecdotes interlaced with possible explanations offered by Price's correspondents and fellow investigators, and the atmosphere of both books is that of the detective at his trade, indeed, Price says he was asked to 'take charge of the case' (*MHHE*).

From the miscellaneous anecdotes and reports that emerge the reader is quickly immersed in a story in which the laws of nature seem horribly in abeyance – the atmosphere is at once sinister and fascinating. Some examples of incidents from the many that are offered will give the reader a feeling for the books. One occupant, 'awoke suddenly and found an old man in dark, old fashioned clothes, wearing a tall hat, standing by her bed. On another occasion, the same figure was seen sitting on the bed' (*MHHE*). 'One early morning in 1919 [other occupants of the rectory cottage] ... saw a black shape, in the form of a little man, running round their bedroom' (*MHHE*). Another occupant, Mr Foyster, recorded in his diary numerous poltergeist phenomena, including violent attacks on his wife, who psychically attracted 'spirit' messages on the walls! Price listed some of the phenomena:

> The phenomena our observers were able to confirm included footsteps and similar sounds; raps, taps and knockings; displacement of objects; 'clicks' and 'cracks'; sounds as of a door closing; knocks, bumps, thuds, jumping or stamping; dragging noise; wailing sounds; rustling or scrabbling noises; 'metallic' sounds; crashing, as of

crockery falling; wall-pencillings; 'appearance' of objects; luminous phenomenon; odours, pleasant and unpleasant; sensation of coldness; tactual phenomena; sensation of a 'presence'; and a fulfilled prediction. One observer says she saw the 'nun'. (*MHHE*)

Finally a planchette message revealed that *Sunex Amures* would burn down the house and this sinister entity finally fulfilled his promise (*MHHE*). All of these strange activities centred on the fate of the spirit of the 'nun' and indeed certain unidentified human bones are finally found in the cellar. The nun emerges during the story as, 'a Mary Lairre ... a French girl of nineteen years of age, who was a novice in a nunnery at Havre, ... and was murdered (strangled) by 'Waldegrave' on May 17, 1667' (*EBR*).

Both books end on a disturbing note of inconclusiveness. Even after the destruction of the rectory the weird phenomena continued and just as Price is ready to leave Borley for good he finds on a photograph of the ruins, the distinct outline of half a brick floating in mid air!

What makes a good ghost story? Price's story of Borley seems to contain the definitive recipe: a coach and *headless* horseman; a ghostly nun who walks the grounds (waiting for her lover?); an old, decayed and isolated rectory (without electricity and with deep, dark and damp cellars that hold a terrible secret); psychic occupants (Marianne Foyster); bizarre occurrences (the appearance of a monster insect in one episode and of an old coat in another); bells that ring without human agency; messages from the dead (via suburban planchette readings); a legendary past (of monasteries and nunneries and a secret tunnel); flying bricks, vanishing and reappearing household utensils and 'apports' (a French medallion and a gold wedding ring). All this on what appears an almost daily basis taking place in and around a 'cold' spot outside 'the Blue Room'. In every respect the case was sensational. Into this sensational setting steps the one person able, like Holmes, to put the thing into perspective: the ghost hunter.

In case the reader may wish to know what a psychic investigator takes with him when engaged on an important case, I will enumerate some of the items included in a ghost-hunter's kit.

Into a large suitcase are packed the following articles: A pair of soft felt overshoes used for creeping, unheard, about the house in order that neither human beings nor paranormal 'entities' shall be disturbed when producing 'phenomena'; steel measuring tape for measuring rooms, passages, testing the thickness of walls in looking for secret chambers or hidey-holes; steel screw-eyes, lead post-office seals, sealing tool, strong cord or tape, and adhesive surgical tape, for sealing doors, windows or cupboards; a set of tools, with wire, nails, etc.; hank of electric flex, small electric bells, dry batteries and switches (for secret electrical contacts); 9cm. by 12cm. reflex camera, film-packs and flash-bulbs for indoor or outdoor photography; a small portable telephone for communicating with assistant in another part of building or garden; note book, red, blue and black pencils; sketching block and case of drawing instruments for making plans; bandages, iodine and a flask of brandy in case member of investigating staff or resident is injured or faints; ball of string, stick of chalk, matches, electric torch and candle; bowl of mercury for detecting tremors in room or passage or for making silent electrical mercury switches; cinematograph camera with remote electrical control, and films; a sensitive transmitting thermometer [etc, etc]. (*MHHE*)

From all this it emerges that the ghost hunter combines the qualities of a Sherlock Holmes, a master spy and a boy scout – he is both a psychic adventurer and a rather well equipped camper (of the 'Famous Five' type). One is irresistibly reminded of this quality of adventure (a cross between E. Phillips Oppenheim and Edgar Wallace) when, after his last visit Price tells us 'although I have investigated many haunted houses, before and since, never have such phenomena so impressed me as they did on this historic day. Sixteen hours of thrills!' (*MHHE*). However, Price combined these elements of the psychic thriller in order to reinforce the message of respectability he wanted to convey. In the second of the two works, *The End of Borley Rectory*, Price brings his narrative to a halt with the repeated, yet contradictory assertions that, firstly science cannot explain everything and secondly it will be able to explain psychic phenomena.

Price's second book ends with quotations linking supernatural phenomena with the laws of thermodynamics (*EBR*), atomic energy (*EBR*) and abnormal psychology (*EBR*). Yet he does not quite end there, for the last chapter presents the evidence of the two books as it was a murder trial and Price 'proves' the strength and coherence of his arguments in a 'literary' court of law. Despite Price's desire for his evidence to be taken seriously, it is entirely based on anecdotes, 'faked' experimental conditions, legend, clairvoyancy and planchette readings. Every time historical accuracy is invoked the text suppresses it.[6] Thus, because 'hard' evidence cannot be found in the records there must have been either a conspiracy to suppress the truth or all evidence was accidentally removed or erased. In every case, the evidence of history and of archaeology is suppressed in favour of the logic of numerous clairvoyant messages and the selection of evidence to fit certain 'physical' phenomena that were reported.

Did these weird events occur? In one sense, there is no need to ask the question in the terms posed by a cultural historian. Our question is why did they occur *when* they occurred and to *whom*. On another level, that of plain fact, rather than perceptual qualification, there are enough clues in the text to suggest that many of the events were possibly 'staged', that some did not occur, that others could be put down to natural phenomena. The way they are *all* placed in one universe suggests a tenuous relationship cemented not by fact but by the fiction of the planchette. These random events are then given a shape by equally random and *variable* planchette messages (even Price agreed that so much was dictated this way that the sitters needed wallpaper rolls) and much of what Price reprints has no basis in anything that *can be checked*. If these are ghosts, then, perhaps they are the ghosts of cultural necessity? Moreover, the way Price constructed his story by claiming for himself only an 'editorial' role (*MHHE*) makes it difficult to see when certain events happened historically and if they really were recorded outside Price's control. Even he admitted that most people left the rectory through natural reasons and not through terrorisation.

What as cultural phenomena do the events of Borley and the status of Price's two books represent? Elsewhere, I have considered this relationship between the sensational and the respectable: that odd mixture of the inexplicable and supernatural and the organised and the social. For want of a better definition I have characterised this attitude as essentially 'lower middle class', a perceptual framework exemplified by, but not specific to, those elements of society on the ragged edge of class division. Here, I am keen to insist that 'class' represents a perceptual space inhabited by a whole spectrum of society and not wholly confined to income. This space is the space of the *disinherited*, culturally and economically. Typically, this is why popular fictions and alternative 'sciences' interest the intellectual and artistic classes as well as those who count themselves bereft of an education. At this period, prior to the Second World War, it is an attitude that is shared by the likes of W.B. Yeats, George Yeats, AE and the circle of the Golden Dawn, as well as the Society For Psychical Research and the 'ordinary' housewife in 'Alma', 'Coronation' or 'Balaclava' villas (or any such decayed suburb) who regularly visited a medium, read the tea leaves or attended a spiritualist meeting to be greeted by her long lost husband with a 'message'. T.S. Eliot satirised these attitudes with 'Madame Sosostris' in 'The Wasteland'.

Because Price appealed to an essentially suburban and southern audience (I suggest) his work should be seen against a background of rapid technological growth, suburban expansion and material progress. In the wealthy home counties of the late 1920s and 1930s (so different from the depressed north), the signs of material advancement could not be ignored. Against this a sense of *disorientation* among certain sectors would lead to the usual vacuum in spiritual needs for which Price's work would provide an ideal panacea: the phenomena (at Borley) could not be explained by science (materialism) but they demonstrated through relevance to the theological backwater of survival after death, that *there was* an explanation and an order which organised, and could not be controlled by, earthly powers.

In an age characterised by the 'mass' and by mass means of control (radio (*EBR*), the loud speaker, the factory floor production line), an age in which commentators noted the 'loss' of individual control and sense of hope (see John Betjeman's 'Slough' or W.H. Auden's 'The Unknown Citizen'), and an age in which bureaucracy and state control appeared unstoppable (and welcome, see Aldous Huxley's *Brave New World*) the 'ordinary' person could be comforted by a non-material explanation of circumstances. Borley's ghosts with their doctrine of survival suggested that one could exist (if only after death!) and preserve one's individualism (if only eccentrically as a 'nun' or 'headless' coachman) and willingly *submit* to an *authority* beyond oneself (via planchette messages). This is the best of both worlds, a theory of compensation that allowed the individual the freedom to be themself only if that selfhood had been granted by the authority of an agency outside the self. I am *not* suggesting (given the period) that Price's work acts as an analogue to the rise of fascism, indeed, given its essential Englishness and normalcy (a story of eccentric rectors in a corner of idyllic Essex) it would seem it acts as a 'mythic' compensation for the uncontrollable nature of world events.[7] The story begins in 1929 and ends during the Second World War. Throughout the narrative, Price insists the events of Borley are a type of 'sign' of other worldliness (a prolonged miracle) that demands explanation. Borley itself is seen as of national importance, little less than a piece of English heritage.

> Borley Rectory stands by itself in the literature of psychical manifestation. Wisely discarding theories of causation (which in these matters are little better than conjecture), the author, Mr Harry Price, sets out to prove by the cumulative evidence of eye-witnesses – recorded in a form which would be admissible in evidence in any court of law – the happening of events at Borley Rectory which it is impossible to explain by the operation of natural law.
>
> The large number of the public who are interested in these things are under a debt of gratitude to him, for without his untiring energy and skilled experience as an investigator, a fascinating chapter in the history of psychical research would have been lost to the world. (*EBR*)

In the end Harry Price never got his department at a university and never became Chair Professor of Parapsychology. For us Borley exists as merely a nostalgic memory, its site left unmarked except for the cryptic sign that once was nailed to the church gate. Ultimately, Price was a materialist who felt (genuinely?) that the domain of science could be widened to include occult subject matter. Despite the 'evidence' at

Borley, the sensational could not be normalised into scientific experience and it remained both peripheral and trivial. A collector of books on magic tricks and a dabbler in the sensational, Price could not reconcile the sensational and the respectable any more than he could reconcile the supernatural and the temporal. For us, Price's life and his two major works represent an excursion into the forgotten, the trivial and the disenfranchised.

Notes

1. Trevor H. Hall, E.J. Dingwall and K.M. Goldney, *The Haunting of Borley Rectory: A Critical Survey of the Evidence* (London: 1956); Trevor H. Hall, *Search For Harry Price* (London: 1978). All biographical details of Harry Price's life from Hall unless otherwise stated.
2. Harry Price, 'The Most Haunted House in England' (Bath: (1940) 1990) hereinafter referred to as *MHHE*; *The End of Borley Rectory* (Bath: (1946) 1980) hereinafter referred to as *EBR*.
3. Belchamp St Paul appears in 'Count Magnus' by M.R. James, in *Casting the Runes and Other Ghost Stories* (Oxford 1987).
4. Paul Tabori, *Harry Price: The Biography of a Ghost-Hunter* (1950).
5. See my essay, 'West is East: Nayland Smith's Sinophobia and Sax Rohmer's Bank Balance' in Clive Bloom ed., *Twentieth-Century Suspense: The Thriller Comes of Age* (London: 1990) pp. 22–36.
6. See Hall ch. 7 and ch. 9.
7. See Price's chronology, *EBR* p. 335.

7 Not like Men in Books, Murdering Women: Daphne du Maurier and the Infernal World of Popular Fiction

Nicholas Rance

In *Reading the Romance*, Janice Radway recalls a time of recession in American fiction. Not surprisingly, they looked about for an alternative source of income. As Janice Radway recounts:

> Gerald Cross at Ace books recalled the consistent reprint success of Daphne du Maurier's *Rebecca*. Wondering whether its long-standing popularity ... indicated that it struck a universal chord in female readers, he attempted to locate previously published titles resembling du Maurier's novel, which he hoped to issue in a 'gothic' series.[1]

This speculation in extrapolating the taste of the reading public or that of the female-reading public was a success. Cross chose *Thunder Heights*, by Phyllis Whitney, as the inaugural title in his 'gothic' line, and Phyllis Whitney shared a literary agent with Victoria Holt, whose *Mistress of Mellyn* sold more than a million copies with Doubleday. 'When other publishers caught on, the boom in gothic sales began.'[2]

Published in 1938, *Rebecca* went into thirty-nine impressions over the next twenty years and was translated into twenty languages. As one of those books cited in *I'll Never Be Young Again* in which men murder women, *Rebecca* has an affinity with the tradition in popular fiction of a paranoid conservatism about women, illustrated by many of the texts of writers such as Bram Stoker, Arthur Conan Doyle and John Buchan. How, then, was such an appeal exerted within a sub-genre of popular fiction, romance, whose readers are nearly all women? There is a relatively placid reading of *Rebecca*, according to which the unnamed heroine, Max de Winter's quietly dependable second wife, triumphs over the memory of her predecessor's wickedness and helps Max to a new and better life. The heroine would then be in roughly the position of Mimi Watford in *The Lair of the White Worm*, which will cheer female readers who are content to be soft and shy like Mimi, and leave sex and excitement to such as Lady Arabella or Rebecca. Alison Light, however, has asserted to the contrary that 'in pursuing Rebecca the girl has identified with her as a positive alternative to herself'.[3] This is a reading which is liable to be more alluring and also one which is hard to eschew. The thesis of a slightly earlier discussion of the novel depends on maintaining that the second wife 'makes no demands to be liberated – she is content to be the domestic half of the monogamous couple'.[4] In *Rebecca*, the heroine breaks 'a little china cupid', as she tries to instal her sister-in-law's wedding present, four volumes on art, in the morning room. If the destruction of the cupid might seem symbolically to distinguish the heroine from the libidinous Rebecca, the heroine's next move does not. The cupid or its fragments are not banished but merely secreted or repressed.

> I glanced hurriedly at the door, like a guilty child. I knelt on the floor and swept up the pieces into my hand. I found an envelope to put them in. I hid the envelope at the back of one of the drawers in the desk.[5]

For Roger Bromley, the heroine is 'thus repressing and sublimating the erotic symbol of Rebecca', but sublimation is not in evidence.[6]

Perhaps the essence of the appeal of *Rebecca* is that the novel may be read in either way, as mood dictates. If the bowdlerised interpretation shows signs of strain as formulated in a critical essay, there will not be an equivalent problem for ordinary readers. Moreover, the author as reader seems to have shown the way. In *Rebecca*, the heroine's libidinous tendencies and the threat which they pose are repressed, to be merely obliquely acknowledged in an overtly gratuitous childlessness. The complexity of Daphne du Maurier's 'I' is the less surprising given the textual and biographical evidence of an authorial identification with the heroine. Though the name of the heroine is withheld, we gather that it is an exotic one. She is complimented by Maxim on having 'a very lovely and unusual name', and replies that her 'father was a lovely and unusual person', which Daphne du Maurier might easily have said of her father, Gerald du Maurier, the eminent actor.[7] According to a recent sketch of Daphne du Maurier and her career, by Martyn Shallcross, the cast of Hitchcock's film, *Rebecca*, referred to the heroine as 'Daphne', which is certainly less of a tongue-twister than 'I' de Winter.[8] Daphne du Maurier told Shallcross that she had thought of her husband's former fiancée, 'a strikingly beautiful débutante', as the heroine thinks of Rebecca.[9] This would implicate her husband (who as Lieutenant-General Frederick Browning in 1944 was to coin the phrase, 'A Bridge Too Far'), as being the inspiration for Maxim, and Shallcross points out that the revolver with which Maxim shoots Rebecca 'is a military one, a Smith and Wesson'.[10] Such a degree of involvement by Daphne du Maurier with her heroine did not preclude an anodyne summary of the plot of *Rebecca* in her autobiography, *Myself When Young: The Shaping of a Writer*. She has referred to self-reliance as more or less a characteristic of the three female narrators in her fiction: 'The only timid one of the trio was the nameless heroine in *Rebecca*, and she found strength of purpose when she discovered that her husband Maxim truly loved her, and had never cared for his first wife Rebecca.'[11]

In fiction published by Mills and Boon, the heroine's battle to see off her vampish rival complements her main mission of eliciting tenderness from the desired male. In one romance published in 1989, the heroine, Jess, has nursed her own Max, in this case Max Beaumont, injured by the skittish stallion which she has imprudently allowed in proximity to the mare. Jess is then able to show that there is a side to her nature apart from nursing and nurturing by riding in Max's stead in the race.

> Leaning forward in her seat, she urged Cloud on. It was as if she and Nina were the only competitors in the race. In one respect, that was true. They were competing against one another in a personal, private race, and the prize was not a silver cup, it was a man.[12]

In *Rebecca*, however, the heroine's victory is a Phyrric one. It is not so much a matter of the destruction of Manderley, which might merely signal the demise of an aristocratic lifestyle which may no longer be sustained, with the heroine embodying and promising a more rooted if less elevated future. This is one way in which the novel has been interpreted, within a historical context of aristocratic compromise and stooping to class alliances in the era from the National Government in the 1930s to the Conservative Government under Harold Macmillan in the late 1950s and early 1960s: *Rebecca* is held to appeal to the common reader as a fable of the aristocracy having to make such common cause.[13] However, the confounding of distinctions of rank in Rebecca is not suggestive of a new dawn. Conventionally in fiction, young children or the promise of young children are a token of the parents being in step with the future. Max de Winter consoles the heroine by invoking the prospect of children: 'We'll start again, once this thing is behind us. We can do it, you and I. It's not like being alone. The past can't hurt us if we are together. You'll have children too.'[14] The story is narrated in retrospect by a now almost middle-aged heroine, and there are no children in evidence. She and Max lead a life hardly conducive to parenthood, existing abroad in a series of skimpy hotels and being rescued from *ennui* by cricket broadcasts. The heroine's incapacity to conceive associates her with her alleged opposite, Rebecca, with her 'malformation of the uterus'.

If the commercial success of *Rebecca* prompted the revival in the mid-twentieth century of 'female gothic' as a popular sub-genre, Daphne du Maurier was herself inspired by the original 'female gothic' of Mrs Radcliffe. The presiding fear in gothic fiction, at least until Mary Shelley's *Frankenstein* with modern and futuristic anxieties and forebodings, is of the return of a malign past. In the fiction of Mrs Radcliffe, the medieval castle refuses to lapse into a mere picturesque ruin: the ghost haunting the castle is a past which will not accept being dead. There may be displacement at work here, which perhaps constituted the nub of the appeal to readers: in the era of the French Revolution, it would seem eccentric to focus anxiety on the possible return of feudalism. That, however, is the relatively comfortable option which Mrs Radcliffe's fiction allows, and as has often been noted, the cursory rationalism in conclusion which puts the ghosts to flight barely dispels the mood of paranoia about a possibly intruding past.

In *Rebecca*, the overtly optimistic conclusion is as fragile and tenuous as in Mrs Radcliffe's fiction. The power exerted by the past and Rebecca is not readily to be dispelled. Interpolated into the dream of Manderley with which the novel begins are narratorial attempts at Radcliffe-like cheer: 'The house was a sepulchre, our fear and suffering lay buried in the ruins. There would be no resurrection.'[15] But the dream itself, the retrospective of Manderley, exemplifies the pull of the past. The housekeeper, Mrs Danvers, has prophesied: 'You'll never get the better of her. She's still mistress here, even if she is dead. She's the real Mrs de Winter, not you. It's you that's the shadow and the ghost.'[16]

It is worth noting how the conception of *Rebecca* was modified or altered in the progress from the chapter plans and snatches of dialogue in Daphne du Maurier's 'Rebecca Notebook', and the apparently final draft of what was to have been the 'epilogue', to the published version of the novel. In the 'epilogue', Henry, as Max then was, has been wracked by contrition or at least remorse.

> We shall never live in England again, that much is certain. The past would be too close to us. Those things we are trying to forget and put behind us would stir again, and that sense of fear, of furtive unrest struggling at length to master unreasoning panic – now mercifully stilled, thank God – might in some manner unforeseen become a living companion, as it did before. We are not unhappy, that I would impress upon you. Henry at least knows something of the peace of God, which, poor darling, he never possessed before.[17]

In the published version, where the material which was to have constituted the epilogue is incorporated into the opening chapter, Max's malaise is much less specified. The only positive or more properly negative guidance is Max's comment: 'I'm glad I killed Rebecca. I shall never have any remorse for that, never, never.'[18]

In the original conception, Henry was to have been injured in a car crash. This would have been the dramatic climax, preceding the 'epilogue', rather than Manderley on fire in the novel as published.

Perhaps Rebecca will have the last word yet. The road narrows before the avenue. A car with blazing lights passed. Henry swerved to avoid it, and it came at us, rearing out of the ground, its huge arms outstretched to embrace us, crashing and splintering above our heads.[19]

The second 'it' in the last sentence is evidently not the car but a tree, but also somehow a conduit of the natural force of Rebecca herself, since the tree, not alluded to as such in what is admittedly a skimpy rough draft, has 'huge arms' with which to 'embrace' its victims. Even with Rebecca compounding her demonic reputation by metamorphosing into a tree, there has to be a hint here of providential retribution: this is what happens if you murder even bad women, and is in keeping with Henry's remorse in the 'epilogue'. The conclusion to the published novel points in a different direction, since Manderley on fire epitomises the havoc which unlicensed female passion will wreak on the great house. There is a lack of focus which is typical of *Rebecca* on details of plot which might distract from the symbolic effect. perversely devoted to Rebecca, Mrs Danvers has decamped, and the reader is free to presume that she has set the house on fire as a parting gift, but such a presumption is not confirmed.

Playing on the lewd connotations of 'salt', the concluding sentence of the novel abstains from safely relegating the consequences of female licentiousness to the past: 'And the ashes blew towards us with the salt wind from the sea.'[20] In what was to have been the epilogue, there is overt reference to the heroine's childlessness, implied to be attributable to injuries sustained by Henry, in particular, in the car crash: there is allusion to 'his maimed body and my disfigurement'.[21] Missing from the novel as published, along with the suggestion of providential retribution for killing Rebecca, is the Rochester-like fate which overtakes Henry, or Maxim as he becomes. Thus the heroine's childlessness is not naturalised: neither, however, any more than Rebecca's 'malformation of the uterus', is such a curse gratuitous.

Rebecca and the heroine are suggested to be mirror-images of one another: this justifies the gothic foreboding about the recurrence of the past. First-person narration is sometimes held to be peculiarly reassuring: in *Rebecca*, as the argument might run, the nameless heroine has her identity encapsulated the more resonantly in the simple first-person singular, the securely delimited 'I', with the connotations of free will

and autonomy informing the bourgeois sense of self. However, Roland
Barthes has enthused over *The Murder of Roger Ackroyd*, by Agatha
Christie (with whom in the 1950s Daphne du Maurier became friendly
and discussed plots and characters), in which customary notions of the
self are confounded by the revelation of exotic depths in the first-person
narrator, Dr Shepherd, who is revealed as the murderer: 'The reader
looked for him behind every "he" in the plot: he was all the time hidden
under the "I".'[22]

Rebecca is in part a detective story. Like that of Godwin's Caleb
Williams, with whom surveys of detective fiction often begin, the
heroine's distinguishing trait is curiosity, and as in 'Genesis', *Paradise
Lost* and Freudian psychoanalysis, the paradigm of curiosity is sexual
curiosity.

> Somewhere, at the back of my mind, there was a frightened furtive
> seed of curiosity that grew slowly and stealthily, for all my denial of
> it, and I knew all the doubt and anxiety of the child who has been
> told, 'these things are not discussed, they are forbidden'.[23]

Mirrors are significant in the mythology of vampires, since one
way to identify a vampire is to note that the suspect casts no reflection
in a mirror: in such a case, the detective looks into the mirror and sees
merely – himself. In *Rebecca*, the heroine has a day-dream and then an
actual dream which are disquieting in rather this way. She looks into
a mirror and sees not her own image but Rebecca's, which is thereby
somehow her own image. In the day-dream which the heroine indulges
about the dead Rebecca returning to her bedroom, the two personalities are yet respectably distinct, 'if she sat there I should see her
reflection in the glass and she would see me too, standing like this by
the door'.[24] In the concluding episode of the novel, as Manderley
burns, symbol both of Rebecca's eroticism and of its inherent tendency,
the heroine has a dream in the approaching car.

> I got up and went to the looking-glass. A face stared back at me that
> was not my own. ... And I saw then that she was sitting on a chair
> before the dressing-table in her bedroom, and Maxim was brushing
> her hair. He held her hair in his hands, and as he brushed it he wound
> it slowly into a thick rope. It twisted like a snake, and he took hold
> of it with both hands and smiled at Rebecca and put it round his
> neck.[25]

In a traditional reversal, the woman is credited with snake-like
qualities for arousing the snake in man. Here, a proper apartness
between the heroine and Rebecca has been dissipated: after the initial
confusion, the heroine does not re-emerge as a separate entity from

Rebecca. Included in the collection, *The Rebecca Notebook and Other Memories*, is an essay, 'This I Believe', written in the mid-1960s. Daphne du Maurier ponders the paradox that 'Each one of us is Perseus, who, cutting off Medusa's head, saw her reflection in the mirror and recognised himself.'[26]

Rebecca is necessarily a figure of melodrama: it would be polite to call her an enigma. According to Maxim, she 'was vicious, damnable, rotten through and through'. On the other hand, she was 'damnably clever. No one would guess meeting her that she was not the kindest, most generous, most gifted person in the world.'[27] The character is constructed by an idiosyncratic male logic. 'Damnably clever' women are liable to challenge patriarchy, which may be ascribed to viciousness. But the appearance of kindness and generosity is a nod in the direction of acknowledging that such an explanation may not be all-sufficient. The choice of the name of Rebecca is calculated to evoke a complex of feeling: strong-minded women, role-swapping, murder, social upheaval. The agrarian riots in Wales in the 1840s were christened the 'Rebecca Riots', 'the strangest series of riots that has occurred in our time', according to Harriet Martineau, who also remarked that 'from the time that Chartist emissaries directed Rebecca's movements nothing went well with her'.[28] The riots were an uprising of small farmers, who always moved by night, nearly always blackened their faces, and frequently dressed in women's clothes. One Thomas Rees was temporarily assumed to be a leading spirit: 'it is said that there had been difficulty in finding women's clothes large enough to fit him until he succeeded in borrowing those of Big Rebecca.'[29] *The Times* accused ministers of preaching on the text: 'And they blessed Rebekah and said unto her ... let thy seed possess the gates of those which hate them' (Gen. xxiv, 60).[30] This is perhaps suggestively close to Rebecca's threat to Maxim, which induces him to kill her, to produce an heir to Manderley who has been fathered by one of her lovers. If the Welsh rioters masqueraded as female, Rebecca alarmingly reverses the process: as Maxim recalls of her at the time of her death. 'She looked like a boy in her sailing kit, a boy with a face like a Botticelli angel.'[31]

A notable preceding fictional Rebecca was the Jewess in Sir Walter Scott's *Ivanhoe*, published in 1819. There is some emphasis on Daphne du Maurier's Rebecca's dark looks: 'her mass of dark hair, standing out from her face like a halo', 'her black hair blowing in the wind'.[32] Not surprisingly, Scott's Rebecca has 'black locks'.[33] The Saxon maid, Rowena, is strictly the heroine of *Ivanhoe*, and wins the eponymous hero's heart: Rebecca cannot compete because of her race, but is more impressive. She is 'of a strong and observing character', an 'apt and powerful mind'.[34] Unlike her successor, Scott's Rebecca deploys her strength in defence of her virtue, as she is pursued and harried by the rogue-templar, Brian de Bois-Gilbert. *Ivanhoe* is then intriguing as a

forbear since its own Rebecca is maliciously demonised in construct-
ing a defence for the would-be rapist.

> If we were told that such a man, so honoured, and so honourable,
> suddenly casting away regard for his character, his vows, his brethren,
> and his prospects, had associated to himself a Jewish damsel,
> wandered in this lewd company through solitary places, defended
> her person in preference to his own, and, finally, was so utterly
> blinded and besotted by his folly, as to bring her even to one of our
> own preceptories, what should we say but that the noble knight was
> possessed by some evil demon, or influenced by some wicked spell?[35]

For Scott, however, relative liberation is compatible with virtue,
and Rebecca is not a demon.

One would guess that the most conscious influence on *Rebecca* was
Ibsen's play, *Rosmersholm*. 'If you want my opinion, miss, it's the dead
who cling to Rosmersholm', remarks the housekeeper, Mrs Helspeth,
to Ibsen's Rebecca West.[36] This Rebecca, of humble origins like the
heroine of Daphne du Maurier's novel, and a guest at Rosmersholm,
has encouraged Rosmer's wife, Beata, to think that her husband and
the visitor are having an affair. Beata obligingly plunges into the mill-
race. This is before the action of the play begins. Rebecca West is then
inhibited from pursuing her design to marry Rosmer, and an analysis
of Ibsen's play by Freud persuasively links the inhibition with guilt about
incest. Inadvertently if carelessly, Rebecca West has already displaced
her dead mother by sleeping with her father. Moved to a half-confession
by guilt, she is also prevented from displacing the dead Beata as the
wife of Rosmer, sufficiently her senior to be a father-figure, as Maxim
is sufficiently senior to the heroine of *Rebecca*: the section of the essay,
'Some Character-Types Met With in Psychoanalytic Work', in which
Freud discusses *Rosmersholm*, is called, 'Those wrecked by success'.[37]
Rebecca West and Rosmer then themselves resort to the mill-race: no
more than Maxim in Daphne du Maurier's novel does Rebecca West
prosper from removing a wife.

In Daphne du Maurier's reworking of Ibsen's plot, the name of
Rebecca is bestowed on the lustful wife (for which *Rosmersholm* provides
a hint: there is a rather casual accrediting to Beata of 'uncontrollable,
sick fits of sensuality').[38] The heroine is in Rebecca West's role of
intruder and rival to the wife. What is intended, presumably, is a
tamed version of *Rosmersholm*: the lustful wife is judiciously executed
by a male rather than dispatched by yet another errant female.
Moreover, unlike Rebecca West and by virtue of the transference of the
fleshly sins of the intruder as well as her name to the wife, the heroine
of Daphne du Maurier's *Rebecca* is designed to testify that not all
females are errant. If there is a return of the repressed in the character

of Rebecca West, however, as Freud suggests, a similar fate overtakes Daphne du Maurier's novel, in which the common origin in the one character of Rebecca and the heroine returns to besmirch the purportedly demure heroine.

In *My Cousin Rachel*, published in 1951, Rachel is promiscuous, responding to a proposal of marriage by conceding a one-night stand ('She had not understood what it was I asked of her at midnight'), and, as if following her proclivity to a logical conclusion, a murderess.[39] This would seem to be so at least until the doubt raised in the concluding pages, by when it is too late in the day to read the novel as being merely about male fantasies of murderous women. Rachel's opposite, Louise, is strictly the good girl and cipher who waits. Thus the reader is comprehensively distanced from countenancing female sexuality.

My Cousin Rachel was a conservative rendering of *Rebecca*; *Frenchman's Creek* has claims to have been a more provocative one. In the novel, published in 1941 and next after *Rebecca*, Lady Dona deserts house and husband in London for Cornwall and a night of passion with a French pirate. 'A heroine who is bound to make thousands of friends in spite of her somewhat questionable behaviour', commented a reviewer in the *Sunday Times*.[40] Daphne du Maurier's so far latest biographer, Judith Cook, remarks that 'reviewers in Britain were non-committal and the book did not have the success of *Rebecca*, although it has remained a firm favourite with readers'.[41] As in *Rebecca*, there are surprises in mirrors.

> She had consented to be the Dona her world had demanded – a superficial, lovely creature, who walked, and talked, and laughed, accepting praise and admiration with a shrug of the shoulder as natural homage to her beauty, careless, insolent, deliberately indifferent, and all the while another Dona, a strange, phantom Dona, peered at her from a dark mirror and was ashamed.[42]

The fling with the pirate follows, who proves himself a philosopher of sorts: 'women are more primitive than men. For a time they will wander, yes, and play at love, and play at adventure. And then, like the birds do, they must make their nest. Instinct is too strong for them.'[43] Licensing primitives occasionally overreaching themselves by playing at love outside marriage, and consigning domestic virtue to the realm of the merely primitive, this was a philosophy too heterodox to charm readers who might claim to have been charmed by *Rebecca* as an anodyne fable.

Though Daphne du Maurier became 'the highest paid woman writer in Britain', her work constitutes, in a phrase which was title to one of her short stories, 'a border-line case' in popular fiction.[44] Mere stereotypes are often a target, as in *Frenchman's Creek* but also in the shorter fiction. The protagonists of some stories are *femmes fatales*, like the Marquise in 'The Little Photographer', who copies the praying mantis in destroying her partner after sexual congress. Daphne du Maurier's spiderwoman tips the photographer over a cliff when he resents the termination of a holiday affair and hints at blackmail. In 'The Apple Tree', a crabbed wife dies and is transmogrified into the tree, which not only produces apples combining leathery skins with disgustingly pulpy interiors, but whose stump trips up and traps the widower until he freezes to death in the snow. Other stories, however, enquire into the male propensity to be nervous of women, which 'The Little Photographer' and 'The Apple Tree', albeit by a female author, seem to duplicate.

The protagonist of 'The Menace' is a purportedly hard-boiled film star, Barry Jeans. When 'feelies' are introduced in the autumn of 1959, Barry's career is threatened since his 'feely' count is found to be a mere Force G. He is exalted to Force A by eating rice pudding and reminiscing about Herne Bay with a Kentish former girlfriend he runs into in Hollywood who shows him snapshots of her grandchildren. Another story, 'The Chamois', similarly suggests that the cult of the he-man is less a demonstration of masculinity than a doomed attempt to assert what is lacking.

> It seemed to me that if Stephen had had his rifle with him he would not have been afraid. The loss of the rifle had unmanned him. All power, all confidence, had gone, and with it, in some sickening way, his personality.[45]

Of 'The Menace' and 'The Chamois', it is reasonable for the blurb to the Penguin collection, *The Blue Lenses and Other Stories*, to claim that they 'throw a different light on aspects of modern sexuality'.

A similar claim may be made for 'The Birds', Daphne du Maurier's perhaps most renowned short story, competing with the vacuous 'Don't Look Back'. It is worth considering 'The Birds' in relation to Freud's essay, 'The Uncanny', containing analysis of Hoffmann's story, 'The Sand-Man'. The nurse in the story, in a passage which Freud quotes, refers to the Sand-Man as:

> a wicked man who comes when the children won't go to bed, and throws handfuls of sand in their eyes so that they jump out of their heads all bleeding. Then he puts the eyes in a sack and carries them off to the half-moon to feed his children. They sit up there in their nest, and their beaks are hooked like owls' beaks, and they use them to peck up naughty boys' and girls' eyes with.[46]

Freud defines the uncanny as 'that class of the frightening which leads back to what is known of old and long familiar', and with particular reference to Hoffmann's story remarks that 'a study of dreams, phantasies and myths has taught us that anxiety about one's eyes, the fear of going blind, is often enough a substitute for the dread of being castrated'.[47] He then establishes how in 'The Sand-Man' the figure of the Sand-Man is recurrently linked with that of the father, and how various elements in the story, such as an anxiety about the eyes being brought into connection with the father's death, or the Sand-Man appearing as 'a disturber of love', 'become intelligible as soon as we replace the Sand-Man by the dreaded father at whose hands castration is expected'.[48]

Like the Sand-Man's children with their owlish beaks, Daphne du Maurier's birds have a penchant for eyes. Not surprisingly, this worries the protagonist, who is a male, Nat, in the story, though not in Hitchcock's film. 'Each stab of a swooping beak tore his flesh. If only he could keep them from his eyes. Nothing else mattered. He must keep them from his eyes.'[49] We have Freud's authority in 'The Uncanny' for considering that 'anxiety about one's eyes ... is often enough a substitute for the dread of being castrated'. In Daphne du Maurier's story, what endows the anxiety about the eyes with this deeper significance, for the reader rather than the characters, is that the birds precipitate a general breakdown of authority and power. There are rumours that the Russians have poisoned the birds (the story appeared in 1952), and a forlorn hope that the Americans, who have 'always been our allies ... will do something'.[50] 'Why don't the authorities do something? Why don't they get the army, get machine-guns, anything?'[51] As the story ends, Nat, who has earlier, 'thrust his poker up as far as it could go' to see whether the chimney is clear of birds, is reduced to deciding that he may as well smoke his last cigarette.[52]

A recent review in *The Guardian* of novels by Terry Pratchett, Ben Elton and Jeffrey Archer exemplifies a traditional wisdom about readers of popular fiction.

> Indeed, the three novels under review seem to lack everything which we self-appointed custodians of the nation's literary conscience tend to extol in a work of fiction: the ironic nuances, the oblique perspectives, the careful shades of thought and feeling. What they painfully lack, in a word, is subtlety. Against this we have to set the fact that they sell by the truck-load. It takes no genius to conclude that most of the book-buying public couldn't care less about subtlety, and that these novels must have other qualities which strike a resounding chord with a popular audience even as they cause reviewers to purse their lips in piqued disapproval.[53]

The review is entitled, 'Schlock therapy'. A trouble with *schlock* is that not all readers will be satisfied by a mere reinforcing of stereotypes. There is liable to be a touch of Rebecca herself in the female readers of *Rebecca*. On the other hand, the Victorians, or the more prosperous among them, were recurrently nervous of what they called opening the floodgates: the French Revolution was cited as an example of what might follow if it was conceded that the slightest thing was amiss with the status quo. An eminent Victorian novelist, George Eliot, was wary of endorsing feminism precisely on the theory of the floodgates. In the face of the deluge, there may be a case for reinforcing stereotypes. If we consider the continuing appeal of *Rebecca*, not only in itself but as a trend-setter in popular fiction, the recipe for success seems to be that readers, along with the heroine, may identify with the passion and freedom of Rebecca, but that readers may also resort to identifying with the heroine in her overt respectability, a demeanour lacking in her successor, Lady Dona in *Frenchman's Creek*. This would not suggest readers of popular romance to be ultra-daring or adventurous: their abandon is prudently within limits. It does suggest them to be less bland than the reading constituency of Terry Pratchett, Ben Elton and Jeffrey Archer, at least as that constituency is presented in *The Guardian*.

Notes

1. Janice Radway, *Reading the Romance* (London: 1987) p. 31.
2. Judith Cook, *Daphne: A Portrait of Daphne du Maurier* (London: 1991) p. 131.
3. Alison Light, '"Returning to Manderley"– Romance Fiction, Female Sexuality and Class', *Feminist Review*, no. 16 (April 1984) p. 10.
4. Roger Bromley, 'The Gentry, Bourgeois Hegemony and Popular Fiction: *Rebecca* and *Rogue Male*', in Peter Humm, Paul Stigant and Peter Widdowson (eds), *Popular Fictions: Essays in Literature and History* (London: 1986) p. 157. The essay was originally published in *Literature and History* in Autumn, 1981.
5. Daphne du Maurier, *Rebecca* (London: 1938).
6. Bromley, p. 163.
7. Ibid., p. 64.
8. Martyn Shallcross, *The Private World of Daphne du Maurier* (London: 1991) p. 62.
9. Ibid., p. 64.
10. Ibid.
11. Daphne du Maurier, *Myself When Young: The Shaping of a Writer* (London: 1978) p. 53.
12. Sue Peters, *Unwilling Woman* (Richmond: 1989) p. 179.
13. See Bromley pp. 151–64.
14. *Rebecca*.
15. Ibid.

16. Ibid.
17. Daphne du Maurier, *The Rebecca Notebook and Other Memories* (London: 1981) p. 43.
18. *Rebecca*.
19. *The Rebecca Notebook*, p. 39.
20. *Rebecca*.
21. *The Rebecca Notebook*, p. 51.
22. Roland Barthes, *Writing Degree Zero*, tr., Annette Lavers and Colin Smith (London: 1967), p. 40.
23. *Rebecca*.
24. Ibid.
25. Ibid.
26. *The Rebecca Notebook*, p. 117.
27. *Rebecca*.
28. David Williams, *The Rebecca Riots: A Study in Agrarian Discontent* (Cardiff: 1955), p. 150.
29. Ibid., p. 189.
30. Ibid., p. 155.
31. *Rebecca*.
32. Ibid.
33. Sir Walter Scott, *Ivanhoe*.
34. Ibid.
35. Ibid.
36. Henrik Ibsen, *Plays: Three* (London: 1988), p. 32.
37. See *The Pelican Freud Library* (Harmondsworth: 1985), vol. xiv, pp. 299–316.
38. Ibsen.
39. Daphne du Maurier, *My Cousin Rachel* (London: 1974).
40. Quoted on the back cover of Daphne du Maurier, *Frenchman's Creek* (London: Pan, 1976).
41. Cook, p. 167.
42. *Frenchman's Creek*.
43. Ibid.
44. Cook, p. 173.
45. Daphne du Maurier, *The Blue Lenses and other stories* (Harmondsworth: 1970).
46. *The Pelican Freud Library*, vol. xiv, pp. 348–9.
47. Ibid., pp. 340, 352.
48. Ibid., p. 353.
49. Daphne du Maurier, *The Birds and other stories* (London: 1977).
50. Ibid.
51. Ibid.
52. Ibid.
53. *The Guardian* (25 July 1991).

8 Horrors and Menaces to Everything Decent in Life: the Horror Fiction of Dennis Wheatley

Gina Wisker

They could see the cabbalistic characters between the circles that ringed the pentacle, and the revolving bookcase, like a dark shadow beyond it, through the luminous mist. An awful stench of decay ... filled their nostrils as they gazed, sick and almost retching with repulsion, at a grey face that was taking shape about seven feet from the floor. The eyes were fixed upon them, malicious and intent. The eyeballs whitened but the face went dark. Under it the mist was gathering into shoulders, torso, hips.

... He knew that his prayer was answered. His fingers closed on the jewel. His arms shot out. It glittered for a second in the violet light, then came to rest in the centre of the circle.

A piercing scream, desperate with anger, fear and pain, like that of a beast seared with a white hot iron, blasted the silence. *The Devil Rides Out*[1]

A hideous, devilish monster lurches into view, serving its Infernal Master, and determined to devour or destroy me. Sign of the cross and it shrivels and disappears, like the wicked witch in *The Wizard of Oz*, who dissolves in ordinary everyday water.

These regular nightmares of mine, emergent at around the age I started reading Dennis Wheatley (read avidly, devoured even, between the ages of eleven and thirteen) were entirely formed, I now realise, upon the formulae of Wheatley's fiction and upon the certainties those formulae reinforced. The titillation of the potential daily presence of true evil is comfortingly matched in Dennis Wheatley's novels by an equal certainty that order and the status quo will be resolved; that honour, honesty and the wartime spirit of Britain can overcome anything nasty lurking in the visible or invisible enemy's plans. The power of assured good triumphs resolutely over evil, and both are equally recognisable.

My father doesn't remember lending me the library books, and probably he didn't. I read whatever came into the house, unselected,

99

unsupervised. It could have been much much worse than Dennis Wheatley: Agatha Christie and selected science fiction! As it was, Dennis Wheatley was, in retrospect, quite a good choice if what you wish to learn and feel is on the one hand that it is entertaining to read a fairly well crafted, factually based (ostensibly) story, and on the other hand, that however monstrous events and people or creatures might be within this world, however formed they might be by genuine evil, there is ultimately and inevitably a triumph of good.

Is it a measure of our sophistication in reading habits that has caused us all as readers to forget we read Dennis Wheatley once? Most of the bookshops I have visited in an attempt to get hold of Wheatley's novels have declared him out of print, but he isn't. There is (as I write) a new edition published by Mandarin paperbacks, and a reasonably priced hardback edition still well in print from Heron Books. W.H. Smith, bastion of popular fiction, couldn't trace his work on their shelves in Cambridge, and returned my downpayment for those supposedly in print, declaring them no longer so. One Cambridge bookshop specialising in ordinary secondhand books said were they offered any they wouldn't touch them. Clearly, popular horror fiction suffers from this snobbery even more than science fiction or romance. And if we do or did read horror, if we do or did watch Hammer films including *The Devil Rides Out* we pretend now we don't or that we didn't.

Re-reading Dennis Wheatley tells us a great deal about the conditioning and expectations of narrative form, the pleasure of reading, the forms of horror fiction, and about the cultural norms which conditioned a generation and which find expression in the text of every Dennis Wheatley novel. Not surprisingly, considering they were written mainly in the 1930s, 1940s and 1950s these books contain attitudes, witting and unwitting, about racism, sexism, the class system, and all sorts of social stereotypes, as well as glaring and quite irritating (or satisfyingly predictable) examples of the ideology of the British people at a particular point in time. For Wheatley is very much a middle-class Englishman's man, and the clarity with which one can recognise the Russian, German or Chinese megalomaniac in a James Bond film is mirrored here as British heroes confront villains and devilish figures whose characteristics resemble those of the 'enemy' we all know. Women are less ornamental than in James Bond and less likely to be a threat to the status quo: they are unlikely to hint at lesbianism (Pussy Galore) or to revel in their promiscuity. Men are men, enjoy the company of women, are likely to have several affairs in passing to assure the reader of their manhood, and are equally likely to be coy about the detail, because this is not the main business of the novel, nor of a man's life, which is essentially action.

Investigating the values and certainties of Dennis Wheatley's popular horror fiction gives us a fascinating perspective on the cultural norms of the time and the ideological implications of all those forces which stress the normative and reinforce the status quo. In looking at these elements, and at 'Wheatley' as a cultural product, it is important to look too at the texture and quality of his writing, how the use of clichéd phrases reinforces the clichéd representations, how the formulae reinforce the security, the certainty that right will win, despite the might of the forces of evil.

Religion, good sportsmanship and a middle-class code of ethics mix solidly with superstition. Right wins, and the formula is comfortingly straightforward: 'As we go past, throw your crucifix straight at the thing on the throne. Then try and grab Simon.' Established religion is here used as a token. Good carries a kind of protective aura, authorised by religion, weapons and chalices. Religious or religiously inspired symbolic objects carry dependable powers, and evil is always megalomaniac, dark and ugly. Those like Simon who have been tricked into the camp of evil by false promises, subterfuge and deceit, can be physically rescued by smart and fast driving. Religion, acting as a talisman, metamorphoses into automotive power, enabling escape through the conversion of belief into technical action. Spirit thus becomes technique.

The car slid forward, silently gathering momentum as it rushed down the steep slope. Next second they were almost upon the nearest of the Satanists. The Duke let in the clutch and Rex switched on the powerful lights of the Hispano.

With the suddenness of a thunderclap a shattering roar burst upon the silence of the valley – as though some monster plane were driving full upon the loathsome company from the cloudy sky. At the same instant, the whole scene was lit in all its ghastliness by a blinding glare which swept towards them at terrifying speed.

Everything is extreme: 'terrifying'; 'ghastliness'; 'powerful'; 'shattering'. Metaphor is out of place, action is paramount, value judgements are clear, and technologically aided, human might is reinforced in its sense of success and power. The 'thing' on the throne might be horrifying because so solidly real, but it can be turned back into the darkness from whence it came; it can become again disembodied.

The great car bounded forward, the dazzling beams threw into sharp relief the naked forms gathered in the hollow. De Richlieu jammed his foot down on the accelerator and, calling with all his will upon the higher powers for their protection, charged straight for the Goat of Mendes upon his Satanic throne.

There is no ambiguity in the language. Masculine power plus technology, founded securely in a knowledgeable understanding of the detail of black magic and the Christian religion based powers of right and good will return the protagonists and the readers to a safe, rational world and will restore the status quo.

What has to be stressed is the basic goodness of those such as Simon and, in *To The Devil a Daughter*, Christina, who have been misled by false powers. They are always rescued, restored to their right judgement. Beneath this lies a very definite and sound sense of what *is* right, and what is British. Here Wheatley relates to the gothic works of the late nineteenth century, *Dr Jekyll and Mr Hyde*, *The Picture of Dorian Gray*, *Dracula* and other works which both consider the forms of decadence, and question what it means to be British. David Punter notes of these texts (but the point would apply to Wheatley too) that,

> they each pose, from very different angles, the same question, which can readily be seen as a question appropriate to an age of imperial decline: how much, they ask, can one lose – individually, socially, nationally – and still remain a man? One could put the question much more brutally: to what extent can one be 'infected' and still remain British?[2]

Strong, assured, British, Wheatley's protagonists rescue infected beings and restore them to normality, their transgressions having been seen in terms of dabbling with magic, or being caught up in its powers through no choice of their own.

In *The Ka of Gifford Hillary*, Hillary is suspected of the murder of his wife's lover, and writes convincingly in diary and statement style to explain that he could not have been so involved, disembodied as he was while it took place. Protagonists are those like the Duke who rescue and clarify, while there is always another central character, drawn from gothic fiction, who is the potential victim. In both *The Ka of Gifford Hillary* and *The Haunting of Toby Jugg* the potential victim ensures our belief by recounting their own tale, certified true by its diary or statement form.

Wheatley's treatment of some familiar characteristics of the fantastic underlines his essential conservatism, the satisfying way in which the status quo, the stability of character, and the rational order are reinforced as they are restored after being challenged. His is a non-subversive use of the fantastic, the product of a writer who ran a secret society at Dulwich school (for which he was expelled), who was first a sea cadet, then inherited the family wine business in which he made a success until the great slump, and who, during the Second World War, actually worked as a staff officer to Winston Churchill assisting in making covert and deception plans. Very much a conservative product of a nationalistic period, Wheatley delivers an ultimately rational and controllable horror to a readership who desire flights of the imagination but wish to have their values reinforced at the end. These values also involve gender, racial, class and other social stereo-typing and prejudices of the pre- and postwar period.

Rosemary Jackson in *Fantasy* defines gothic fiction as it, 'tended to buttress a dominant, bourgeois ideology by vicarious wish fulfilment through fantasies of incest, rape, murder, parricide, social disorder. Like pornography, it functioned to supply an object of desire, to imagine social and sexual transgression'.[3]

We can see gothic, of which horror is a descendant, as an outlet for the frustrations and doubts of society where fears can be safely played out, the pressure of unresolved tensions relieved and released. Wheatley's horror writing is of this kind, but it is on an even tighter rein. Jackson argues that the fantastic undermines concepts of the 'real', of character, of ideological fixities and norms; it challenges social stability. Cixous sees the characteristics of the fantastic, the use of multiple subjects, the confusion of states of being, defamiliarisation and the undercutting of norms as an essentially creative and liberating force because it all upsets 'logocentrism, idealism, theologism, the scaffolding of political and subjective economy'.[4] This is creative and liberating not merely in an anarchic sense, because the de-stabilising of social and philosoph-ical and political beliefs springs from, and promotes, a healthy enquiry of, and perspective on, what is asserted as 'social', 'normal' or 'given'. Such a perspective is post-Marxist, post-feminist, post-Lacanian, and offers a useful contemporary approach to reveal the contradictions implicit in Wheatley's work and the ways in which he uses gothic and fantastic elements to actually bolster up the social fabric. Such ques-tionings of the stable order are always dangerous in Wheatley's novels, always the actions of those who have taken the left hand way, or been lured into contemplating taking that way. He operates a cultural con-servatism which designates the forms and products of fantasy as dangerous and anti-civilisation, yet of course he uses these in the fabric of his plots. He points out how difficult it may be for the ordinary rational person to believe the fantastic and horrific events, and this very rational apology secures the acceptance of the details of the uncanny, the mon-strousness which follows and the horrors which take place in the lives of ordinary people (readers like you or me).

In this year ... how many people, I wonder, believe in the Devil? I mean as a definite personality with hoofs and horns and a barbed tail, waving a pitchfork and breathing brimstone over everything? I suppose a few very religious and backward people do; lonely, timid spinsters living in remote country districts, particularly in Scotland and down here in Wales, and the older generation of peasants in central and Southern Europe.
    I can't myself. (*The Satanist*)

The argument is rationally and commensensically based but we are actually mistaken and the Devil is ever powerful. In fact, he has just sent an emissary to this narrator, sound as he obviously is in mind and body,

> but, unless I am suffering from delusions, I can only suppose that either I, or this room have recently become the focus for the activities of one of his innumerable lesser satellites. How otherwise can one possibly explain the shadow, or the stark terror that has gripped me rigid in a paralysis of fear, on each of the five occasions that I have seen it – and, God forbid, may do so again tonight.

Like the narrator, we are wide open to belief with these rational explanations and this straightforward tone, but we need to be assured that whatever horrors do emerge, they will be returned to the dark from whence they came, before the book closes.

Dennis Wheatley's readers can enjoy the *frissons*, and feel comforted in the destruction of the potential undermining, subversive forces, as the fantasy is both explained factually and controlled by good, straight, white Christian men of power.

Other ways in which his work differs from that of many horror writers is his direct talismanic use of religion as a powerful active force for good. In his *Fear: a History of Horror in the Mass Media* Lee Daniells makes an interesting case that,

> One of the prerequisites for the emergence of horror as a distinct genre was the secularisation of society. Whilst religion held sway, the supernatural world would seem as natural as, if not more so than, the scientific. This meant that surprise and amazement at the odd and inexplicable could not be separated out, and treated as exceptional and as a possible subject for bravura and delicious daring.[5]

Once religion declined, however, the explanation of these fears, their everyday familiarity, came under question. What could not be explained by a powerless religion or by its successor, science, lurked in the recesses of the mind to emerge in the explosion of horror writing. 'And all the emotions that surrounded dark and death, and bad luck, and the uncontrolled areas of human life could be leaked away, aroused but controlled, in their own special genre, horror.'[6]

Wheatley's horror provides this psychological safety valve for the unspeakable fears, but it doesn't let the reader take full escapist flight. Readers are kept safely in mid-twentieth-century Britain with a Church of England Christianity at their beck and call, backed up with some Roman Catholicism if something a little more incantatory and censor swinging is necessary. The ritual and the magical elements in religion are necessarily reasserted with crucifixes that prove souls sold to the Devil are burnt or choked when touched by them, and with miniature holy grails and the Lord's Prayer to ward off evil beings.

In Wheatley the rational is used to reinforce religious or quasi-religious belief, and to detail factual information about magic and superstition and to scientifically explain why horrible things take place and horrible forces triumph. Ultimately, it is through rational knowledge that these evils can be overpowered. In Wheatley, evil is socially attractive but there is no complex psychological basis for it. It appears as an external enemy force which can be beaten with its own weapons, a good, religiously inspired magic instead of a wicked, black magic.

There is nothing psychologically gothic about Dennis Wheatley's fiction. His horror is of an entirely different sort, and the pace, tone and tenor of his novels depend on a different legacy, that rather of the adventure story and spy thriller: a kind of Captain Hornblower tale in which might and good are always right and always win in the end. None of the terrors are deeply psychological, Freud and Jung and their colleagues and inheritors have no place here.

A recognisable social setting both renders the evil frightening because everyday in the real sense, belonging to your colleagues and neighbours and relatives and just around the corner, and also *very safe*, because once the powers of might and right have worked against that evil, it leaves no trace. Nevertheless Wheatley has it both ways suggesting that the desire to seek out and call up evil is ever present in society and that a return is ever possible.

This essentially ironic product of a very rational and logical argument, and Wheatley's constant comments that the left-hand way coexists with a right-hand way are of a part with the mundanely factual and detailed descriptions and explanations he offers of occult activities from hypnotism to numerology, ESP and various much more obscure rituals. The drive for power in these novels overides any psychological insights. Power is a *material* presence though occultly produced: it is at once mundane and supernatural, factual and objectively present. To defeat such power one needs physical prowess and cunning rather than psychological insight. It remains residually attractive.

The Duke explains in *The Devil Rides Out:* 'others have cultivated the powers of Evil, and among whites it is generally the wealthy and intellectual who are avaricious for greater riches or power, to whom it appeals'. And Tanith, in the same novel, is clearly driven to a kind of *jouissance*, with *frissons* of delight, at the thought of powers beyond the normal. She is partly to be forgiven because, like so many of the pretty women in Wheatley's novels, she is under some sort of wicked dastardly spell, partly sold already to the Devil. Truly naturally evil women are necessarily ugly women. Tanith, knowing her time is limited on earth because she has learned she will die, describes the attraction of the power of the left-hand way, and its social frame of reference:

> Religions and moralities are man-made, fleeting and local; a scandalous lapse from virtue in London may be a matter for the highest praise in Hong Kong. ... One thing and one thing only remains constant and unchanging, the secret doctrine of the way of power.

and for her:

> Unfortunately the followers of the Right hand path obsess themselves only with the well-being of the Universe as a whole, whereas those of the Left exercise their power upon living humans. To bend people to your will, to cause them to fall or rise, to place unaccountable obstacles in their path at every turn, or smooth their way to a glorious success – that is more than riches, more than fame – the supreme pinnacle to which any man or woman can rise, and I wish to reach it before I die.

The author's disapproval is obvious from the reversal of the normal clichés 'rise and fall' to 'fall and rise'. Mention of living humans conjures up pictures of human sacrifice, hinted at throughout the book, especially when skulls form part of a later ritual on Walpurgisnacht. Tanith sounds like Milton's Satan, daring beyond normal human powers, and dangerously so. Her position as potential victim, cursed with a shortened life, bound to be tricked into losing her soul early in the horrid rituals though she has been promised power, causes the reader as well as the Duke and Rex, to forgive her and to explain away her sick commitment. After all she is a beautiful woman even if she has some rather odd looking friends.

The pursuit of power in Wheatley's novels is always played out within a fast-paced thriller. Usually there are many adventures along the way to uncovering and overcoming the evil manifestation. Wheatley's finest novel *The Devil Rides Out* does not follow any of the rules of horror fiction, with the slow lead ups and threats, moments of terror and then deliciously threatening calm. From the first to the last page, about 300 pages later, it grips the reader in a headlong flight and fight against evil. All the rollicking good yarn characteristics of an adventure tale are there. Whenever Simon, the victim, is caught by the forces of evil, promising him new power and insight, his solid good friends rescue him and the rescues become more and more difficult as the book progresses. The reader wonders about the actual powers of this knowledgeable right, and hints are given that it might not be able to overcome the evil, but we have no real fears.

Traces of medieval chivalry mixed with a Sherlock Holmes investigative nature make up the Duke de Richlieu, an aesthete whose choice wine drinking and cigar smoking are the embodiment of masculine values. His companion and side-kick is his son-like friend Rex, ugly and built like a bull, yet a jolly good chap.

Rex, giant-shouldered, virile and powerful, his ugly, attractive, humorous young face clouded with anxiety, the Duke, a slim, delicate-looking man, somewhat about middle height, with slender, fragile hands, and greying hair, but with no trace of weakness in his fine distinguished face.

Tanith's power hunger is explicable in her predicted short life. When she is rescued from giving herself to the dark rites, she amazingly has life restored to her and the ugly, powerful, honest giant Rex solves all her problems with promises of a long life to be spent with him: 'If you want them, my days are yours.' Marriage, one suspects, is a much more satisfactory resolution than gaining the powers of the left-hand way. Wheatley mingles romantic fiction with the adventure story here. In *The Satanist*, Mary, presumed dead after escaping various rites, is rescued by Barney, whom she believed hated her but who of course loves her. Near dead, she smiles and 'Then their icy breath mingled as their lips met in a long kiss.'

Wheatley rewards the good even by bringing them back to life, and the family unit is restored, wedding bells no doubt about to sound too. Closure is satisfying; the status quo is restored, and readers who have stretched their credibility with the tales of horror and of religious faith can, like those who wake from a dream, explain enough of it with realistic details and factual, rational explanations.

Their escape mimics that of the reader's from the novel. The Duke cannot explain everything, but provides a satisfying blueprint.

'Even the greatest seekers after Truth have done little more than lift the corner of the veil which hides the vast Unknown, but it is my belief that during the period of our dream journey we have been living in what the moderns call the fourth dimension – divorced from time.'

Wheatley uses some of the characteristics of the gothic, but in David Punter's categorisations, he is well in the camp of the realists as one of the writers who, 'agree that the world is indeed largely and usually as the realists perceive it; but that at rare moments it is quite different, and that these moments are of peculiar, epiphanic importance'.[7] He does not question the established bourgeois dominant world view; these fantastic and horrific moments are revelatory rents in its fabric and only the really solidly dull characters are resistant, and that only temporarily, to recognising the force of facts about the supernatural and the forces of the left hand of evil. The status of reality is not questioned. If the gothic writer insists that realism is not the whole story then Wheatley falls very much into Punter's realist category because he ultimately can 'smooth out the moments of terror and vision which comprise experience and render them into a unitary whole'.[8]

Wheatley's horror 'takes us on a tour through the labyrinthine corridors of repression. Gives us glimpses of the skeletons of dead desires and makes them move again' but the reality principle operates more cleanly and completely in Wheatley because the unfinished gothic quality is overcome and closure is accomplished. Villains disappear or die, and the good guys marry or perhaps shake hands in very British fashion. All ends well: Gregory Sallust marries Erika in *They used Dark Forces*, John goes off with Christina in *To the Devil a Daughter*, Rex with Tanith in *The Devil Rides Out*, Barney with Mary in *The Satanist* and the fine wine drinking older men remain manly and knowledgeable.

The adventure-story form mixes with that of horror fiction to provide a very British Empire version of gothic which celebrates sound technology, fears potentially blasphemous scientific experiments, and recognises that evil is tapped by social greed and desire for power, but can be controlled with factual knowledge and common-sense reason.

Wheatley never thoroughly embraces the fantastic with his horror fiction. The assertion of rational explanations with a hint of faith ensures the security of the familiar and of dominant signifying practice. The fantastic is the source of the horror: hooves, blood, goats, devils, apocalyptic horsemen and all. And yet even in its most bizarre and outré moments evil displays its own amenable common sense and it is this logic of common sense *within* evil which will produce its final destruction.

Wheatley's *The Devil Rides Out* was filmed by Hammer, released in 1967 and directed by Terence Fisher. It starred the marvellous Christopher Lee, veteran of so many Hammer horror films. Fisher and Wheatley seem well matched in their aims and intentions in film and book. If later Hammer films emphasise the link between violence and sex, Fisher's insist on retribution for sexual transgression and attraction: 'One of the consequences of Fisher's moralism is that the fatal attractiveness of evil is inevitably undermined in all his films by his insistence on punishing the seductive'.[10]

For the reader as for the audience, it is a very dubious moralism when carefully investigated. Reading Wheatley, like watching a Fisher film, is an activity which raises questions of reader response, reader collusion and corruption. Readers who, along with Wheatley, condemn the evil they read about, and react with moral indignation at the sickness of the sexual seductions and perversions hinted at, get the benefit of the *frisson and* the satisfaction of resulting moral condemnation. With the horror, as with the sexuality, we can dabble at secondhand, repeat the careful warning instructions and condemn the evil.

Critical reading of Wheatley's horror is so bound up in awareness of him as a cultural product of a period which celebrated all things male, middle or upper class, straight and very British, that it is sometimes as difficult to avoid parody as it is for him to avoid cliché and stereotype. There is a peculiar Britishness about the security of the values of goodness, of the assurance of fists and the powers of the established church to defeat anything dark, dangerous and nasty. Evil people are visibly so, usually deformed, not British, and those who are like ourselves and in the hands of the satanists are clearly drugged or hypnotised or persuaded against their better judgement: thus curable. A strong sense of right and wrong, health and sanity prevail above and beyond the darkness which lurks and twitches behind the social curtains. Horror here is socially courted, supernatural but on a par with the supernatural powers of good. It is not psychological.

Dennis Wheatley made horror fiction a very popular 'populist' fiction, and a very British popular fiction at that. If we wince at the language, we must admire the pace of the action, the vitality and the excitement. His author's note to each book captures the way in which his horror fiction so completely enters into the realms of our everyday lives. He always starts with a warning. If his readers meet any man or woman of the black magic secret arts:

I feel that it is only right to urge them, most strongly, to refrain from being drawn into the practice of the Secret Art in any way. My own observations have led me to an absolute conviction that to do so would bring them into dangers of a very real and concrete nature.

Read, and beware! Order will triumph.

Notes

1. Books by Dennis Wheatley referred to in the text: *The Devil Rides Out* (1934); *To the Devil a Daughter* (1953); *The Satanist* (1960); *The Ka of Gifford Hillary* (1956); *The Haunting of Toby Jugg* (1948); *They used Dark Forces* (1964).
2. David Punter, *The Literature of Terror: a History of Gothic Fictions from 1765 to the Present Day* (London: 1980) p. 240.
3. Rosemary Jackson, *Fantasy: the Literature of Subversion* (London: 1981) p. 175.
4. Hélène Cixous, 'The Character of Character', trans. Keith Cohen in *New Literary History* vol. 5: no. ii Winter (1974) pp. 383–402.

5. See Lee Daniells, *Fear: a History of Horror in the Mass Media* (London: 1977).
6. Martin Barker, *Haunt of Fears: the Strange History of the British Horror Comics Campaign* (London: 1984) p. 127.
7. Punter, p. 406.
8. Ibid., p. 407.
9. Ibid., p. 409.
10. Ibid., p. 361.

9 The Abolition of Man?: Horror in the Science Fiction of C.S. Lewis

Dennis Butts

He had read his H.G. Wells and others. His universe was peopled with horrors such as ancient and medieval mythology could hardly rival. No insect-like, vermiculate or crustacean Abominable, no twitching of feelers, rasping wings, slimy coils, curling tentacles, no monstrous union of superhuman intelligence and insatiable cruelty, seemed to him anything but likely on an alien world. The *sorns* would be ... would be ... he dared not think what the *sorns* would be. And he was to be given to them. Somehow this seemed more horrible than being caught by them. Given, handed over, offered. He saw in imagination various incompatible monstrosities – bulbous eyes, grinning jaws, horns, stings, mandibles. Loathing of insects, loathing of snakes, loathing of things that squashed and squelched, all played their horrible symphonies over his nerves. But the reality would be worse: it would an extra-terrestrial Otherness.

Out of the Silent Planet (1938)

Any amount of theology can now be smuggled into people's minds under cover of romance without their knowing it. *Letter* (9 July, 1939)[1]

Although such writers as J.G. Ballard and Darko Suvin have suggested that the basis of science fiction is atheistic, any list of famous science fiction would have to include such religious novels as Walter Miller's *A Canticle for Leibowitz* (1960). Indeed Tom Woodman has argued that since the ultimate theme of science fiction is man's attempt through science to come to terms with the cosmos he inhabits, implications often develop from it that go well beyond a purely anthropological or sociological approach to religion, and he cites numerous works by such writers as Ray Bradbury, Philip K. Dick and Chad Oliver to support his argument.[2]

It is not surprising then that Clive Staples Lewis, a world authority on romance from the Middle Ages onwards, as well as a popular Christian apologist, should use the form of science fiction for religious purposes. Born in Belfast in 1898, Lewis and his older brother spent endless hours reading and making up stories, even before his mother's death when he was only nine. Educated mainly in England where he was unhappy and lost his Christian faith, Lewis won a scholarship to Oxford, but his studies were interrupted by the Great War, where he served in the trenches and survived being wounded. When he returned to Oxford in 1919, he took a double First in Classics, and then a First in English, and obtained a Fellowship at Magdalen College. In 1931 he rejoined the Church of England and for the rest of his life produced a stream of works of Christian theology, beginning with *The Pilgrim's Regress* in 1933. During the 1930s Lewis and a circle of close friends calling themselves 'The Inklings' began meeting in Lewis's rooms to hear each other's works, and it was here that J.R.R. Tolkien's *The Hobbit* (1937) and Lewis's first science fiction novel, *Out of the Silent Planet* (1938) were read. *The Allegory of Love*, a study of medieval poetry, had won Lewis the Hawthornden Prize in 1936, and by the 1940s he had attained enormous popularity as a Christian apologist, particularly after the success of *The Screwtape Letters* in 1942 and many broadcasts for the BBC. The other volumes of his science fiction trilogy followed – *Perelandra* in 1943, and *That Hideous Strength* in 1945. Lewis's *Preface to Paradise Lost* (1942) and *English Literature in the Sixteenth Century* (1954) sealed his reputation as a critic and scholar, and he was appointed Professor of Medieval and Renaissance English at Cambridge in 1954 at the time when he was making a new reputation as the writer of such outstanding children's fantasies as *The Lion, the Witch and the Wardrobe* (1950) and other chronicles of 'Narnia'. Lewis died in 1963.

Altogether Lewis wrote over 40 books, including autobiography, children's stories, literary criticism, novels, poetry and theology. With the other members of 'The Inklings', particularly Tolkien and Charles Williams, he has become something of a cult figure, the subject of numerous biographical and critical studies.[3] But while his children's books, literary criticism and theology are extremely well known, his science fiction trilogy deserves further discussion. There are three full-length books: *Out of the Silent Planet* (1938), *Perelandra* (1943) and *That Hideous Strength: a Modern Fairy Tale for Grown-ups* (1945). Although each of the books may be read independently, they are connected by the presence in all three of the same hero Ransom, and by the re-appearance of two villains, Weston and Devine; there are also strong thematic links.

We first meet Dr Elwin Ransom in *Out of the Silent Planet*. He is a distinguished Cambridge philologist enjoying a walking holiday, and looking for shelter for the night, when he comes across an old school acquaintance Devine in company with an eminent physicist, Professor Weston. Although they appear friendly at first, Weston and Devine drug Ransom and take him to Malacandra (Mars) on a spaceship developed by Weston. They propose to offer Ransom as a sacrifice to the Martians, whom they have already met on an earlier flight, in exchange for gold which is mined on the planet. On Mars, Ransom manages to escape from his captors, however, and is befriended by the sorns, who, far from being cruel and vengeful as he had expected, prove to be gentle and intelligent. Oyarsa, the god-like intelligence of the planet, interviews Ransom about the struggle between goodness and the evil Oyarsa on earth, and reprimands Weston for his blind faith in scientific evolution. But in the end the humans are allowed to return to earth in their spaceship. Ransom is told that great changes are coming to the cosmos, and that he and Oyarsa may meet again.

In *Perelandra* Ransom is summoned by the Oyarsa to the planet Perelandra (Venus), which he discovers largely consists of an ocean covered with floating islands. Here Ransom meets a beautiful Green Lady, waiting for her Lord to make up the sole human pair on the planet, and he realises that she is completely innocent of evil. But the scientist Weston again arrives in a spaceship, and soon reveals himself as the instrument by which the evil Oyarsa from earth has escaped in order to strike against the unfallen world of Perelandra. Weston (or the frightening Un-Man into which he soon turns) tries to tempt the Lady to disobey the ban of Maledil (God) on residing on the 'fixed lands' of Venus and, although Ransom strenuously opposes the Un-Man's arguments, he feels unable to halt Weston's powers of persuasion, until he realises he must fight the Un-Man physically. Ransom fights Weston the next day and, after a great struggle, kills him. The Oyarsa of Malacandra and of Perelandra greet Ransom, and he has a vision of the entire universe in a great cosmic dance with Maledil at its centre. Then Ransom returns to earth.

Lewis's creation of the secondary worlds of Malacandra and Perelandra is done with enormous invention and variety. The description of Malacandra in *Out of the Silent Planet* is packed with detailed information about the geography and history of Mars, its flora and fauna, its culture and religion, and especially about its remarkable inhabitants, the hrossa, the sorns and the pfifltriggi, as well as the supernatural eldila and Oyarsa. (The philologist Ransom also gives us a good account of the Malacandran language which he soon acquires.) The unfallen world of Venus is presented with even greater richness. Although Lewis's writing strains for effect at times, he is after all attempting the impossible, and his descriptions of the planet's blue waterfalls, floating islands, and weird but friendly creatures – a small dragon, singing beasts, man-loving sea-horses – are often delightfully realised.

At first *That Hideous Strength* looks more like a completely new beginning than the concluding part of a trilogy. Unlike the earlier books, it is completely earth-bound, and opens as if it is going to be a very worldly story about a conflict between careers and marriage told in the realistic mode. Mark and Jane Studdock's marriage is falling apart, as Mark throws more and more of his energies into pursuing his career first at Bracton College in the small country town of Edgestow, and then at the nearby National Institute of Co-ordinated Experiments. He learns from Lord Feverstone (formerly Devine) that the Institute – NICE, for short – is planning no less than to re-organise society on scientific lines, a project for which he feels some sympathy. But, as he becomes more involved in the inner workings of the Institute he discovers that its real purpose is to create a world of pure brain through hideous biological experiments, and tries to withdraw from the organisation. At the same time, however, his dissatisfied wife Jane, seeking an explanation for some disturbingly violent dreams she is experiencing, joins a small group in the village of St Anne's, consisting of a few eccentric humans and a tame bear, Mr Bultitude, who are led by the Director, Ransom. Jane discovers that her dreams are in fact true stories revealing the Institute's evil plans. In a final conflict, the Arthurian magician Merlin emerges from Bragdon Wood to join Ransom's group and the planetary gods, who destroy the Institute and all its works. The story ends with a great coming together in love – Venus is literally over St Anne's – and Ransom taking his leave of the earth.

All these stories clearly operate within the conventions of romantic fantasy. The heroes and heroines are involved in great adventures, often quests, in which they encounter many horrors, in ways that clearly relate to a literary tradition which includes not only Homer, Spenser and Milton, but also modern writers of fantasy whom Lewis also admired such as George MacDonald and H.G. Wells. Ransom's initial dread of the grotesque sorns on Mars clearly derives from such stories as *The First Men on the Moon*, and Professor Weston's convulsive collapse into Un-Man in *Perelandra* owes something to Satan's sudden disintegration into a serpent in Book X of *Paradise Lost*. All of these elements are there to make the reader's flesh creep, none more so than Jane's description of her encounter with the diabolic decapitated head of the criminal Alcasan in *That Hideous Strength*.

> I thought I saw a face floating just in front of me. A face not a head, if you understand what I mean. That is, there was a beard and nose and eyes – at least you couldn't see the eyes because it had coloured glasses on, but there didn't seem to be anything above the eyes. Not at first. But as I got used to the light, I got a horrible shock. I thought the face was a mask tied on to a kind of balloon thing. But it wasn't, exactly. Perhaps it looked like a bit of a man wearing a sort of a turban. … What it really was, was a head (the rest of a head) which had had the top part of the skull taken off and then … then … as if something inside had boiled over. A great big mass which bulged out from inside what was left of the skull. Wrapped in some kind of composition stuff,

but very thin stuff. You could see it twitch. Even in my fright I remember thinking, 'Oh, kill it, kill it. Put it out of its pain.' But only for a second, because I thought the thing was dead, really. It was green looking and the mouth was wide open and quite dry. ... Well quite suddenly, like when an engine is started, there came a puff of air out of its mouth, with a hard dry rasping sound. And then there came another, and it settled down into a sort of rhythm – *huff, huff, huff* – like an imitation of breathing. Then came a most horrible thing: the mouth began to dribble. ... Then it began working its mouth and even licking its lips.[4]

Even a bald summary of the plots of Lewis's science fiction trilogy makes it clear that the stories are intended to convey meanings and resonances beyond the purely narrative, though Lewis himself certainly never underestimated the importance of story *qua* story. The opening of *Out of the Silent Planet* is almost allegorical, as C.N. Manlove observes, as Ransom, with that precisely chosen name, makes his way through a landscape that inevitably reminds us of *Pilgrim's Progress*.[5] What emerges as the story develops, however, is that Lewis is not simply using Ransom's adventures on Mars as a way of suggesting a Christian view of the universe in general, but that he is exploiting the form of science fiction in order to attack Professor Weston's ideas of scientific progress in particular. For in the final confrontation between Oyarsa and Weston, the Professor makes it perfectly clear that he has not travelled to Mars to steal its gold like Devine, but to claim the planet and ensure the survival of the human species, even if this means destroying the Martians or other races. 'Our right to supersede you is the right of the higher over the lower', Weston brazenly tells the Martians. 'It was against this outlook on life, this ethic, if you will, that I wrote my satiric fantasy', Lewis explained later.[6]

Perelandra develops this idea in a more oblique but even more pessimistic way. The central drama of the novel clearly focuses upon Ransom's struggle to prevent Weston's achieving a Second Fall on Edenic Perelandra by tempting the Lady to disobey Maledil. But Weston's justification for his actions are disingenuous. He disclaims his previous interest in colonising other planets and eliminating their inhabitants, and now asserts his belief in the value of evolution and the forward movement of life towards an ultimate spirituality. But when Ransom questions the quality of that spirituality, Weston equates it with an amoral Life-Force, obedience to which will permit lying, treachery and even murder. Soon, in fact, Weston is revealed as an Un-Man, the agent of Devil on Venus, and someone Ransom has to fight literally to the death. It is increasingly a part of Lewis's belief by this time – a time when Britain was surrounded by the forces of Nazi Germany, we must remember – not that all scientists or believers in evolution were literally agents of the Devil like Weston, but that anyone who worshipped a being or a principle which Christians regarded as evil (the necessity of murder for example) was behaving diabolically. This happens when people believe a doctrine which asserts that an individual, whether a Green Lady or a human being, fails to matter. As Noel Annan says in his study of Leslie Stephen,

> When Stephen says that the moral code on which social welfare depends changes as society evolves, he does not tell us why nor how high-minded men are entitled to break the code in order to make it 'higher'. It is not evolution which sanctifies our conception of right or wrong; it is the very reverse – morality gives meaning to such words as 'progress' and 'welfare'.[7]

Annan might have been writing about the fictitious Professor Weston himself.

In February 1943 Lewis gave a series of lectures at Durham University, later published under the title of *The Abolition of Man*, in which he took these ideas even further, incorporating many of them into his last novel, *That Hideous Strength*. In these lectures Lewis argued that from the beginnings of literature until the middle of the twentieth century a system of values – what he called the *Tao* to show its universal expression – was accepted by everyone. These were the generally agreed standards of right and wrong, esteem for certain virtues, hatred of cruelty and dishonesty, and so on. But Lewis argued that this system of values was no longer taken for granted, and he pointed to an increasing belief in relativist or subjective values, which he suggested, amounted to a rejection of the *Tao*. But if the *Tao*, the sole source of all value-judgement, was rejected, all value would be rejected, he claimed, and the abolition of man as a moral being would have been achieved. Man's attempts to set up new value-systems in place of the *Tao*, however well-intentioned, always came down to the power of some men to make other men do what they wanted, and this power would be enormously increased by the adoption of scientism and scientific techniques in the twentieth century. Thus, in *The Abolition of Man* Lewis selects for particular attack teachers who preach relativist values, scientific planners, and popularisers of evolutionary ethics such as C.H. Waddington, whom he ironically quotes as saying 'an existence which is essentially evolutionary is itself the justification for an evolution towards a more comprehensive existence'.[8] Although he may seem to be attacking easy targets at times, Lewis really did believe that the abolition of Man was at stake.

Much of this is to be found dramatically expressed in *That Hideous Strength*. The Institute for Co-ordinated Experiments aims to apply science and scientific principles to the re-organisation of society, and intends to include the sterilisation of the unfit and experiments on criminals among its practices. Opponents are bribed, bullied or murdered. Civil disturbances are deliberately created and newspaper reports of them skilfully manipulated so that the Institute's own special police force can take control. And the guillotined head of the criminal Alcasan is resuscitated in order that alien macrobes can control the earth with the help of an élitist minority from the Institute.

But the macrobes who speak through Alcasan's head are really Dark Eldils (or devils), and they turn on the leaders of the Institute at the end to demand adoration and further sacrifices in a bloody and annihilating conclusion. The Institute's leaders are easy, if unsuspecting, victims for the Devil to take over, and it is no coincidence that one of them actually quotes Waddington's views on developmental evolution at the beginning of chapter 14, for, as we have seen, it is Lewis's view that the fallacies of evolutionary ethics makes their proponents particularly vulnerable.

The elements of horror in Lewis's trilogy of science fiction novels, which expand as the seriousness of the whole work increases, have to be seen then as completely at one with the meanings the books endeavour to convey. Ransom's fears of the sorns in *Out of the Silent Planet* prove to be unjustified. Indeed it is a feature of much of Lewis's work that creatures who at first appear odd or frightening often prove to be friendly, such as the web-footed Marsh-Wiggles in the Narnia series. But Weston's transformation into Un-Man in *Perelandra* is a powerful expression of the evils of atheistic scientism, as Lewis perceived them. And in *That Hideous Strength* the horrors abound with not only the obscene treatment of Alcasan's head, but the physical torturing of Jane, the bestial slaughter at the banquet, the deaths of Filostrato, Straik and Withers, and the great earthquake which engulfs Feverstone and the whole of Edgestow at the close.

Lewis pulls no punches in his vision of the cosmic and moral evil that he feared. Yet paradoxically it is not always the great set scenes with violence so fully described on a large scale which are the most disturbing. Supernatural evil is often difficult to evoke, however emphatic the writing, and the actual effect of an over-insistence upon horrors is sometimes 'not to magnify but to muffle', as F.R. Leavis observed about Conrad's treatment of evil in *Heart of Darkness*.[9] (There is surely something of this in the over-detailed description of Alcasan's head.) Lewis's attempts to articulate fear and horror are often more effectively realised by microscopic suggestions rather than by macrocosmic catastrophes. The narrator's fears of going insane as he walks through a normal English landscape on a dreary evening at the beginning of *Perelandra*, the fears of a decaying mind, are every bit as disturbing as the great clash of forces which is to follow, and Weston's systematic and apparently *petty* tearing apart of the trail of brightly coloured frogs on Venus tells us more about his moral sickness than pages of supernatural horror.

Lewis's novels raise other questions, too. J.B.S. Haldane, the distinguished scientist, attacked the stories in an article entitled 'Auld Hornie, F.R.S.' in the *Modern Quarterly* in 1946. Haldane protested not only against the poor science in the novels, but against Lewis's hostile treatment of scientists in general, and for associating them with racism and national socialism. Haldane suggested that Lewis was simply reactionary, unwilling to interpret any attempt at social improvement as other than evil. These are serious points and not completely refuted by Lewis's (unfinished) 'A Reply to Professor Haldane', in which he legitimately claimed poetic licence for his inaccurate science, but argued that he was not attacking scientists *per se* but trying to defend traditional values. And in the end Lewis repeats his arguments from *The Abolition of Man* that when parties replace traditional values with belief in an impersonal force, such as Nature or Evolution, they are in danger of abrogating all ordinary moral values and becoming devil-worshippers. Although Lewis admits that the *Tao* allows developments from within the system of traditional values, and talks about the possibilities of a new 'Natural Philosophy' in *The Abolition of Man*, he remains vague about this, and is short of examples of what he regards as desirable social change.[10]

Lewis's tales are told with great skill, and the descriptions of planetary landscapes and the human and non-human struggles often evoke horror and excitement with considerable power. The meanings the stories articulated raise serious questions, too, about evolution and science and religion which one would like to have heard discussed by theologians such as Dietrich Bonhoeffer or Teilhard de Chardin as well as Professor Haldane. But there is no doubt that, as A.N. Wilson has said, 'Though Lewis's cooking may be tough, you never forget the flavour.'[11]

Notes

1. C.S. Lewis, *Out of the Silent Planet* (London: 1938) pp. 49–50; *Letters of C.S. Lewis*, ed., with a Memoir by W.H. Lewis (London: 1966) p. 167.
2. Tom Woodman, 'Science fiction, religion and transcendence', in Patrick Parrinder ed., *Science Fiction: A Critical Guide* (London: 1979) pp. 110–30.
3. See, for example, Humphrey Carpenter, *The Inklings: C.S. Lewis, J.R.R. Tolkien, Charles Williams and Their Friends* (London: 1979); Paul H. Ford, *Companion to Narnia* (San Francisco: 1980); Roger Lancelyn Green and Walter Hooper, *C.S. Lewis: A Biography* (London: 1974); Clyde S. Kilby, *The Christian World of C.S. Lewis* (Abingdon: 1965); C.N. Manlove, *C.S.

Lewis: His Literary Achievement (Basingstoke: 1987); A.N. Wilson, *C.S. Lewis: A Biography* (London: 1990).

4. *That Hideous Strength: a Modern Fairy Tale for Grown-ups* (London: 1945) pp. 220–2.
5. C.N. Manlove, pp. 25–6.
6. C.S. Lewis, 'A Reply to Professor Haldane', in *Of This and Other Worlds*, ed., Walter Hooper (London: 1982) p. 101.
7. Noel Annan, *Leslie Stephen: the Godless Victorian* (London: 1984) p. 288.
8. C.S. Lewis, *The Abolition of Man or Reflections on Education with Special Reference to the Teaching of English in the Upper Forms of Schools* (London: 1943) pp. 50–1.
9. F.R. Leavis, *The Great Tradition: George Eliot, Henry James and Joseph Conrad* (London: 1950) p. 177.
10. J.B.S. Haldane, 'Auld Hornie, F.R.S.', *Modern Quarterly*, vol. 1, Autumn (1946) pp. 32–40; C.S. Lewis, 'A Reply to Professor Haldane', pp. 97–109.
11. Wilson, p. 191.

Part III: It's Alive!

10 Scared Shitless: the Sex of Horror

John Nicholson

> In the world of fantasy, in dreams and in tales of horror, things happened which were the work either of evil spirits or of perverted sexuality. Could it be that the lonely fantasies of masturbation ... were taking over the collective fantasies of religion? ... The horror story stood at the meeting of the ways, its ambiguous fascination explicable either in sexual terms as fear of parents or in religious terms as fear of the wrath of God and the works of the Devil.[1]

Horror has a special relationship with its audiences. Unlike science fiction which rarely acknowledges feelings, let alone sex, horror relies on emotions. Horror is an emotion and it must arouse a reaction. Horror awakens hidden fears and desires. While science fiction uses the intellect as a tool, horror engulfs the reader. Science fiction explores the possibilities of technology and investigates the unknown to bring order. Horror neither explores nor investigates. It experiences – or rather its readers react.

In 1973, horrors were everywhere and unavoidable. Horror fiction also got a shock. The one film which transformed public consciousness had profound effects on their business. *The Exorcist* created ripples still felt nearly 20 years later. In 1990 and 1991 the British courts were saturated by cases about children supposedly attacked sexually and satanically.

The second taboo transgressed irrevocably in 1973 was the public confession and insistence by women that they masturbated – and enjoyed it![2] Indeed the idea was so horrible that when *The Exorcist* showed a young girl on the verge of puberty exhibiting sexual proclivities the public accepted the explanation that she must be demonically possessed. Suddenly there were tangible proofs of the existence of the Devil, if not God.

The novel which began it all was quite explicit – more than the film – which is a point this chapter will elaborate. The girl, Regan, was portrayed as suffering the stereotypical fate of masturbators: she became an addict. She masturbated so compulsively and with such relish that she had obviously lost her mind. She masturbated all the time, especially in front of others. When she is examined medically and psychiatrically 'she pulled up her nightgown, exposing her genitals. "Fuck me! Fuck me!" she screamed at the doctors, and with both her hands began masturbating frantically'.

She had begun to 'go wrong' when she urinated in front of her mother's guests. She defecated in front of authority figures. 'The priest heard the sound of diarrhetic voiding into plastic pants'. Her contempt for proper behaviour was inhuman. She forced her mother's face into her genitals. She used a crucifix as a dildo. She vomited on priests and spewed verbal filth at visitors.

At least this is how she behaved in the book. The film could show only some of this. It was a landmark because it showed *any* of it. Bad language in a major film in 1973 still evoked controversy – but from the mouth of an innocent young girl? We must remember that the battle for films to show female pubic hair was only won at the end of the 1960s while 20 years later male genitals have not become a regular feature of main-house films.

The image hit some nerve because a glut of films and books followed about young girls needing exorcism – in 'fact' as well as fiction.[3] All exhibited the same signs: sexual perversity in terms of abnormal ejaculations. Horror provided the perfect excuse for audiences to consume scenes of girls pissing, shitting, vomiting and masturbating to orgasm. There was an obvious displacement by association since all these acts guarantee a person has lost control of their body. They were therefore possessed since no girl in her right mind would do any of these things.

Horror had long been a coded language. After *The Exorcist* a whole new area could be included. The element of domination had been a staple of horror but now it was linked to sexuality. Hollywood was inventing a new vocabulary for unacceptable behaviour.

The chief confusion of sexuality has received little comment though it is the basis of the horror. The novel claimed to be based on a true case but in real life the child was a boy. So it transpired that 'no girl in her right mind' had done these things. But then neither had the boy. Why the sex change for the book and film? Could it be that sexually outrageous acts by a boy would not need supernatural explanation? Faced with the publicly admitted horrific behaviour of women, Hollywood supplied an answer.

According to its publicity the film evoked a parallel response in its audiences. The stunt of having emergency staff to save the terrified moved up a notch. Cinemas had to cope with patrons being physically overcome. Stories spread of vomiting, possession, even death in the auditorium.

Another effect of the impact of *The Exorcist* was the immediate obsolescence of the previously shocking. The languorous looks and heaving bosoms (even when bared) of Hammer films lost any claim to credibility. They looked silly. Suggestiveness that there might be something going on when vampires bit victims could only cause laughter in audiences rapidly used to on-screen acts of explicit sexual abnormality.

Besides, if the plot of films with lesbian vampires was stripped of period costume the situations were derisory. Victorian society might have been horrified by the possibility of predatory lesbians but it did not scare the West after the sexually liberated 1960s! Instead of drippy Victorian maidens in some Ruritania, the audiences could identify with the 'all American girl next door'. Yet *The Exorcist* retained the religious framework of the Hammer films: a priest could still banish the Devil.

Three years after the success of *The Exorcist* another box office smash began with a pubertal heroine being disgraced when she wet herself publicly. *Carrie* revolved around a young girl who was so innocent – another pure all American girl next door – that she didn't know the blood trickling down her legs meant she had started to menstruate. Her schoolmates humiliated her again by drenching her in blood in front of the whole school. Nasty, explicit and never before shown and only possible in the context of horror. Again, the girl was just leaving her state of bodily innocence which was regarded as the proper moment for her to awaken sexually. But Carrie, like Regan, was so aroused that she awoke other psychic powers. Regan was able to levitate, move objects without touching them and twist her head round on her neck. Carrie got her revenge by unleashing a psychic fury which destroyed much of her town. If there was any doubt that female sexuality in the context of horror was breaking taboos in the same year as *Carrie* another main-house film *The Man who Fell to Earth* gave audiences a close-up of a girl urinating through her knickers. She had discovered she had been having sex with an alien, a monster. The depth of her horror was plain to see. However there was no need for any supernatural explanation for her act. Her behaviour was entirely natural and under-standable. (That also excused the watching audiences.) Everybody admitted the physical effect of being possessed by fear. This was a huge admission however. Mrs Radcliffe's heroines may have been frightened out of their wits but we had never needed the soggy pants.

If *The Exorcist, Carrie* and *The Man who Fell to Earth* were not strictly exploitative horror there could be no doubt about *The Last House on the Left* which came out the year before *The Exorcist*. Certainly not a main-house release, indeed it was run out of the exploitation circuit in disgust, the film offered a familiar plot: a girl being victimised. Why the outrage? The teenager was forced to commit sexually degrading acts such as having sex with her friend, female. So what? She was instructed to piss her jeans while the tormentors – and audiences –

watched the stain spreading. The revenge by her parents was a bloodbath, raising the question as to who were the monsters. The atmosphere was realistic, documentary, and lacked any suggestion of supernatural forces. The sexual degradation had only sexual motives: the tormentors wanted to see the girl wet herself. The context of sexual perversion was as unacceptable as satanic possession was acceptable.

The scale of the change in horror between 1973 and 1983 can be seen from a list of hits from the main houses and cult circuits.[4] Here were post-apocalyptic worlds full of inhuman monsters: suburban houses with white sticky stuff coating the walls, rape by tree trunk, a woman in the subway writhing as muck streamed from between her legs, a fat transvestite eating a fresh dog turd, a woman vomiting devotionally into a toilet and a musical starring a drag queen from outer space. After these what price Bela Lugosi?[5]

Or the horror novel? How could writing compete with images such as *Videodrome* where the hero inserted a video cassette into the gaping vagina-like slot in his chest?

Both special effects and the sheer daring of horror cinema left the horror novel bereft of imagery. American horror writers responded to the challenge by joining the cinema. After the success of *Carrie* all Stephen King's work was rushed on to the screen. Indeed the author himself was seen as an actor!

How did American horror and cinema horror affect British horror writing?

The English have a propensity for horrible thrills. For 30 years Hollywood horror was dominated by Hitchcock. The mixture of Daphne du Maurier and Laurence Olivier in *Rebecca* provided a yardstick for the psychological thriller – set in England. Hitchcock's last film, *Frenzy* also revolved around a very English location: the capital's fruit and vegetable market, Covent Garden. There was irony in this vegetarian setting for dead human meat. A hint of cannibalism? One image or supreme nastiness remains: the killer in the back of a lorry getting a corpse out of a sack then snapping its rigor mortis finger to remove a ring. Maybe this gives us a clue as to why the English are so good at horror. Hitchcock represents a particular sort of horror, a nastiness rather than the sexual repression we have noted in the Americans. It is horror based on revulsion – like Shaun Hutson who can be relied on to provide a scene with slugs or some such clamminess. There is a nightmare sense of being at the mercy of something monstrous, a merciless relentless all-destroying power.

In society which elevates secrecy and self-control is it surprising that the lure of the forbidden and unknown makes people obsessed with repression and abnormality? English society is so clearly at the mercy of invisible forces, if only the class system, that there is an endless supply of stimulants for conspiracy freaks and occult enthusiasts.

Both share a sort of perverse worship. They believe there is a vastly superior power which controls everything and everybody. Paranoia is the last refuge of the powerless.

———

Clairvoyance, remote viewing, precognition are early signs that the mind can manipulate, even destroy, physical and biological objects. Right now secret researches are being made in special laboratories by military and intelligence agencies because the psychic war will soon be on!

Thus Melanie in *Premonitions of an inherited Mind* by Andrew Laurance. This is the first in a trilogy. It indicates how the action has moved on. From the 1960s British audiences had grown used to the idea of a secret war. James Bond, the secret agent with a license to kill had spawned not only films but nightly doses on television. Soon these agents became weirder: *The Avengers, Adam Adamant, The Man From Uncle* and a glut of lesser breeds, created a public acceptance. A topography of paranoia and kinkiness lurked under the surface. A cupboard in a drycleaners was the doorway to a world of bunkers and gadgets. Soon they were given a new generation of special powers not just lasers disguised as cigarette lighters. They were trained to use psychic abilities as weapons, like the comic-book heroes X Men who could see through solids, burn with their glances and touch or fly without mechanical aid. These agents did not rely on fists but ESP.

Andrew Laurance's trilogy introduced an element which could not be shown, or even be implied on screens. Melanie explains, 'The orgasm creates the energy which enables one to leave one's physical casing.' Hence she provokes her astral projection by 'masturbating feverishly' in a mirror. 'If you try to reproduce yourself a mirror helps.'

In *The Link*, volume two, the hero becomes aware of his psychic powers and of the powers competing to harness him. In a series of episodes he sees 'messengers', a pair of children about seven or eight years old, who materialise as they are coupling.. They are not ghosts but the astral bodies projected by the real children. When he meets them in the flesh he asks the boy's mother, Melanie, if the children copulate to trigger their projection. 'Their bodies actually experience the pleasure of orgasm, otherwise they wouldn't do it.'

We have already met Melanie in the first book where she deliberately get pregnant then kills the father. Clearly we have moved beyond the satanic excuse for childish sexuality given in *The Exorcist*.

The Scar offers a female who revels in her sexuality and the power it gives her. First published in 1981, *The Scar* was one of eight novels by Gerald Suster. A beautiful teenager, Helen, moves into town. Soon everybody she befriends dies horribly. With the help of her sexual dupe, a resentful punk, Helen kills the élite of Thatcherland who hypocritically desire her. There are none of the social ironies of American horror as in the films of Romero, Craven or Speilberg. Helen is descended from a witch mutilated and murdered by her victims' ancestors. The revenge by seduction echoes *I Spit on your Grave*, a plot which reappeared regularly throughout the 1980s. Surprisingly nobody seems to have noticed that the traditional image of a serial killer is female. What is noteworthy is how *The Scar*'s twist, of making the villain a woman, enables a parade of female sexual powers. Helen is not only powerfully sexed – she chooses her partners and initiates sex – but also is the controlling partner.

> He wanted her body to acknowledge his as master and to crown him king with screams of pleasure she couldn't suppress. Yet even as he thrust he was alert to the suspicion, not that he was penetrating her but that she was enclosing him.

Helen enjoys her orgasms. She comes before, during and after fucking. She has orgasms without partners. Is she a masturbator driven mad by Satan? Hardly. Firstly she gets aroused by evil. Secondly she enjoys it. She dies unrepentant and satisfied.

Yet if Helen is a monster so is her killer. He too is a descendant of The Witch Finder General. He is killed by a policeman as he is about to kill Helen's little daughter who also bears the witch's scar.

Suster set *The Offering* in another idyllic English village. The ancient curse is the power inside an artefact. It is the centrepiece for a secret cult (conspiracy) of female worshippers continuing practices which activate psychic powers. These are fed by the sacrifice of men's genitals. A sect of castrating women.

Striker is the name of the narrator who discovers his psychic power while at an English boarding school when he causes the death of the headmaster. The story is remarkable for its description in passing of a non-mysterious horror: the way the English treat their children. In New York, Striker is taken up by a secret group researching 'mutants' (humans who have evolved). A detailed scientific explanation is given for the powers. It turns out the mutant monsters are really being manipulated by the government, by monster powers.

As usual it is hard to avoid thinking of film equivalents: *Scanners* by Cronenberg, *Firestarter* from Stephen King's novel and *The Fury* from a novel by John Farris and, indeed, Suster's early books read more like film scripts. His next titles, *The Block* and *The Force*, were longer (*The*

Force is 367 pages) and more ambitious. Both are complicated and set in institutions: an apartment building and a large firm. They have large casts which only draws attention to the lack of characterisation.

By contrast, *Necromancer* shows a novelist's skills. Robert Holdstock later moved from the horror genre to develop the fantastical themes touched on in *Necromancer* and appeal to a different audience with *Mythago Wood*. At the other extreme he showed he was capable of potboilers by writing a series under a pseudonym, *The Night Hunter* by Robert Faulcon. In five books which were issued in two batches, he exploited some themes he had previously treated seriously. The plot was absolute stock: a struggle between goodies and baddies, chases and psychic powers. The blurbs capture the tone: 'One man against the monstrous evil of the occult'; 'Both the evil and the innocent were summoned to the hellborn gathering'; 'Beneath the earth a spider-web of ancient evil – soon to be awakened.' There was scope for set episodes (and perhaps a television spin-off?) dealing with specific local colour: the Ghost Dance Red Indians. The main figure was a sort of psychic private eye. The powers and the procedure were the usual: psychic and sex. The story raced along and provided readers with a cracking good yarn.

Necromancer's plot contains familiar elements but Holdstock is original in his ideas and treatment. He develops the secret research into dormant powers by relating it to Earth mysteries.

He did not acknowledge that there might be some unknown forms of energy eluding detection except in the tentative relationships of stones, leys and underground streams. He did accept that, under certain circumstances, known energy forms could be elusive. And it was people like dowsers and sensitives ... who might be the 'machines' of a new technology, a technology for reading more from standing stones than that which the eye could see and the mind could imagine.

There is a reference to *The Stone Tape*, a television play, which had dramatically illustrated the notion of memories as ghosts trapped inside the stones of buildings.[6] The ancient surviving artefact is in a church. A megalith is embedded in the earth and its tip, projecting above the floor and converted into a font, is still active. At times people commit suicide to fill the font with their blood. A baptism goes wrong when a baby's head hits the font. The child lives, although pathologically withdrawn, and its mother believes its spirit is trapped inside the font. An American scientific researcher, whose open-minded attitude is quoted above, investigates. By contrast the father is an Englishman whose proper behaviour, emotionally dead, extends to an inability to refer to his wife by her name. He habitually calls her 'my wife'. He regards her belief about their son being trapped inside the font as madness. He believes the boy is trapped inside himself. The daughter, almost 16, is on the verge of expulsion for aggressive behaviour. She is open about her sexuality but suffers from nightmares that make her wet herself in arousal and terror. The boy, who refuses to speak or walk, expresses himself by biting through his finger: a happy English family.

A psychic describing herself as a necromancer is enrolled to 'tap' the stone. She recounts how touching stones overwhelms her, 'a strange sort of orgasm. It was beautiful in a cruel sort of way.' There is a struggle between psychic forces. In this case the villain is a demon imprisoned in the stone. It is manipulating people and killing them or making them kill themselves. It possesses the boy who behaves destructively and swears – just like Regan. Yet we get no compulsive masturbating, pissing or shitting. No filth, just normal vomit. The demon feeds on fear, a sort of psychic vampire, 'possessed by something we don't really understand, except in such words as Ancient God, Dark Power, and Supernatural Force'. This evil is imprisoned by ritual use of a code or spell – a prayer – what would to Christianity be an exorcism. However the key can turn the opposite way and unlock the prison releasing the forces of havoc. The resulting devastation is total.

Soon ancient stones and sites became regular plot devices. In *The Worm Stone* the way the ancient evil re-enters the world is explicit. The heroine described the start of her possession. She copulated during a picnic at a site.

It sounds silly, but I had some sort of vision, hallucination, God, I don't know. I'd started to come. It was incredible, I've never come so strongly in my life. It was beautiful. I expect you could feel it. I was right in the middle of it and it felt as though it would go on for ages when it stopped and I had this awful feeling of emptiness and everything went blank. I thought, Oh God, this is stupid – I'm going to pass out in the middle of my climax. And then I saw this thing.

By the early 1980s English horror novels were again showing signs of becoming clichéd. They were again relying on a kind of antiquarianism escape clause. The Hammer vampire or Poe curse had been replaced by another sort of curse or psychic vampirism. The supernatural was being replaced by the unnatural which reflected the paranoia that science had unleashed monsters.

––––––

Everybody in Britain knows Stephen King but few have heard of Guy N. Smith? Yet he is probably Britain's most prolific and biggest selling horror novelist with more than 30 titles. These include many series on the theme of unnatural creatures. *Killer Crabs, Origin of the Crabs, Crabs on the Rampage*. The *Sabat* series is about witches and there is also a set of werewolf novels.

In 1981, Smith produced *Warhead* whose front cover showed a skull with a missile sticking into its mouth while the tip poked out of the top. The ultimate penetration by the ultimate weapon? The legend offered: 'The old gods were threatening mankind with the ultimate holocaust.' The blurb tells potential buyers, 'But there was another power that could destroy utterly. Created by man it lay dormant but always ready.' More ancient psychic demons? No. 'Underground, fuelled and targeted, it lurked in secret launch silos.'

The mixture now includes psychic forces, mad science and an equation between the nuclear armageddon and Earth mysteries. Had the End of the World happened before and were the ancient sites something to do with saving Earth? If it is necessary to re-awaken powers through procedures, usually sexual, then certain places can help because of their potency. Setting aside the arcane mixture which sustained mystical and Fortean magazines for more than a quarter of a century, we have here much in the way of sites as ancient power points which can be re-activated by the correct combination.

Melanie and Helen, like Regan and Carrie, not only have special powers linked to sex but their abilities are inherited. Here the British and Americans diverge. The newcomers to the continent have no archaeology. Instead the original inhabitants are familiar with the land. People have an ancient genetic power which is still inside waiting to be revived.

During the hippie period interest in LSD was in terms of it being a new type of drug. It was a 'psychedelic' or consciousness expanding mechanism. Psychedelics would chemically trigger off latent powers. The leap was into biology. These abilities were supposed to be in the silent part of the mind (the silent majority) where they lay dormant. They were benevolent lurkers at the threshold. Mankind had once been as intelligent as aliens from outer space. It could communicate again if it restored its whole intelligence. In the meantime a secret few descendants had never lost those powers, witness Melanie and Helen.

In real life this genetic dream relates to another English obsession: genealogy. Such an obsession in origins and continuity was upheld and disturbed by the power of sex-induced Earth mysteries.

The paranoia of the nuclear age suggested that man was interfering in God's work. Proof was the fear of biological monsters. For every lost continent full of giant apes there were plagues of mutant creatures swarming over the planet: killer crabs and slugs were the latest in the genealogy which included freak plants like triffids. Nature could become monstrous just as supernature, the biological heaven, could produce angels with non-human powers. The chemically induced new human, the psychic mutant, was the other side of the same coin.

The new intelligence was not just evolutionary but could give birth to a new species. 'Our consciousnesses linked up, formed a new entity that was not human, and wasn't inhuman either.'[7] If this was what was going on in experiments conducted by Havard personnel in 1963 what might not happen once the drug was used by anybody? The advocates preached it would spread like an infection, a virus. Was this the biological counterpart of the domino theory?

———

By the 1980s horror had become big business. Here was a viral infection spreading out of control! In the late 1960s it had been like belonging to a secret society to admit you read horror. Few publishers and fewer shops bothered. When Bram Stoker, in his early twenties was working in one of the Popular Book centres (half price back when returned), he ran a side line: The Vault of Horror. Realising there was a market he spread his importing of American paperbacks to include science fiction. Within six years he had moved twice and expanded tenfold. By the 1980s horror was on every paperback list and in every town. Horror had its own section, even a livery: every cover was black. Was horror turning into a huge industry like science fiction?

The kinky and criminal – the refusal to obey nature's laws – were stock in horror. Likewise sexuality in children could be described in the guise of perversity. Odd and inexplicable behaviour were allowed with the excuse of horror. In reality, they were only odd and inexplicable because people refused to admit they were neither. Instead they preferred much more bizarre explanations.

Alan Garner's books for youngsters revolve around awakening special powers: supernaturally and sexually. His first books in the 1960s were creepy precisely because the sexuality was unstated. *The Owl Service* (1973) was as cryptic as *The Turn of the Screw* being full of 'strange goings on' with sexual hints. By 1975 in *Red Shift*, his characters were more explicitly drawn and reflected the changed social climate.

A pair of young lovers slip back and forwards in time. They are lovers in the physical sense too. At the start of the book the girl betrays her pregnancy by being dramatically sick. However hers is no demonic filth manifesting. Her behaviour is natural while the horror is the monstrous attitudes of her parents who regard her as a monster for behaving naturally. In 1976, *The Story of the Weasel* was set in *Turn of the Screw* period dress. A brother and sister are an odd couple. She loves him and they consummate. She has their child. The reviewers enthused about 'sadism, madness and mutilation. ... dark gothic doings ... add ... immeasurably to their erotic and mysterious power'. *The Wasteland* (1983) had similar undertones, including incest and a baby.

By 1981, a young girl did not have to be demonically possessed to exercise sexual powers. The main character in *The Birthday Treat* is a twelve-year-old girl. Admittedly she is an American who has to live in England. Nevertheless her adventures are a long way from Regan. She is secretly destroying her neighbourhood. She engineers assaults on the children in her group, often lethally. To help her she needs the help of a boy. He sets his price: she must show him her pants. As she does so she wonders how much more cruelty she can inflict. Looking at the agitated boy 'something like an enormous smile began in her stomach, rose up fluttering her chest, blossomed on her face'.

The prestigious Maugham award for 1976 went to a collection of short stories which was 'rapturously received ... dark and dangerous ... gruesome ... perverted lives'. Because they were literature people unaware of horror, they dutifully read a story about a 14-year-old boy's sexual awakening told in a dead pan tone familiar to horror fans. He finally learns how to fuck and orgasms inside his younger sister. She corrects him after his ignorant attempts. 'I know where it goes. I know where the hole is.' The other stories contained elements which were as familiar to horror readers as they were exotic to followers of literature. The author was Ian McEwan.

McEwan's second collection provided more shocks for such readers. Perversions were the staple presented in a matter-of-fact way which evoked horror. Literature lovers were introduced to a nurse who initiated a sleazoid into her 'wants' and his unacknowledged tastes. She sexually degrades him, pissing on him during sex. Literature now included females who openly played sexual games previously so horrific and perverted they needed the excuse of satanic possession! Women enjoyed behaviour regarded as perverse. They didn't have to be possessed by demons or terrified out of their wits – they pissed for erotic effect. McEwan's stories are full of such horrific behaviour. The ultimate sexual degradation? She and his other lover-nurse strap him down to operate on him, to emasculate him surgically. Hitchcock or exploitation drive-in gore-fest?

The Cement Garden was McEwan's first full-length novel. It is a psychotically nasty place. A family has become isolated and when the last parent dies the children keep her by walling up her corpse in the cellar. They cement over everything – the physical repression reflecting their emotional state.

The eldest children, Julie, who is 17, and Jack the narrator, who is 14, play 'The Game' with Sue who is 12. They all pretend Sue is a specimen from outer space. The Game 'climaxes' in them taking turns to masturbate Sue. As the boy gets older he prefers to withdraw to masturbate thinking 'of Julie's pale brown fingers between Sue's legs'.

Jack and Julie have their own games. He terrifies her 'coming to get you'. Julie 'stares at the huge filthy gloves' which overpower her so much she loses control. 'One hand plucked at the coarse material of the glove. As I moved forward to be in a better position to hold her down, I felt hot liquid spreading over my knee.'

Julie performs a Regan-like exhibitionistic act in front of the family. Though it is received as innocent and delightful its effect on Jack is undeniably sexual. When Julie performs a cartwheel,

Her skirt fell down over her head. Her knickers showed a brilliant white against the pale-brown skin of her legs and I could see how the material bunched in little pleats around the elastic that clung to her flat, muscular belly. A few black hairs curled out from the white crotch. Her legs, which were together at first, now moved slowly apart like giant arms.

Eventually matters reach a conclusion. Julie's frustrated man friend smashes the cement to expose the rotting corpse. His thuds coincide with the thrusts of Julie and Jack consummating to the delight of their siblings. As they finish they hear the police cars. The horror, the real world, is about to break in. In McEwan's world, as in *The Weasel* or *The Birthday Treat*, there are no external horrors. No bug-eyed monsters, no supernatural forces, simply the unnatural. Nastiness and creepiness take place in the setting of real life. The unnatural creatures are children.

The sexual element of horror and vice versa, was now in the open. The coded language of pubertal girls doing perverse sexual acts no longer automatically proved they were possessed by unearthly forces. Were they evil or just perverts?

Hollywood and American horror novels did offer a new twist. Heroines did not have sexual feelings so when they experienced orgasm without a partner they were being raped psychically. Involuntary climaxes were the stars of *The Entity* and *The Searing*. The climaxes of the victims in *The Institution* are so physical they gush out as their life-blood. The victims in *Whispers* are not responsible for their climaxes because they are controlled by behavioural code words. Even the mother in *Poltergeist* was assaulted when she lay on her bed wearing no skirt. Invisible forces lifted her sweater and opened her thighs so audiences focused on her heaving crotch.

Nancy Friday produced more documentary confessions during the next 20 years culminating in *Women on Top*. This was the generation after Regan and Carrie with women who no longer felt guilt. Here was a parade of perverted women in real life. Their sexual imaginings were recounted in a matter-of-fact way. On the contrary these scenarios, like horror stories, were useless unless they provoked an emotional and physical effect. Successful business women detailed how they regularly spent hours photographing themselves with dildoes in their anuses. And that was apart from the fantasy.

The narrator of Iain Banks's *The Wasp Factory* is a 16-year-old boy who is the sole human in a world of totemic animals, a monster among monstrosities. The story is set in one of those lost places, like *The Cement Garden* or *The Wasteland*, which are on the edge of the world. In this case it is a desolate cast-off Scotland. The few humans in the nearby village ignore the narrator and his solitary parent. He has the characteristics of the other flora and fauna: left-overs, social debris like the carcasses which litter the waste land. The narrator lays a mythology over the topography of despair. He maps it out with personal fetishes: skulls on posts on which he ceremonially urinates. We are inside a mind of madness, childish, cruel, nasty and perverse. As savage and barbaric as Kurtz in *Heart of Darkness* who goes native. It does not come as a surprise to learn the boy has already killed humans.

Two years after I killed Blyth I murdered my younger brother Paul for quite different and more fundamental reasons ... a year after that I did for my young cousin Esmeralda. That's my score to date. Three. I haven't killed anybody for years and don't intend to ever again. It was just a phase I was going through.

The complicated mythology of tortured creatures relates to his attempt to make his own order or creation out of the perversity surrounding him. His own life is officially ignored, his parents did not register him, so he attends no school.[8]

He suffered a ghastly denial as a child when a dog bit off his genitals. Consequently he is reduced to urinating like a woman, squatting. This he does even when drunk in public, followed by copious vomiting. No satanic possession but too much beer! There are more loathsome twists to this story – the childhood mutilation is a lie. His father is the mad creature–torturer who made tiny marzipan genitals to deceive his daughter.

The Wasp Factory earned raves and disgust but Banks would move away from the horrific and perverse towards the fantastical or science fiction in his later novels.

––––––

By the mid 1980s a new British horror had emerged. If there is one element which can be isolated from Alan Garner, *The Birthday Treat*, *The Story of the Weasel*, *The Wasteland*, *The Cement Garden*, *The Wasp Factory* – it is perversion and murder in the world of children. Could this have any relation to the previous observations about the twisted way the English treat their children? Is there any relation between these horrors and another sort of horror which emerged next, noticeably among British writers? Can we see any social echoes in the cross-over of stock from horror to literature, years before they were claimed for *American Psycho*?

Many of the writers mentioned in this chapter are lesser-known even in the horror genre. Nick Sharman certainly merits that comment despite the brave puff, 'Stephen King and James Herbert ... have a chilling challenger ... Nick Sharman'. *The Switch* was a workmanlike horror about a girl and her parents being taken over, possessed, literally. 'Hauntings' are revealed as a conspiracy to inhabit their bodies. People who interfere are killed mysteriously. It turns out that the doctor is the villain. She is central to the conspiracy as are her son, daughter and husband. The son intends to 'switch' the spirits of his dead father and sister into living bodies. He chooses these victims because the heroine's father had caused their deaths in a car crash. The youth's mediumistic powers are related to his sexual feeling for his sister. They were lovers and are having a baby.

Apart from some twists on the idea of possession (as a type of forcible re-incarnation) this story is useful as an example of another sort of switch. The real world is fantasy while the person accused of imagining things knows the truth. People who realise there is a conspiracy are killed or dismissed as mad. Consequently when the switch occurs there is a moment of shock horror: the extent of the evil is revealed. Also the extent to which the ignorant dupes have been accomplices.

This is a staple device in horror. The misunderstood messenger is treated as mad, evil or alien. To the normal world the truth is mad, outlawed, criminal, perverse, monstrous, horrific – because the normal world is mad, illegal. Yet there is a further dimension familiar to every horror fan: the reader's relationship to this quandary. The reader is another powerless onlooker, part victim, part accomplice. The readers know but can't warn, therefore they are part of the perversion before the reversal. Not that the reversal is inevitable. Horror doesn't always end happily. The truth doesn't always triumph. The powerless onlookers are forced to watch the approach of the inevitable catastrophe. They share the plight of the solitary mad person or alien. The horror of being right but treated as wrong, of not being believed, will end if the warning is heeded and everybody wakes. Then they will see a monstrosity has been in control – of minds, bodies, towns, countries. ... The reversal is total and revolutionary. The real villain is the authority figure, normality.

Normality is evil while the truth is a troublemaker. This situation provides plenty of opportunities for paradox and bitter irony. The fake control, the loss of contact with reality, the separation of the mind from feelings are clinical symptoms.

The glut of 'slasher' movies and books had a strange echo. In real life in the early 1980s a new phenomenon was identified: the serial killer.

Suddenly everything transformed. Many of the plots described in this chapter are about figures who must now be re-categorised. The narrator of *The Wasp Factory* is a serial killer. So is Helen in *The Scar*.

In novels, killers were no longer used simply as plot devices. Another shift took place – from the supernatural we had moved to the unnatural creatures, now the focus became sharper. Most remarkably the change came from England. We have seen how English novelists explored a previously taboo area: childish sexuality. The perversity they found now surfaced in another form. Between 1982 and 1984 a surprising number of novels appeared in England with a plot that was very different. The peculiarity was that these novels shared the same new plot! All were strangely horrible and concerned lethal perversity.

That so many writers attempted to portray the mind of a ghastly murderer at the same time may be dismissed as coincidence. It is certainly uncanny. The less sceptical may wonder if there was some malaise in Britain in the early 1980s. Again it may be coincidental that the second term of Thatcherism began in 1983 after a war fought for national pride. The characteristic shared by these fictional killers is their total split from the rest of the world coupled with their ferocious belief in their moral imperative. *Jacqui, The Banquet, The Sandman, The Wasp Factory, The Cement Garden, The Watcher* and McEwan's short stories all depict moral disorder of pathological proportions which must destroy all opposition or doubt. There is no alternative. Most of the accounts of atrocities are narrated in the first person to increase the sensation of being inside the mind of the killer. All are eager to make the readers appreciate them. They do not seek understanding but recognition. They deserve recognition. They regard themselves as normal, proper, even as benefactors.

They share the same tone of sweet reasonableness as they recount ghastliness. Yet one can sense how thin is this surface. Underneath swirls burning rage! They are motivated not by lust to murder but by moral indignation. They are driven by self-righteousness to a perverse degree. The Yorkshire Ripper, active between 1975 and 1981, claimed he was simply 'cleaning the streets' of immoral – and therefore worthless – women.

Come the Night was originally published in 1984 as *Chainsaw Terror*. A boy peeps on his parents as they row in their bedroom. The wife is leaving and the husband prevents her. He attacks her brutally, finishing by stabbing her to death with a shard of mirror. Then he cuts his own throat. 'He felt his bladder give out, the warm urine running down his leg and then, as blackness finally swept over him, his sphincter muscle failed'. Readers accept this as pathology. Of course everybody knows the ultimate loss of control is death. Except we have come a long way from the introduction of such matters as a sign of satanic possession. We have accepted such behaviour as natural when terrified. We have even acknowledged some people find sexual pleasure in perversion. Now we see it as the proof of death. Soon such descriptions will be obligatory in horror.

The boy goes in to look at the charnel room. 'The stench which flooded over him was almost palpable and he recoiled momentarily, coughing as the pungent coppery odour of blood and the even more powerful stench of excrement assaulted his nostrils.'

He withdraws into himself. He is self-possessed. When his sister comes home to this scene she goes into a state near catatonia. Both victims separate themselves from the outside world in mutual support. After five years the sister begins to re-build a normal life with a boyfriend. The brother's focus however is on his sister. He becomes aroused just watching her preparing a meal. When she has a bath he watches her through a peephole. After she takes her sleeping drugs he creeps into her room to sniff her underwear. He knows she will not wake as he uncovers her to look at her naked body.

He cannot face the possibility of his sister leaving so he re-enacts the scene he saw performed by his parents. Again we get *schadenfreude*, both by the characters and the voyeurs, the readers: 'her clothes drenched in blood, she noticed the puddle of urine between her legs'. Realising she is dying she deliberately focuses on her lover, her brother, hacking away until he beheads her,

> [she] noticed that he had a strong erection. He looked at the blood splattered body of Maureen and found that the throbbing between his legs was even more powerful but he tried to force the thoughts to the back of his mind. He had other things to do.

He embarks on a programme of street cleaning. He brings prostitutes home to show them the rotting head of his sister. As they react he thrusts his tool into their bodies. The sexual confusion means the tool he uses is a chainsaw. Their bodies explode literally in a total body spasm.

Jacqui is presented in the form of a monologue, taking us inside the mind of a monster. As he talks to us he builds up layer on layer of horror. His version of normality is so far removed from that of the world – and presumably of the readers – that the suspense becomes unbearable. He keeps telling us that he had to kill his girlfriend and as he recounts their story he continually emphasises how right his behaviour was compared to hers. The readers listen powerless to warn the unsuspecting victim that she is living with a monster and her death is inevitable. The supreme irony is the madman's respectability. He never tires of emphasising how his behaviour is proper while the girl is disgusting.

God knows how she was cramming a five month pregnancy into skintight jeans, the poor baby must have been stifled. ... When I laid her out in her tomb I bought beautiful things for her, a long black silk skirt and a beautiful honey coloured silk blouse.

What 'tomb'? Her corpse lies at the bottom of his kitchen's deep freeze for a year. Having investigated all ways of disposing of the body the madman picks 'the ancient Egyptian' method: embalming. He takes out the corpse, thaws it and cuts it open. The innards are thrown into a wine-fermenting plastic drum.

'If you put it in a horror movie and showed it to the Ancient Egyptians, they'd have wondered what you were going on about.' *The Sandman* delves even more deeply into horrors and irony.

I have killed 18 men and women ... I am an artist. My work has been shown on TV and acclaimed as a national scandal. The popular press has followed my career with feverish enthusiasm. My work has been reviewed in several languages. I am celebrated.

The killer is much more self-conscious and critical than in *Jacqui*. He knows he is doing evil and is philosophical, almost religious about his 'work', his mission. He sees himself as a manifestation which comes in many shapes and guises. He is an incarnation. Is he therefore possessed? He considers himself rational and fully aware. He chooses to kill. When he was rehearsing he saw himself as a conjurer who makes people disappear. He wandered the streets and, in his imagination, chose victims.

My moment to reveal an imaginary revolver or knife. Blades sprang from the tips of my shoes. Acid spat from my buttonhole. My thumbs were loaded pistols. I slaughtered men and women at random. ... It was a macabre game for a bright young man.

As the Sandman he brings sleep. He sets himself up to begin his work in earnest. He has a laugh at the expense of the stereotype of the habitual or serial killer.

Killers, I knew from my boyhood visits to the cinema, dwelt in basements ugly as caves, full of broken bottles and bundles of damp newspaper. They crouched at smeared windows and stared up at the feet of the people who passed on the street above. ... The rooms I chose ... were small and pretty. The chairs were sweet and plump ... here I would sit and contemplate murder in comfort.

Soon he is massacring strangers in batches: 'In that moment I felt as huge as an angel watching over the slumbering world.' The Sandman's alienation grows from isolation in a seaside boarding-house with a mother who gets madder. His companion, a girl slightly older than him, sets her mark on his sexuality. She delights in being dominated and progresses to other perversions until she is killed by her husband, a butcher, who puts her carcass in his freezer.

The madmen in *Jacqui* and *The Sandman* live happily ever after. They could be your neighbour.

Though the author of *The Banquet* is a woman the only voice to speak in the first person is a man. This is not because the woman is the victim – her thoughts are reported. There is an intense feeling between them which makes them consenting. 'Perhaps he will kill me, she thought, her eyes wide and strange, perhaps he will. And she was more exhilarated and terrified than at any time in her life.' As we have seen horror fiction has no shortage of females who kill either or both sexes. Likewise for real life murderers gender is not an issue. The thrill is dominance.

In *The Banquet* the pattern is classic. The predator, the lover, stalks a victim. The irony in this novel is that the processes are seen as so similar as to be interchangeable. The vocabulary is full of metaphors and similes for passion *as eating*. True love is all-devouring. Their love affair follows the traditional route: 'at first ... a rapport ... eager and fragile, then deepening to a consuming passion'. The girl also realises their desire to unite is literal. 'Our frenzy of possession could only be eased by a total consumption of one another – mind, flesh and soul.' They inhabit a world of sensual pleasures, joy, laughter, good living. There is no sexual oddness, no nastiness, no perversion. There is no agent of death, no crazy with a chainsaw or knives. Only appetite.

In fact he doesn't kill her. She falls down stairs and breaks her neck. Yet the logical climax follows. The lovers have their ultimate banquet, uniting in a love-feast. 'Set out beside him was a small covered dish.'

The Banquet is by the author of *The Story of the Weasel*. Both novels describe love in a world set apart. In *The Banquet* there is an echo of childish perversity. A 15-year-old girl suddenly appears at an adult party and, Regan-like, performs an act of perverse exhibitionism. It turns out it was in revenge for being sexually abused by her uncle.

––––––

These writers, Slaughter, Gibson, Rush, Swift, Banks, McEwan, Garner, are not regarded as horror writers. The horrors they describe are increased precisely because the context of horror is removed. Similar scenes may have been stock in horror but there was the escape clause of *condemnation*. These new writers offer a world *without* moral judgement. Regan and Carrie could not be further apart from little girls who help their brothers with 'I know where it goes'. But there is a further notch. These novels are presented as real life, unlike much horror. This is how people really behave. The use of the confessional – documentary device increases this impression. If these stories were not literature they would belong in the outer regions of exploitative pulp.

This point can be expanded by thinking of Dennis Wheatley who dominated the horror and satanism area from 1935 with *The Devil Rides Out*, until the 1970s when he edited the *Dennis Wheatley Library of the Occult* containing more than 40 titles for Sphere paperbacks. Wheatley left no doubt that the people and antics he described so often and luridly should be condemned. The same stern prurience dominated *The Exorcist* which otherwise dealt in subject matter that could only be found in highly specialised perversion or pornography.

The most powerful of these madman novels is *The Watcher*. It stands between the psychic horrors and the interior horrors of killers. It was first published in America in 1982 and is set in the New York area. However it was written by an Eton and Oxford Scotsman.

The trigger as always is simple, trivial and unremarkable. The hero becomes alienated by chance as he is outside his house. Looking up at a window he watches his wife undressing. He imagines how it would be for a voyeur, 'I was an alien pair of eyes. She was unknown, forbidden territory, inviting exploration. Like some Peeping Tom scarcely able to believe his luck I concentrated my whole gaze on that bathroom window, determined to miss nothing.' It turns out she knew he was watching and had deliberately exhibited herself. Both are sexual conspirators.

But he is in an alien world, a world where he is no longer himself. A world where his actions are horrendous. Next morning he leaves his sleeping wife, goes downstairs and butchers their dogs. He puts the bits in a box as a present for her and leaves.

He has a sort of breakdown or, in non-psychiatric terms, sees visions. He hears noises at night in his anonymous boarding-house room. It vibrates to the rhythm of a masturbating young woman behind a screen in the corner. '"Fuck me" she howls against the din, "under the tail, sweet Jesus!" Faster, faster, rocking violently, to and fro, in, out – slipping it to herself, she reaches her solitary climax in a long defiant snarl of ecstasy.' He goes to look and finds instead the maggot squirming body of a ten-year-old girl with a vent in her abdomen, 'loose grayish knots of intestine spilled over into her hardly pubescent groin'.

Under hypnosis he 'releases' at least six personalities (he is possessed in the non-supernatural sense). The idea of multiple personality was becoming the new explanation for serial killers. They were not possessed by devils and not schizophrenics like Jekyll and Hyde, nor psychotics – they were inhabited by many personalities.

These six personalities span time. The most recent is a half-breed Cherokee. The hero tracks him down and discovers that he really existed. More extraordinarily the Indian vanished at exactly the same instant the hero was born. This re-incarnatory instant coincides with another death and birth: the dropping of the atomic bomb on Hiroshima. Are the personalities sequential and is there any other link? He realises the Indian believed he was A Watcher, a sort of cosmic guardian. The hero therefore inherits this role: of watching for signs that the world is ending, this time for certain. He learns that the first incarnation was tricked into parting with a talisman. This must be recovered to save Earth. There is knowledge of an act so monstrous it generates a need for atonement. This need takes on a life of its own. It is a psychic creature which ignores time and space. It can possess persons or places.

Of course this mystical interpretation is at odds with the psychiatric version. *The Watcher* operates on different levels of reality. Not only does it play off the contradictory views of events by letting the readers hear the hero's own voice and then the psychiatrist's notes but it also puts readers in a new variation of suspense. They have to make their own choice about what is real. Gradually and subtly we notice the two accounts of the same events diverge until we are not sure who is telling the truth. We are courted by rival conspiracies. We become peepers as we see what is in the secret notes of the psychiatrist who is manipulating the patient with the collusion of his wife and friendly doctor. This paranoia, of the reader, is increased by the hero's account of how he uncovers another secret side to the psychiatrist. He finds a hidden library containing works of deviance: sexual and religious. An illustration shows a nun committing fellatio while being penetrated by a girl with a dog's head. The Watcher's visions also involve mixtures of a half dog, half woman. Are the psychiatrist and his female assistant planting this deliberately or do they belong to some ancient sect of heretical perverts?

The young dog-woman is the key between the conflicting realities. Does she come to his seedy rooming house to betray the psychiatrist or is she part of the psychiatrist's conspiracy against The Watcher? Does she really come or is it all part of his fantasy about her? Their coupling synthesises many strands, real or imagined. She has doglike attributes: hair down her spine and she behaves like a bitch in heat. 'Moisture ran down the inside of her thighs, gushing out of her like a stream'. She emits 'grunts and cries' as she 'began to circle around ... on all fours nosing and nipping and licking me all over'. He grabs her hair, bites her neck and mounts her 'doggie style'. They set up the room as a sex aid where they behave like animals. He watches her from behind the screen with 'one hand curled between her thighs and her livid tongue lolling out of the corner of her mouth, lips all frothy with white stuff' and howling.

To The Watcher her visit is real and 'exorcises' the confusion he had when he first used the room. His sense of mission reinforced he attacks the psychiatrist. He knows the psychiatrist is the re-embodiment of the figure who, for centuries, has tried to thwart his mission to save Earth. But he realises 'who would believe me?' in preference to the authority figure? What he asserts is so unimaginable it will be regarded as the fantasy of a madman. The climax leaves the choice to the reader. The Watcher goes off to fulfil his messianic role.

The ultimate horror must be the extinction of all life: doomsday. Horror often deals with this fear in metaphoric terms. In 1987, *The Power* took Armageddon as its literal starting point. The author, Ian Watson, was introduced to readers as being involved in real life with social and disarmament politics and *The Power* has a very recognisable English setting: a 'wimmins' peace camp outside an American nuclear base, hunt saboteurs, student activists. Watson's next novel approached The End from an ecological angle.

The Power makes full use of horror effects. Whereas *The Watcher* dealt in psychological 'subtleties' in terror and played with the reader. *The Power* is unequalled for its parade of sexual confusion as a metaphor for evil. Jenni, the 35-year-old heroine, is a sexual mess. This manifests itself in her confusion about her natural functions. On the toilet she feels a long sausage slide out of her. Moments later in the kitchen she has to squat urgently to pour out a mess on to newspapers quickly spread on the floor. There is no doubt this is shit so what was 'the toilet thing'? She realises it must have been 'born' from her vagina. This perverse monster takes to stalking the countryside and murdering!

But there are other killers lurking in the hedgerows. If Jenni, the respectable primary school teacher conceals horrors so does the picture-book English village.

> Behind almost every other herd of cows there seemed to lurk some item of the next world war. To city dwellers the extent of doomsday packaging was virtually invisible. Not in the green and pleasant land, once you looked beyond the scenery.

Behind the facade of essential England we find the now familiar association of the nuclear holocaust with some atavistic religious rite. The blurb's appeal has nothing to do with libertarian politics and everything to do with horror: 'An ancient Power awakes. ... A modern evil mushrooms into apocalypse. ... Cocooned in a nightmare world the village of Melfort waits, as The Power feeds on the death and destruction, fuelling its gross appetite.'

The monstrous happens. Jenni witnesses a bomb explode, the nuclear war is taking place. Jenni's response is natural, she pisses herself in terror like the woman faced with the unthinkable in *The Man Who Fell to Earth*. In post-apocalyptic England perversion is the norm. A priest's decapitated head vomits, Regan-like. Except in Jenni's functionally confused world vomit takes second place. The mouth vomits excrement.

Survivors, the undead, stagger zombie-like, keeping up a parody of normal life and even spending the evenings in the village pub. Their loss of human status is signified by their loss of control over their natural functions: they leak urine and excrete continually like incontinent babies or seniles. People turn to Jenni to save them. Didn't she have a miraculous birth, the Madonna of the Toilet? We get a scene that could never be filmed. Jenni has to copulate with a dead man. *It* insists Jenni makes its penis erect otherwise the act can't happen. To help herself she uses her secret masturbatory fantasy: being forcibly masturbated by her college friend, a nurse. The climax is a collector's item. A bucket full of shit whizzes up a well – or Jenni's throat. As it surfaces (shit? vomit?) it ejaculates out of Jenni's mouth over her partner.

Horrible certainly. Yet it is essential to stress that all this perversity is not simply for effect but is the result of a very complicated ideological plot. English political attitudes had become perverted by the late 1980s.

By the end of the book Jenni reaches a sort of peace. When she sees another nuclear flash she pisses herself again. However this time she is not disturbed and lets nature take its course. The sun will dry her out. She wanders off with her dog happily nuzzling her unsavoury crotch. Though this is not the attitude of the book, Jenni's new behaviour is unnatural: she is reconciled to her perverse nature.

Is it possible to go further? If so what will we find – about horror or about the English? English horror writers had found material which certainly put their books beyond anything which could be shown on screens.

At the same time as the burst of killer novels already mentioned appeared, there was a publishing event more noted in retrospect. In 1984, three anthologies of short stories by Clive Barker were issued. Next year came three more. They had a catchy serial title *Books of Blood*. A year and 30 short stories later Clive Barker was hailed as the new hope of British horror. His growth continued to be extraordinary. Within less than five years he had diversified with full-length novels which crossed genres. More significantly he broke out of books and into films, following the example of American horror writers.

By the age of 39 Clive Barker is already an industry. English horror is out! This chapter gives indications of how this became possible.

Instead of a sudden monstrous growth, Clive Barker inherits the legacy of a host of British writers inside and outside horror. In a review of Barker, *Private Eye*, suggested Barker was offering a new twist on an old theme: hatred or fear of women. Perhaps there is more. Barker is exploring perversion under the guise of horror. This is not a horror of sex but the sex of horror. Barker's regular reports of fear causing loss of control, signalled by bladder and bowel, or the hint of ambiguous thrills in torture, are replacing satanism with sex.

Between 1975 and 1985, English horror found its own areas beyond cinema and American horror. It explored small enclosed worlds ruled by a perversity which was far too strong for screens. Though the presumed messiah of English horror, Clive Barker, left England and moved into film. Nevertheless experimental writing is now *indistinguishable* from horror. Small presses such as Creation/Annihilation with their stables of writers chart even more ghastly regions.

Personalities and bodies merge and devour each other. Bowels, bladder, blood are everywhere. *Red Hedz* is typical of their work: 'Like some obscene practical joke: there was TOO much blood. ... Innards. Faeces. The stench was horrendous. Sickening ... a domestic ... abattoir.' The police have trouble establishing an identity for the remains. Literally. They know it is human but 'there was only one body immediately visible; the other person we found sat huddled into a corner of the living-room, covered in the victim's blood. Staring. Seemingly hypnotised by the slaughter.' In Creation Press's anthology from its first year, *Cease to Exist*, the last contribution gives us a paedophile serial killer as the 'hero'. All the horrors rise up to form a creature which advances devouring everybody. The two monsters face each other. The thrill killer faces his reflection. 'He felt as if he was on display, some prime side of beef up for raffle.' By now readers of this chapter know what to expect. Does it still shock? 'His erection wilted, so much useless meat. His sphincter loosened as the shit in his bowels turned liquid. Diarrhoea seeped out and traced the line of his arse, warm as a finger.' The monster metamorphosises its 'meat' to produce a cunt out of which protrudes an erect penis. 'As it fucked him into unconsciousness, he speculated idly on the relationship between sex and death.' He names it: 'Passion'.

English horror moves from one century into another producing work of a uniquely English character.

Notes

1. Derek Jarret, *The Sleep of Reason: Reality and Fantasy in the Victoria Imagination* (New York: 1989).
2. See for example, Shere Hite, *The Hite Report* (New York: 1975) and Nancy Friday, *Our Bodies Ourselves* (Harmondsworth: 1979).

3. See for example, Malachi Martin, *Hostage to the Devil* (London: 1988).
4. See for example such films as *El Topo* (1972); *Wicker Man* (1973); *The Texas Chainsaw Massacre* (1974); *Shivers* (1975) and many others.
5. The career of David Cronenberg is indicative of the discussion here.
6. Nigel Kneale also created *Doomwatch* which foreshadowed much ecological horror.
7. Jay Stevens, *Storming Heaven: LSD and the American Dream* (London: 1989).
8. England 1991: This chapter was completed in December 1991 as the media told of a case in darkest Surrey, a place not associated with remoteness or bleakness. An eleven-year-old boy has never been to school or registered as born. He and his mother lived surrounded by more than two dozen carcasses of pets and 'thousands of maggots'. They were surrounded by neighbours who gave interviews which showed no puzzlement at their own behaviour.

   Later the same evening television offered a documentary about Dennis Nilsen who chopped up at least 15 young men. He buried the remains in the back garden of his respectable suburban house. What of his bleak background? Or his neighbours who complained at the smell – he boiled human heads. The man who came to inspect the blocked drains found human flesh and bone – flushed down the toilet. The remains in the garden and drain are so muddled as to be impossible to identify let alone count.

   Next day a man in charge of homes for disturbed youngsters is found guilty of systematically raping and buggering boys and girls in his care. Then an even bigger scandal is uncovered. In another complex of homes the staff were acting as pimps for the top authorities including senior police.

   The child abuse paranoia has come full circle. Case after case is being thrown out and parents are being exonerated of sexually abusing their children for satanic purposes. Instead it is being revealed that there was a conspiracy against children. It was run by the authorities appointed to care and protect those children. Even Nilsen was an official in charge of helping young men.

   These three stories are from the same week. They are all true. Real life horror in England at the end of the twentieth century.

11 Horrible Writing: the early Fiction of James Herbert

Alasdair Spark

James Herbert has the strange distinction of being one of the most read, and simultaneously one of the least written about contemporary British authors. In sales terms at least, the covers of his novels accurately describe him as 'Britain's number one horror writer' and since his first, *The Rats*, was published in 1974, Herbert has produced at least one horror novel a year. Any perusal of his yardage on bookshop shelving reveals his popularity, and in this sense he is the British equivalent of Stephen King. Later editions of his novels carry the following citation from King on the cover: 'James Herbert comes at us with both hands, not willing simply to engage our attention; he seizes us by the lapels, and begins to scream in our faces.'[1] Which is perhaps why Herbert has had neither the critical attention (even in studies of the genre) nor the movie and television adaptations which so typify King's success. It must be frustrating for Herbert that many casual readers believe that both *The Rats* and his second novel *The Fog* have been filmed. However, John Carpenter's *The Fog* (1981) shares a title, but has no other relationship with Herbert's novel, while *The Rats* is often confused with the two American 'rat' films of the early 1970s *Willard* and *Ben* – the latter best remembered for the eponymous theme song sung by a teenage (and still black) Michael Jackson. So, despite his success, Herbert remains elusive: while paperback editions all share a photograph of the author on the back cover, his face half-lit, brooding upon the horror within, its very artifice seeming to comment on Herbert's lack of identity as little more than a name on a cover.

Herbert is clearly a less capable, more one-note writer than King (King also describes him as 'modern pulp') and he freely admits in the intro-duction to the 1989 edition (and the fourteenth impression) of his second novel *The Fog* (1975), that his early work was crude. Herbert explains that nevertheless he has resisted re-writing or polishing the novel, since its very crudity is an index of horror writing of the time and 'refinement might well sap its strength'.[2] Self-deprecatingly, he adds that practice must have taught him something about writing, and it is appealing that unlike so many American horror writers he does not

147

read as if he emerged fully formed from a university creative writing programme – though it is dispiriting to think that his learning experience should have been so lucrative. Certainly his later novels, such as *The Magic Cottage* (1987) or *Creed* (1990), are better constructed, better plotted, better characterised, and improved in almost every technical feature, although Herbert's titles continue to be horror-denominative as in *Shrine* (1983), *Moon* (1985), *Sepulchre* (1988), *The Jonah* (1981), *The Spear* (1983) or *The Haunted* (1988).

The later novels are more restrained in their depiction of horror (simply put, there is less of it, less often and less graphically described), perhaps an index of Herbert's desire to be taken seriously as a author – and one is reminded of the similar authorial yearnings of that other great popular success, Jeffrey Archer. For the critic, there is an inevitable tendency to regard the later novels as more worthy, but this is unfortunate, for it does hide Herbert's significance as one founding father of a new generation of British horror writing characterised by explicit and graphic description. Herbert very much broke the ground for 1980s horror by such as Ramsay Campbell, Clive Barker, Graham Masterson and Shaun Hutson, and almost single-handedly his success established a new form of mass-market paperback horror fiction. Accordingly, the focus of this article will be upon Herbert's cruder first novels, *The Rats* and *The Fog*, to examine what made them so influential, and to assess the basis of their horror.

The Rats was published in 1974, and it met with immediate popular acclaim (two sequels, *Lair* (1979) and *Domain* (1984) followed). A reviewer in the *Salisbury and Winchester Journal* is quoted on the inside cover.

Should be given an award as the most gruesome book of the year. If the thought of large rats with blood stained teeth and piercing eyes makes you squirm, don't read this book ... enough to make the fearless have nightmares.

The *Sunday Times* agreed, writing of 'the gruesome set pieces and brilliant finale [which] put it in a class of its own'. Both reviewers located the appeal of the novel in the gruesome, referring to Herbert's graphic descriptions of mutilation. *The Fog*, at almost twice the length, was Herbert's first horror-epic, giving the reader more mutilation for the money. In his chatty study of horror, *Danse Macabre* (1987), Stephen King itemises three emotional tiers of horror writing: terror, horror and revulsion.

I recognize terror as the finest emotion, and so I will try to terrorize the reader. If I find I cannot terrify, I will try to horrify, and if I find that I can't horrify, I'll go for the gross-out.[3]

By terror, King apparently means the implied threat of the unknown; by horror, its revelation; and by revulsion, graphic description. In itself, this delineates a formula by which many horror novels move towards a crescendo, but in herbert, it applies less to the structure of the novel as a whole than to individual chapters – as in the *Rats*, where progressively chapter after chapter finishes with a graphic description of a rat eating a victim. To give an example, in the following the narrator describes the climax of an attack by the mutant rats on a London underground train:

A scene from hell: he saw bloody-covered limbs; torn faces; ripped bodies. A man stood almost opposite him, against the wall, stiff and straight, his eyes lifelessly staring, it seemed into his own, while three of four rats gorged themselves on his bare legs. A fat woman completely naked, cried pitifully as she beat at two rats clinging to her ample breasts.[4]

Overwhelmingly, the rhythm of Herbert's fiction is founded on such regular 'gross-outs', what Herbert himself described as 'violence for violence's sake'.[5] Despite such intensity, as Noel Carroll points out in *The Philosophy of Horror*, two paradoxes remain at the heart of horror fiction: 'how people can be moved (e.g. be horrified) by that which they know does not exist [and] how people can be attracted to that which is repulsive'.[6] Carroll argues that the resolution of these twin paradoxes is deeply rooted in the act of reading horror, since

We are attracted to the majority of horror fictions because of the way that the plots of discovery and the dramas of proof pique our curiosity and abet our interest, ideally satisfying them in a way that is pleasurable. But if narrative curiosity about impossible beings is to be satisfied through disclosure, that process must require some element of probable disgust, since such impossible beings are, ex-hypothesis, disturbing, distressful, and repulsive.

Both *The Rats* and *The Fog* are discovery narratives of this type, in which the central horror is unveiled to the characters and to the reader via two narrative structures: the separate vignettes of horror, each an escalated description of bodily mutilation; and the central narrative of the protagonist, detailing his battle with the horror, and also his battle with authority, for a parallel horror exists, located either in the refusal of the authorities to recognise the threat (*The Rats*), or in the discovery that the horror has in fact been created by the authorities (*The Fog*). Of course, the threat of *The Rats* is somewhat more plausible than that of the madness-inducing fog; there was much discussion at the time of a mutated poison-resistant super-rat. But what makes Herbert's rats repulsive is their taste – veritable hunger – for human flesh, and their noxious, foul sewer-diseased state, such that a single bite is fatal.

The peak of horror comes at the climax of *The Rats*, and concerns the discovery by the hero (Harris) of the mutant King Rat, a scene which Herbert describes as follows:

Its whole body seemed to pulse spasmodically; it was almost hairless, a few grey threads clinging sparsely; it was completely white or perhaps grey-pink, impossible to tell in the poor light, and its veins showed through obscenely, throbbing in time with the body movement. It reminded Harris of a huge, dismembered, bloodshot eye. He swallowed hard to stop the rising sickness. He looked into the sightless eyes. There were no pupils, just yellow gleaming slits. The head waved from side to side, seemingly sniffing the air. The stench from the creature was foul, putrid – almost poisonous.

Description such as this – with its declaration that the horrible is best evoked via description – remains the key feature of Herbert's horror to this day. While such description does not vaguely compare to horror of the detached prose of Bret Easton Ellis what differentiates this genre prose is the focus on the foul, the putrid, the verminous and the noxious. Within the genre, the early Herbert now seems tame to any reader accustomed to the harder core descriptions of Clive Barker (it was Barker who said 'you can never show too much') or more so Shaun Hutson, but this was not so in 1974, and as a teenager at the time I can recall the parental disfavour shown toward such, and therefore their precise taboo interest for a teenage audience. Horror fiction was not yet the mass market paperback genre it would become – King, Herbert, *The Exorcist, The Omen* and the like would make it so – and my recollection of pre-Herbert fiction is of anthologies such as those edited by Herbert Van Thal. Some speculation about Herbert's readership is in order here: in my local public library most were shelved in the young adult section, and from one 13-year-old informant it would seem that Herbert was and is most popular among early teen males, an audience for whom he is a collectable author – although a considerable investment is required to buy and keep pace with Herbert's ever expanding canon.

The printing history of *The Rats* is revealingly typical of Herbert: 24 editions printed between 1974 and 1988, and it is not unreasonable to consider this both an index of successive generations of Herbert readers, and of the upward re-pricing made possible by such a consistent and reliable market. One interesting question here lies in the order of reading – it would be interesting to know where the majority of new readers begin, whether with the most recent novel, and then a review of Herbert's canon, or in some other order based upon word of mouth about individual novels. Bearing upon this, my young informant also tells me that James Herbert is generally considered a better (that is, easier?) read than Stephen King, though many readers graduate to King as they get older.

Given Herbert's focus on discovery and description, one of the ironies imposed by the endless re-print status of *The Rats* (and indeed many other such instant classics of the horror genre) concerns its contemporaneity – or rather its lack of it. *The Rats* was written in 1974, and its referents (of which more later) are clearly rooted in the period of the Heath Government, the miners' and other strikes, the 'Three Day Week' and the like; all providing contextual details of a time which must be before the birth of many of Herbert's current readers. Ironically, due to subsequent Conservative administrations, history has passed by *The Rats*. The location for much of the novel is London's East End and docklands, particularly Stepney and Poplar, and the book is full of descriptions of a physical fabric now gone, or at least eclipsed (call them neo-anachronisms): today one obvious denomination for Poplar is as a station on the high-tech Docklands Light Railway. Atop the initial domain of the rats now stands the Canary Wharf development. Equally, one segment of *The Rats* details an attack on a group of vagrants – elderly, meths-drinking, pre-cardboard city vagrants that is. In strict terms, *The Rats* is now a historical novel, though it is doubtful that many readers would describe it as such. This historical erosion is also true of *The Fog*, which contains neo-anachronisms such as a Fleet Street where newspapers are still printed, but most especially in its climax, which takes place in a London gas-works, and involves the detonation of a gasometer full of town-gas – obsolescent since North Sea Gas was first introduced. Since the central appeal and evocation of Herbertian horror is that 'It' (rats, fog, demons, devils or whatever) might happen here and now as you read these words, a tension exists which at some point must become acute, and will eventually de-nature the immediacy of the horror, much as the mention of shillings and pence, or Morris Oxfords might. Furthermore, given that the focus of Herbert's horror fiction is almost always British, this matters to a degree which it might not in fiction with a less familiar American locale. That such appears not to have happened yet with Herbert's early novels, is both a commentary on the discrimination of his audience, and implies that presumably there is an incentive in horror reading to ignore these contradictory details as far as possible, whether obvious in locale or more subtle in social history, in order to validate the horror and hence be horrified.

The central appeal for the teenage reader presumably rests in graphic description of the transgressive and the taboo, both in terms of horror and sexuality. Descriptions of sexual activity are recurrent in Herbert as in much contemporary horror, and in *The Rats* and *The Fog* heterosexual and homosexual intercourse can be found, though the latter is much more coyly presented. Herbert does not directly link sexuality and horror in *The Rats* but presumably the below is just as stimulating (and a fantasy?) to the readership as are descriptions of mutilation: 'She moaned with pleasure, and reached for him. ... His hand crept slowly between her flimsy panties and soft skin, finding her private silky hair, and then down, between her thighs, his fingers becoming wet from her.' There are several similar passages (including a lesbian scene) in *The Fog*, but the novel provides a more direct linkage, since the horror of the virus-laden fog is that it acts to release controls and inhibitions. Several horror passages concern rape and sexual mutilation, and the most notorious scene in *The Fog* concerns an attack by a group of 'fogged' schoolboys on their (male) gym teacher:

> They tore the track suit trousers from his body, and turned him over onto his back, grabbing and kicking at his exposed testicles. Several tore off their own shorts and vests, and began rubbing at their already enlarged penises. One of the smaller boys jumped on the teacher, and tried to enter him as if he was a woman, but was dragged off and beaten to the ground by the others.

Sexual violence against young women and especially the threat of rape has, of course, been one of the chief foci for horror explicitness since the 1970s, perhaps most notably in so-called 'slasher' films such as *Halloween* and the *Friday the 13th* series. Given Herbert's likely readership, it is interesting that in *The Fog* he dwells horrifically on male rape and homosexuality. The above scene continues into an orgy led by a repressed gay teacher (eventually his erect penis is amputated by a deranged school caretaker armed with a pair of garden shears). Herbert's focus on the school, emergent male sexuality, and especially latent homosexuality, is striking and so appropriate to Herbert's readership that one wonders at its deliberateness (I have been unable to discover if Herbert ever taught). In *The Rats* the hero is a schoolteacher, one of the major attacks is upon his school, and the chief victim is the headmaster – he is not given a name.

As already noted, the basic horror structure of both *The Rats* and *The Fog* is twofold: a series of short chapters which progress from an ordinary, often domestic situation, to a revelation of horror, in the form of a graphic account of mutilation, violence and death; and secondly, the narrative of the hero's revulsion and his struggle to defeat the horror. In the first, Herbert's vignettes present the reader with a gallery of working-class, middle-class and upper-class types from a repository of caricature, perhaps with its roots in popular film and television – some can only belong in *Carry On* films. At times this can be comically grotesque, with a good example in *The Rats*.

Stephen Abbott sat in the darkened cinema and stole a quick glance at his girlfriend's face, illuminated by the cinemascope screen. He was bored with the film, partly because the big, craggy cowboy on the screen was too old to act like superman, and partly because he wasn't wearing his glasses. Vikki didn't know he wore glasses sometimes, and he thought it might spoil their relationship if she did. She'd probably go off him too, if she ever found out about his two false front teeth: he had to be so careful in their 'snogging' sessions that her probing tongue didn't dislodge the plate.

Naive or deliberate, sadly Herbert's authorial yearnings have stripped his later fiction of such delights. As it happens, Abbott, Vikki and indeed the entire cinema audience are soon to be eaten alive by the rats, with Abbott dying as 'The End' is projected on the screen.

Presenting this series of individual and class portraits, one reading of their fate would be that the rats get their dinners, and the victims their just desserts. For instance, in the opening segment, a salesman is devoured after losing his job, following the revelation of his homosexuality; in another a baby is eaten after her young mother leaves her unattended; a group of East End vagrants, including a prostitute – intriguingly named Mary Kelly after one of Jack the Ripper's victims – are attacked; and the lustful young man above in the cinema. However, reading the attacks as punishment for transgression will prove unsatisfactory, since in fact Herbert's victims are not presented unsympathetically – and if they were, the reader would presumably cheer on the rats. For instance, the homosexual referred to above is described as follows:

Guilfoyle had fallen in love. He knew the dangers. He'd heard stories of middle aged men and young boys, knew their vulnerability. But he was happy. For the first time, after making love to another man, he felt clean. Purged was the feeling of guilt, gone was the feeling of self-disgust. He felt free, and alive, more alive than he'd ever been.

The rats then eat him, but it is difficult to see this as retribution for his transgression. That Guilfoyle (and note the effeminate name) dies, comes as a result of the gossip and censure of his colleagues, which drives him from his job and his home, and condemns him to the vagrancy which then makes him vulnerable. Likewise, the young mother who leaves her baby for a moment, is not condemned by Herbert – again it is the poverty of the surroundings which makes her leave the room – to borrow some tea – and her baby (it is defended for a while by Shane, the family dog). Undeniably, this is all written naively, but I believe Herbert's intention is clearly and necessarily sympathetic. Much the same can be said of *The Fog*. There is one difference in that the fog does not act itself, rather it liberates violent tendencies and sexual repressions. But in doing so, it does purge its victims – indeed, John Holman (whole-man?), the hero of *The Fog* has undergone the fog-madness and survived, to be strengthened as a result. Since evoking sympathy for those attacked involves presenting them as already victimised, the rats might almost be considered comparable to their victims – at least the early ones – as isolates and outcasts, living at the margins of society. That the rats finally extend the circle of their appetite to the whole city, and to all classes and areas, therefore, ironically counts as a revenge by those they have initially eaten.

In *The Rats* the protagonist is a school teacher named Harris (he is never given a Christian name) whose narrative occupies a good two-thirds of the novel. He progresses from teaching at the school where a pupil is one of the first attacked, to virtual leadership of the government unit combating the rats. One of the central problems a discovery narrative such as *The Rats* faces is to plausibly hold the hero at the centre of the action, once that action has become general. Herbert achieves this by making Harris part of the 'Ratkill' team by virtue of his local knowledge of the streets and canals of dockland, and once inside the team, his anti-bureaucratic common sense leads to the final solution to the rat plague, the evacuation and gassing of all London (a rather lame climax this). In the team, he competes with various ineffectual civil servants, led by the fussy, upper-class 'under-secretary' Foskins (again, note Herbert's emblematic naming); at the close of the novel it is Harris who finds and kills the mutant King Rat in his lair, after Foskins has tried and failed. The same narrative is largely true of *The Fog*, except that the hero Holman is already located within a government team, though he is painted as already a rebellious uncooperative member. That Herbert should begin his career with this type of narrative, a focus on a devastated London, with its gallery of class differentials, and all the incidental details of the army and the like, is unremarkable. It is at the core of the British horror landscape, and Herbert has himself acknowledged the debt his first novels owe to H.G. Wells's *War of the Worlds*, John Wyndham's *Day of the Triffids* and Nigel Kneale's *Quatermass* series.[6]

Where Herbert does strike a different note from the role models provided by Wyndham or Kneale is in the class credentials of his heroes. Harris's working-class background is central to his status in *The Rats*. He is in his early thirties, a child of the East End, educated at college, who has returned to teach at his old school – significantly he went to art college, that 1960s institution which bred Mick Jagger and John Lennon. Herbert paints him as a working-class graduate, unhappy in a stuffy middle-class profession. Herbert describes him as 'still a student at heart, a rebel against the powers that be' and his politics are clearly signalled as working-class Labour. For instance, Harris hates the conformity of the staffroom.

> He unfolded *The Mirror* to look at the headlines. He usually read the paper on the bus on the way to school – he loved to leave it around the staff room, to the disapproval of his colleagues who thought any newspaper other than *The Times* or *The Guardian* were comic books.

Harris is that archetypal figure of postwar Britain, the working-class rebel, but at the same time he has been to college, and is a responsible teacher. Herbert signals Harris' politics as follows:

> As a teacher, he was directly under the control of a government body and was often exasperated by 'committee' decisions, but he knew there were fair-minded men and women who really did care amongst the committee members, who fought hard to get the right decisions. He'd heard many stories of individuals who had fought the government ban on free milk for kids, for instance. Of men and women, including teachers, who had all but lost their jobs because of their opposition.

The reference to free milk is revealing – and now ironic, remember 'Thatcher, Thatcher, milk snatcher?' – and the politics suggested of the fair-minded men and women are clearly Labour. *The Rats* was published in 1974 and presumably written at the time of the Heath Government, and in the novel the Conservatives are in power. Herbert writes positively of the criticisms made by Labour during the rat crisis,

> the party in power, never really cared about the living conditions of the working class people, and had neglected to clear slums, allowed filth to pile up in the slums, and had never implemented proposed plans (proposed by Labour when they were in office) for a completely new network of sewers to cope with London's vast waste problem.

It would be tempting to see a simple relationship here, with the mutant rats spilling out of the East End slums as symbolic of the working class, and the madness induced by the fog of their repressed brutishness, but as the above suggests, Herbert is not to be so easily read. The politics of the two novels are not conformist and clearly depict some of the victims as genuinely victims. In *The Rats* – at least in the East End – people become victims as a result of a London which 'for all its modernity, its high standard of living, could still breed obnoxious, disease carrying vermin'. To that extent, the rat attacks in the West End which close the novel are a politics of the ripped throat which is ultimately indiscriminate. Herbert makes his analysis explicit with the location of the rat lair and the first rat attacks in docklands.

> What disgusted [Harris] more? The vermin themselves – or the fact that it could only happen in East London? Not Hampstead or Kensington, but Poplar. Was it the old prejudices against the middle and upper classes, the councils that took the working classes from their slums, and put them into tall remote concrete towers, telling them they'd never been better off, but never realising that forty homes in a block of flats became forty separate cells for people, communication between them confined to conversations in the lift, was it this that really angered him?

One might quibble that Labour councils were just, if not more, responsible for such urban planning, but it is notable that Herbert locates the problem not in the traditional terraced slums, but in their modern replacement, the tower block which has destroyed a working-class community.

What Herbert is suggesting here is the authenticity of this working-class community, with Labour as party-political register of such. If the menace of the rats is not to be found in a symbolic representation of a threatening working class (except possibly as an agency of their revenge), but instead in violation of their community, where is it to be located? First of all, Herbert's authenticity is predominantly male and white. I have been able to discern only one coloured or ethnic minority person in either novel: in *The Fog*, Samson King, briefly appears, as a maddened London Transport bus driver. *The Rats* and *The Fog* are undeniably chauvinistic and, by and large, the women in both novels fall into the familiar categories of shrews, nags, whores or dutiful, dependent, loving wives and girlfriends. If any just victim for the rats is nominated, it is the promiscuous vagrant prostitute, Mary Kelly, whose life is presented as a catalogue of license. In *The Fog* the range of characters is generally more extensive and women are somewhat better represented – one is a scientist and a member of the team – but even so, most women are individualised because of their nagging, their pulchritude or the eccentricities of their deaths – as in the old lady who is eaten by her dozen pet cats. Both Harris and Holman have girlfriends (Judy and Casey), and if Herbert does suggest some credit for women in these novels, it is in the girlfriend's assigned role to comfort and soften the hardness of the hero, but the two women are all but indistinguishable.

Secondly, Herbert supplies the answer to the location of menace when it is discovered that the rats are in fact a mutated tropical strain, introduced into England by one Professor Schiller. Improbably he rented a house in Poplar to continue his experiments, and it is there that the King Rat is found. In contrast, the fog is British made (and it works!) invented by a Professor Broadmeyer. The symbolics of the rats as foreign/non-English are pre-figured in a day trip Harris makes to Stratford.

> Walking towards the Royal Shakespeare Theatre he saw that many of the old streets had managed to retain their old charm, after all, but it was the throngs of people, the multi-racial accents that destroyed any hope of atmosphere.

Again, Herbert is complaining about the violation of a traditionally cohesive local–national identity. Despite the implied reference, no racist description follows the above, though the implication about ethnic minorities in the United Kingdom seems clear; instead American tourists, that familiar target for all Little Englanders, are caricatured. What Herbert seems to criticise here is another loss of authenticity, through the commodification of English identity, and the violation of community, and hence history, or rather Herbert's equally imaginary version of history. A key moment closes this chapter, as later in the day, at an Olde Worlde pub in Stratford, Harris speaks to his girlfriend: '"This isn't so bad is it?" He turned to study a large square timber coming from the floor and supporting the low ceiling. He reached out to let his fingers run along the deep grain. Plastic. "Shit".'

It is striking that all Herbert's books are about Britons, British institutions, British cities – nowhere in these two novels is there any mention of overseas reaction to these catastrophes – and reflect upon the dissatisfactions of modern British life. This does not exclude criticism of the working classes, if they transgress the boundaries of Herbertian authenticity. He writes of two obviously northern tourists as follows:

> A thin sallow-looking round-shouldered man in an open-necked, short-sleeved floppy shirt, camera hanging on his flat chest: 'Are you coomin', Ilda?' The droning reply from a plump bespectacled woman emerging from a shop doorway, clutching a dozen Stratford-on-Avon postcards. 'Wait oop, wait oop'.

Therefore, what the rats symbolically represent is not the working class, but fears of their contamination and loss of their supposed authenticity, completing the destruction of an identity at threat in other ways. Herbert is quite deliberate in suggesting this, putting into Harris's mind the following: 'He'd had a feeling of revulsion towards the people, not as individuals, but en masse. Strangely enough it had been slightly akin to the revulsion he'd felt towards the rats.' What Herbert writes here is a representation of a working-class politics that

did exist in the 1970s – it led the Labour party to oppose the Common
Market and the dockers to march in support of Enoch Powell – but
essentially what Herbert has done is to appropriate for his violations
a political complexion necessarily sympathetic to a white male view
of working-class life.

The political complexion of the government in *The Fog* is not made
clear. What is, is the lies and corruption of a government which
created the fog as a weapon, then failed to confine it securely, and then
finally abandons the people of London and the South East to it, while
they sit in a bunker under Whitehall. Holman's background is less clear
than that of Harris, but he too is a disaffected graduate, feeling the same
tension with his working-class roots. In the bunker Holman recognises,

> many familiar faces, familiar only because he'd seen them in the
> media. He was puzzled as to what possible value most of them
> could have in this situation. The fact that they were very wealthy
> made him extremely suspicious. Had they bought their way in. Or
> had they done certain favours for government officials, their price
> a ticket for survival on the Doomsday?

In some of the vignettes in *The Fog* madness empowers, acting to
release latent hatreds, and enable victims to enact revenge upon
husbands, wives, employers, colleagues, even policemen, for past frustrations, but it is the bunker which forbids them from attacking the
true source of their frustrations and their madness. As in *The Rats*, it
is implied that fog might exact a legitimate revenge upon its makers
via the maddened population. Holman ponders public reaction to
the fog and the probable government explanation:

> Who would they blame? The Russians, the Chinese. Maybe some
> other countries for a change. ... What excuse would the government
> give? Pollution. Would that play its part? God knows he'd found
> enough evidence of the damage pollution could do in his job, but
> nothing of this magnitude, obviously. And the public weren't stupid
> anymore. The media had broadened their minds, given them an
> insight, however vague, to things that years ago would have been
> completely unheard of, let alone believed.

Therefore, at the close of the novel, Herbert makes it clear that
Holman's mission is not over, it is not merely to defeat the fog, but to
expose the truth of its origins: 'the people are going to find out exactly
how it happened'.

Herbertian horror in *The Rats* and *The Fog* operates through two
unfolding narratives of discovery: one of horror and one of responsibility, and both are conveyed via the interweaving of Herbert's two char-

acteristic structures, the horror vignette and the hero's struggle. The horror operates at several linked levels, first of all, in the facts of violence, especially the mutilation of the human body which it produces; secondly, in the fact that Herbert conveys this, not by implication or omission, but by graphic description modelled on the horror genre's traditional concern with the foul; thirdly, that sympathy for the victims of the horror rests not just upon reader identification, but upon the violation of a set of relationships that Herbert necessarily presents as cohesive (or historically having been so); fourthly that this victimisation must be measured against a communal order which has already been violated by government authority, either by neglect or by lies; and fifthly, that this horror might even represent legitimate violence if directed against the agents of this pre-existing violation. The central feature of the two novels, the explicit description of violence, bodily mutilation, the foul and the noxious has remained a distinctive feature of Herbert, and of British horror fiction, but *The Rats* and *The Fog* now seem untypical horror novels, either of Herbert or the mass market. Both are novels of social catastrophe, not the supernatural, and it is my impression that British horror has progressively moved in this direction. Given the mass experience of Thatcherism in the 1980s, this may seem odd, and to the horror genre's loss, but perhaps it does speak to the stated ideology of the decade that the focus of horror should have concentrated on the individual. Carroll suggests that in the 1970s the disruptions of Watergate and depictions of the Vietnam War may have been responsible for the revival of the horror genre in film and novel, and in the 1980s a requisite postmodern loss of cultural and personal anchorage was responsible for the focus on violence to the body.[7] From a British perspective, perhaps the same formula could have its initial terms substituted by strikes, urban development, immigration and the Common Market. As I have argued, Herbert does speak, however naively, to some of the tensions of 1970s Britain, most especially those relevant to a depiction of the working classes. For this reason, his early naive fiction has a significance which will outlive its notoriety, and perhaps the message of this is that critics ought to give a best-selling author such as Herbert more attention.

Acknowledgements

I should like to thank Francis Simons for his assistance in researching this article.

Notes

1. The citation comes from Stephen King, *Danse Macabre* (New York: 1987) p. 407.

2. James Herbert, *The Fog* (London: (1975) 1989) p. 6.
3. King, pp. 22–3.
4. James Herbert, *The Rats* (London: (1974) 1988) p. 89.
5. Herbert, quoted in King, p. 410.
6. Noel Carroll, *The Philosophy of Horror* (London: 1990) pp. 160–1.
7. Carroll, pp. 209–11.

12 At Home all was Blood and Feathers: The Werewolf in the Kitchen – Angela Carter and Horror

Gina Wisker

A house full of locked doors that open only into other rooms with other locked doors, for, upstairs and downstairs, all the rooms lead in and out of one another like a maze in a bad dream. 'The Fall River Axe Murders'[1]

Angela Carter's sense of horror is based on the grotesque, the bizarre and excessive, a kind of baroquely overlaid nightmare which has uneasy echoes for us. She investigates the stuff of myth and dreams and in doing so unearths rather unpleasant, perverse sexual fantasies, digging further behind the suburban mind to identify the interest in the werewolf tale, the fairytales of Bluebeard and his wives and Beauty and the Beast. In investigating our subconscious horrors, Carter brings a chill to the domestic and the everyday. Opening a kitchen drawer in the Carter kitchens of our minds, we are always like Melanie in *The Magic Toyshop* likely to meet something horrid:

Melanie hummed to herself as she hung cups from their hooks and propped the plates. She opened the dresser drawer to put away the knives and spoons. In the dresser drawer was a freshly severed hand, all bloody at the roots.

The details are domestic and realistic, the episode and object monstrous, inexplicable, though Uncle Philip is a sort of urban Bluebeard in his own way, and Melanie has been thinking of Poe. In Carter's horror, the mazes of the ordinary mind in the ordinary house are entered to reveal gothic torture chambers and spiral staircases leading down to dungeons.

In 'The Fall River Axe Murders' Carter looks at the catalysts, the events and moments which made murder inevitable in the claustrophobic middle-class normality of the Fall River, Massachusetts Borden

161

household. She does not linger on the blood. Threat permeates the descriptions: of ties which 'garotte' their virtuous wearers and the oppressive constricting clothes the women wear in this sweating, constrained household. Carter investigates. Her probing of details reveals gaps and silences, 'what the girls do on their own is unimaginable to me' and of Emma, Lizzie's sister that, 'she is a blank space'. (*Black Venus*) The iron-backed, capital-accumulating father, the repressed, stifled sisters, the air of suppurating normality; these permeate Carter's descriptions of this fated family, our knowledge of whose violent fate lurks and drips over every restrained comment, calm as the clichéd 'still waters' of Lizzie's nature as she drives hatpins into her hat or weighs the axe which slaughtered her pigeons to make a pie for her stepmother.

Horror in much of Angela Carter's writing captures a sense of a potion containing the monstrous and the everyday. Lizzie Borden is a figure for this, and we are reminded that given the right circumstances and the appropriate kind of suburban claustrophobia, we might all erupt and give our family 40 whacks with an axe.

Carter explores those locked rooms. The mazes and corridors and doors of conformity and normality which we use to confuse and hide away our destructive drives, and our nightmares are replicated in the twists and turns of the fiction's realistic artifice, while networks of imagery hint, suggest and occasionally dramatically reveal the sources of the terror, the disgust and the horror. There are blood, feathers and much worse, in all of Angela Carter's kitchens. 'The structure of fantastic narratives is one founded upon contradictions.'[2] There are many recognisable realistic details, dates, times, typical clothing and furniture in the text. The places are familiar, and at the same time the surreal and the symbolic provide another layer of meaning. Metaphor combines with metonymy and the oxymoronic mixture is the fabric of her language.

Carter's fiction disinters and utilises the stuff of dreams. The fiction proves dreams palpably 'real', and so shows itself as psychologically based horror which owes much to Freud, Jung and to Melanie Klein. Her dream – and magic-based landscapes are rendered tangible because, she insists, dreams are part of our lives, and related to the myths we use to describe and direct our lives, 'There is certainly confusion about the nature of dreams which are in fact perfectly real: they are real *as* dreams and they're full of *real* meaning as dreams.'[3]

Like Bruno Bettelheim, whose work influenced *The Bloody Chamber*, Carter uses dream and fantasy material to reflect inner experiences and processes, ways of rendering and coping with the palpable conscious world and the reactions of the unconscious.

The break with the notion of a straightjacket of the real releases energies leading to a fuller understanding of how meanings are created, values constructed and versions of worth and of reality validated over other versions. Fantasy is a useful mode 'Because it is a narrative structured upon contraries, fantasy tells of limits, and it is particularly revealing in pointing to the edge of the "real".'[4] And as Jackson says, 'breaking single, reductive "truths", the fantastic traces a space within a society's cognitive frame. It introduces multiple, contradictory "truths": it becomes polysemic.'[5]

Horror, gothic and the use of fantasy combine in Carter's work. The collapse of boundaries and divisions, between the animate and the inanimate is a regular element of fantasy, while one chief tool of terror is the reduction of man to an object, a machine, a doll or an automaton. This is a frequent characteristic in an Angela Carter story or novel. In her examination of sexual politics and their psychological motivation and their social representations, she repeatedly presents scenarios where women are manipulated as marionettes (*The Magic Toyshop*), or preferred as tableaux vivants: disempowered objects of desire, as in the hideous living-sex museum of Madame Schreck in *Nights at the Circus*, or preferred dead and kept as mementoes in Bluebeard's castle. She allies her examination of the basis of terror and horror with an interest in sexual power and perversion, and so it is that the ones rendered immobile and automated are usually women in the hands of men, manipulated by power or for money; it is a logical enactment of the 'living doll' image.

The most consistently developed example of the recurring automaton, puppet or doll image in Carter's fiction can be found in the early 'The Loves of the Lady Purple' (*Fireworks*) where the doll who enacts the quiet circus professor's violent erotic fantasies, comes to life and finally repeats them in reality, draining him in an act of vampirism.

The Asiatic professor reminds us of Carter the author.

> The puppet master is always dusted with a little darkness. In direct relation to his skill he propagates the most bewildering enigmas for, the more lifelike his marionettes, the more godlike his marionettes and the more radical the symbiosis between inarticulate doll and articulating fingers.

He acts as intermediary between audience and the dolls, the 'undead', here deliberately described in the language used to describe vampires. The puppet master's dolls are a mixture of magic and realism; the stories they enact speak to the audience of a certain repressed and unspeakable reality and the more extreme, bizarre or perverse the incidents in which they are involved, the closer the recognition of those selves and secrets the readership keep behind their own locked doors.

The professor has no language which can be understood and his apprentice is deaf, his other foundling helper dumb, but the Lady Purple blazons her messages in her actions accompanied by the appropriately weird but untranslatable stories of the professor. As Queen of the

Night, the Lady Purple, object of all the professor's sexual fantasies, is 'filled with necromantic vigour' with the vitality of the professor passing directly through into her, draining him while she embodies that traditional perverse twinning of sex and pain, the erotic and power. She is 'a distillation of those of a born woman ... the quintessence of eroticism'. Nightly she acts out the story invented of her life, lusts and eventual reduction to a marionette. The stylised, symbolic puppet characters and sexual scenarios are equally figures 'in a rhetoric' where the abstract essence of erotic woman can be bought, used, manipulated and later shelved. The constant oscillation between the language of artifice and the language of the real, tells the story Lady Purple enacts, as if it were a true record.

Ironically her power is emphasised as one who encourages the acting out of fantasies which then reduce her lovers to objects. 'She, the sole perpetrator of desire, proliferated malign fantasies all around her and used her lovers as the canvas on which she executed boudoir masterpieces of destruction. Skins melted in the electricity she generated.' For those watching the show she embodies the object of their desire as well as their fears, rendering them ultimately safe because of the awareness of artifice. This mimics the activity of horror fiction: embodiment, audience enjoyment, and a sense of release and security. The interest, the drive, the fears do not disappear. Indeed, Carter suggests they return nightly.

Modern horror tales emerged as a genre with the secularisation of society and the leaking away of religious explanations of the odd and inexplicable.[6] Science also could not explain all that was unusual and strange, so a space for these expressions was found in the genre of horror which itself was enabled to ask questions about the power of religious controls as well as the dangers of science. Things 'out of control' and objects 'come to life' emerge as the main example of these expressions. As Martin Barker puts it looking at the lobby surrounding the horror comic censorship of the 1950s in *A Haunt of Fears*.

It is the sense of helplessness in the face of unpredictable objects and processes that make such narratives work as horror. In this .. they come closest to film horror, where the classic motifs – dark nights, unknown threats, and ritual incantations to control the forces of evil – are just what leave us deliciously shuddering when they are well manipulated.[7]

Lady Purple is a thing come to life, and a thing out of control. She is more than that though, for she is the embodiment of the perverse and lustful thoughts and dreams both of her creator the professor and the audiences who enjoy watching a doll act out sado-masochistic fantasies. Her coming to life is ironically the downfall of those who have thus positioned her (the professor and future male victims in the brothel). She also embodies the frighteningly circular and inevitable re-enactment of myth. Lady Purple is a vengeful fetishistic object, sado-masochistic and horror fantasy combined.

Fetishism is the stuff on which pornography thrives and Carter takes further into social critique her manipulation of fantasy and horror's technique of confusing the boundaries between animate and inanimate, objects of desire and object to be controlled and destroyed. In *The Magic Toyshop* is a palimpsest of popular fictional forms, fairytales. myths, girls' own paper stories. Through examination of Melanie's adolescent construction of herself in the semi-pornographic art modes in which woman is represented by great painters and writers, Carter examines how the myths of our femininity, our sexual being come to be fashioned upon us and come to be that part of us with which we willingly collude, blind to their reifying implications. These implications: rape, violation, pregnancy, are indicated in the positioning of Edward Bear 'swollen stomach concealing striped pyjamas' and Lorna Doone, 'splayed out, face down in the dust under the bed' – remnants of childhood. Moreover, we are also presented with the sacrificial tone of the virginally white bridal pictures of Melanie's mother.

> Her mother exploded in a pyrotechnic display of satin and lace, dressed as for a medieval banquet. ... A wreath of artificial roses was pressed low down on her forehead. ... She carried a bunch of white roses in her arms, cradled like a baby.

She is a meal to be devoured, a firework display, and when Melanie tries on her mother's dress it acts as a malevolent object, drowning and capturing her.

Bunty, Judy, Schoolfriend and *Girl* stories often concentrate on the 'little mother' who stands as a surrogate for her siblings when their parents are, as are Melanie's, killed in a plane crash. Plucky tomboys also abound. Melanie pictures herself in all these roles, and rejects them, but still awaits the kiss of a prince charming to awaken her from herself into a role he designs. In the working-class East London toyshop there is a wicked uncle, no stepmother or wicked aunt, and it is his designs on Melanie which cast her in the role of the traditional female victim, manipulated into a rape victim through his control. Uncle Philip is a child's nightmare figure, a character from a fairytale by the Brothers Grimm.

> Uncle Philip never talked to his wife except to bark brusque commands. He gave her a necklace that choked her. He beat her younger brother. He chilled the air through which he moved. His

towering, blank-eyed presence at the head of the table drew the savour from the good food she cooked.

His menace is both physical and psychological and the spell he casts over the household renders them mute and powerless.

The moment in which Melanie, reified by her role as Leda in Uncle Philip's puppet version of that high art pornographic favourite, Leda and the Swan, is overwhelmed by the monstrous wooden and feathered swan, which is both horror and pure farce. In her mixture of the horrific and the humorous, Carter resembles Roald Dahl, whose short stories have similar twists to hers, and who similarly re-writes 'Little Red Riding Hood'. Dahl comments, 'What's horrible is basically funny ... in fiction I mean.'[8] Angela Carter's delicate mixture of slapstick, irony and the machinations of Sadeian horror typifies her stylistic strategies; an ornate overlay of Western myths and representations, funny, fantastic and frightening. It is deeply revelatory about the forms and intentions of Western art from the National Gallery and Sadlers Wells to the toyshop. Melanie last recalls 'Swan Lake' when her father took her to see it. The embrace of the plywood and feathered swan is a mock up of the many languorous godlike embraces between a loving Leda and an elegant swan found in the world's great art galleries, celebrated in hauntingly beautiful tones by Yeats in 'Leda and the Swan' where phrases such as 'terrified vague fingers' and 'feathered glory' suggest that the aesthetic enjoyment overcomes the sense of the strange and horrific; a version of a grotesque, power myth rape many women readers find bizarre.

Carter's version emphasises the otherness, the disempowering and the horror.

All her laughter was snuffed out. She was hallucinated. She felt herself not herself, wrenched from her own personality, watching this whole fantasy from another place; and in this staged fantasy, anything was possible. Even that the swan, mocked up swan, might assume reality itself and rape this girl in a blizzard of white feathers.

Horror here is a direct effect of the dramatic embodiment of despotic patriarchal power writ large and backed up by the collusion of that other patriarchal power base – high art. Carter's debunking of this high art, patriarchy's dubiously intellectually tarted up sadistic power games, empowers us all to reveal the unpleasantnesses, the potential sick violence, underlying everyday mythic representations of sexual relations.

The dangers are no less real despite the slapstick rendering of events, but Carter's irony and slapstick humour provide themselves with a liberating vehicle to expose and defuse such powers. 'Like fate or the clock, on came the swan, its feet going splat, splat, splat.'

In *Nights at the Circus*, male fear, horror and fascination at female sexual parts are figured in the geography of Madame Schreck's brothel, where the girls work in the basement.

> Madame Schreck organised her museum, thus: downstairs, in what had used to be the wine cellar, she'd had a sort of vault or crypt constructed, with wormy beams overhead and nasty damp flagstones underfoot, and this place was known as 'Down Below', or else, 'The Abyss'. The girls was all made to stand in stone niches cut out of the slimy walls, except for the Sleeping Beauty, who remained prone, since proneness was her speciality. And there were little curtains in front and, in front of the curtains, a little lamp burning. These were her 'profane altars' as she used to call them.

The offhand, everyday Cockney tones of the winged, iconic aerialiste Fevvers renders these traditionally gothic horrors almost domestic, but visions of a visiting judge who ejaculates when black hooded and when a noose is placed round his neck, and of clients who revel in the gothic nightmare of clanking chains, who are turned on only by recumbent, seemingly dead women, and all the trappings of a mixture of Poe and de Sade illuminate the dubious interrelationship between a love of horror and a perverse sexuality: a desire to brutalise women. Women, of course, collude in their own dehumanisation. Fevvers's avarice leads her into the clutches of the determinedly male, sadistic Duke, whose own brand of mastery consists of reducing his objects of desire to just that, a miniaturised, gilded objet d'art. The Grand Duke represents sterile power.

> His house was the realm of minerals, of metals of vitrification – of gold, marble and crystal; pale halls and endless mirrors and glittering chandeliers that clanged like wind-bells in the draught from the front door ... and a sense of frigidity, of sterility, almost palpable.

It is a gothic horror threat of potential disempowerment and reification since all therein is artifice and glitter.

Murderous histories, sexual mutilations of women, and the *frisson* of total control of the human by rendering it entirely useless, pure art ornament and entertainment: the Duke's collection embodies his vile proclivities.

Fevvers's earlier encounter with Christian Rosencreutz, whose sexual perversity was related to his wish to gain new powers by sacrificing what he feared, is an echo of a familiar gothic encounter with Rosicrucianism. Carter replicates the seductive powers, the *frissons* of horror, and exposes a basis of horror in desires to dehumanise, to control, to fix, pin, collect and, perhaps, destroy the adored object. Humour, irony and slapstick undercut and disempower the perpetrators of torture, terror and death in her work and female victims soar above what could destroy them, using for their own ends the very images and forms which could otherwise represent them in a constrained sense.

Fevvers's own canny common sense enables her to turn the Duke's lust against him and she escapes into the Fabergé model of the trans-Siberian railway: a celebratory moment when magic and realism confusingly and amusingly unite. Fevvers escapes, a feathered intacta, icon of dreams, 'bird' woman and yet her own person. The last laugh is on the loving journalist Walser who wishes to pin her down with facts, and on the readers who want her metaphors explained, but who are left instead realising that the best thing to do with myths and metaphors is to reclaim them for our own variety of interpretations, rather than accepting any fobbed off on us by a patriarchal culture.

Reclamation is the key also for Rosaleen, the Red Riding Hood figure in *Company of Wolves*. The grotesque horror of being eaten alive by a lascivious wolf is replaced by the turning of the tables, as she celebrates her own sexual powers, burns her own clothing, becomes a werewolf herself and so tames the beast, thus proving her mother's comment, 'if there's a beast in man it meets its match in women too'. It might seem trite, or even dangerous as some have suggested that Carter merely repeats much of the sexist psychology of eroticism, but it is a way of suggesting reversal, using irony and the technique of 'the pulling of the plug' on a socially constructed version of horror based on a pornography which always renders the woman as victim.

Slow mental and physical torture, claustrophobia, a living death ... this is the stuff of her horror and recalls Poe as it does the Jacobean. But her vision is more ironic and amused. Her aims are related to reversal, there is a consistent drive towards celebration and carnival. In the midst of being almost eaten by the big bad wolf, Red Riding Hood/Rosaleen is empowered by her awareness of the strength of her own virginity, as well as that of her emergent sexuality. This is a reclamation of the body as a site for woman's empowerment. Virginity in myth 'normally' renders a woman both magically safe and ideally fitted to be a sacrificial victim, in a system which sees virginity as a commodity. Here Rosaleen celebrates, her clothes burned by choice in her granny's fire, a werewolf herself?

Fires such as that in *The Magic Toyshop* are purgatorial: the evil die, the good are doubtless rescued. This is in the true tone of Shakespearean late Romance which suggests tragedy and horror but ultimately avoids or overcomes it. There are hints of death by drowning, of tragedy entering our living rooms when Tiffany, the Ophelia-like spurned innocent stripper in *Wise Children* disappears, but she escapes and lives again. Twins are produced from pockets, dead uncles reappear twice as large and filled with largesse. Reunions and unifications replace the open endings of some of the earlier works. Carnival towards which all Carter's work has long leant, triumphs over horror in her most recent work *Wise Children*.

Carter's best horror writing is more suited to the art of the short story than to longer fiction. Like Poe she goes for 'unity of effect', telling individual, perfectly controlled tales which retell and often revalue a myth or legend, which develop and embody a particular lurking perversity or nightmare, and which explore the horrific sources of real events. As in traditional gothic tales, we are terrified because the atmosphere threatens us, the familiar is our familiar nightmare. Beautifully, fatally, realistic, encyclopedic details combine with the immediate, mythic, nightmarish and surreal. In *The Company of Wolves*, we are told that,

> at night, the eyes of wolves shine like candle flames yellowish, reddish, but that is because the pupils of their eyes fatten on darkness and catch the light from your lantern and flash it back at you – red for danger; if a wolf's eyes reflect only moonlight, then they gleam a cold and unnatural green, a mineral, a piercing colour.

The movement of nightmare is enacted with a rich mixture of visual and psychologically threatening imagery:

> If the benighted traveller spies those luminous, terrible sequins stitched suddenly on the black thickets, then he knows he must run, if fear has not struck him stock still.
> But those eyes are all you will be able to glimpse of the forest assassins as they cluster inevitably around your smell of meat.

And her language draws the reader in and implicates them as it reproduces a fascinating and compelling mixture of terror and the *frisson* of joy at such terror.

The title story of *The Bloody Chamber* is one such perfect gothic tale in which we are seduced and drawn in as slowly as the victim, the virginal wife of this art collecting Bluebeard. The language of food consumption, aesthetic pleasure and avaricious cruelty dominates her descriptions of him, his wooing and her collusion. Threat drips slowly from every crevice. His is 'possessed of that strange, ominous calm of a sentient vegetable life, like one of those cobra-headed funereal lilies whose white sheaths are curled out of a flesh as thick and tensely yielding to the touch as vellum.' His desire she perceives but does not understand though the 'choker of rubies, two inches wide, like an extraordinarily slit throat' presages the total ownership he has in mind while his 'sheer carnal avarice' watching her in gilded mirrors positions her both as consumable meat, and art object. Mirrors, billowing gauze curtains, indecipherable imprecations from (traditional, gothic) menials, huge beds and lilies: these gothic familiars draw in and thrill the reader, who wants yet to cry out a warning.

Carter's intertextuality provides a smile of recognition, 'All the better to see you' says the lupine, leonine, vampirish, art/wife collecting descendant of Browning's Duke who keeps pictures and relics of previously, mysteriously, dead wives. The ravishment is surreal, particularly as he removes all her clothes except the choker, and mirrors reflect every move:

> Rapt, he intoned: 'Of her apparel she retains/Only her sonorous jewellery'.
> A dozen husbands impaled a dozen brides while the mewing gulls swung on invisible trapezes in the empty air outside.

Carter investigates also the notion of the 'pleasures of the flesh' and here reveals a link between pornography and horror: man as flesh, skin covering meat, the source of the horror of cannibal tales and movies like *The Silence of the Lambs*. 'The strong abuse, exploit and meatify the weak, says Sade'. (*The Sadeian Woman*) 'She knew she was nobody's meat' is a challenge Rosaleen holds up to the wolf, though necrophagy (exposition of the meatiness of human flesh) and cannibalism lurk behind Bluebeard's delights at his new wife. 'I saw him watching me in the gilded mirrors with the assessing eye of a connoisseur inspecting horseflesh, or even of a housewife in the market, inspecting cuts on the slab.' This terrifies but attracts her, as she recognises her own potential for corruption. His sexual 'appetite' and then his 'taste' for her she mistakenly feels will protect her when she investigates the locked rooms of his house in his absence. We know versions of the story, know she will find the remains of dead ex wives. As with many gothic horror tales of castles, locked doors, horrid secrets, threatening husbands and marital violence, walled up wives, spiders, jewelled daggers and necklaces, the very familiarity produces a *frisson* for the reader, and the familiarity here of the old tale captures and captivates us. Languorousness, inevitability, these entrap the reader as they entrap the bride about to be turned into a 'meal' for her murderous husband who swings a cruel sword, and forces her to dress in white as the sacrificial victim, to his lustful power. The warrior mother rescues the bride with the aid of the new servant. The story becomes a romp, but its horror has a sexual and social basis we won't forget, and which returns in many another of her tales.

In *The Sadeian Woman* Carter notes, 'Sexuality, stripped of the idea of free exchange, is not in any way humane; it is nothing but pure cruelty. Carnal knowledge is the infernal knowledge of the flesh as meat.' The potential of devouring lurks behind 'The Tiger's Bride' but the proud voyeuristic beast is tamed with the girl's love and her recognition of her own tigerishness. In 'The Lady of the House of Love', a female vampire strikes a familiar terror, her necessary plan involving the capture of male morsels. Her room is funerary, pungent with smoke and elaborate, and in true vampire fashion her seemingly virginal beauty is evidence of her desires as, 'In her white lace negligee stained a little with blood, the Countess climbs up on her catafalque at dawn each morning and lies down in an open coffin.' Metamorphosis takes place as she turns into a nocturnal creature sniffing out lesser prey. Change and the question of what it means to be human, that fearsome ingredient of Victorian horror of the *Dr Jekyll and Mr Hyde* type, but with its roots further back in the Jacobean horror of wolfish brothers carrying legs of corpses over their shoulders in *The Duchess of Malfi* – these crowd many of Carter's short stories. Here the rococo strangely juxtaposes images and descriptions which conjure up a night world of horror.

> the voracious margin of huntress's nights in the gloomy garden, crouch and pounce, surrounds her habitual tortured somnambulism, her life or imitation of life. The eyes of this nocturnal creature enlarge and glow. All claws and teeth, she strokes, she gorges; but nothing can console her for the ghastliness of her condition, nothing.

Employing what David Punter calls 'the dialectic of persecution', Carter's gothic investigates the extremes of terror, leading the audience gradually into realms which are nightmarish and horribly familiar.[9]

Influences on Carter's work include Isak Dinesen, who continued gothic interest in decayed aristocracy, and as a feminist writer, filtered society's problems 'through a pervading and ironic self-consciousness' much as does Fevvers, and the protagonist of *The Bloody Chamber*.[10] Another main influence is in the nightmarish, surrealist and psychologically fired night wanderings of transvestite characters in Djuna Barnes, particularly the highly Jacobean *Nightwood* (1937). *Nightwood* belongs to a tradition of lesbian gothic writing, which highlights the sexuality implicit in such horror figures as vampires, werewolves and zombies. Richard Dyer comments that,

> a number of ... writers on the horror film have suggested, adapting Freudian ideas, that all 'monsters' in some measure represent the hideous and terrifying form that sexual energies take when they 'return' from being socially and culturally repressed. Yet the vampire seems especially to represent sexuality ... s/he bites them, with a bite that is just as often described as a kiss.[11]

Werewolves are favourites in *The Bloody Chamber* collection, their sexuality emphasised as handsome young men who leap in front of girls, men with eyebrows meeting suspiciously in the middle; men who want to eat you up and devour you sexually. The main vampire is a woman in 'The Lady of the House of Love' who lures in wandering men who, 'led by the hand to her bedroom … can scarcely believe their luck'.

Investigating her relationship to other postmodernist writers we find many parallels with the American gothic of Purdy, Pynchon and Coover. Recognition of this appears in her epigraph to *Heroes and Villains* which comes from Leslie Fiedler's exploration of the American gothic, *Love and Death in the American Novel*.[12] The epigraph runs: 'The Gothic mode is essentially a form of parody, a way of assailing clichés by exaggerating them to the limit of grotesqueness.'[13]

One of Carter's main stated aims is demythologising, unpicking and unpacking the myths and legends (those fictions) which shape and control our lives, whether safely contained in a fairytale or shaped around us in newspaper articles, adverts or television stereotypes. The human mind forces experience into familiar shapes so that it can comprehend it, but in so doing it simplifies into stereotype and myth, which themselves seem then to us to have safely embodied the less pleasant of those experiences, mental or physical, by objectifying and fictionalising them in this way. Stereotypes, myths and fictions are shorthand, but they exercise a control on the expressions and forms of the everyday world. Carter particularly intends to demythologise the fictions related to sexuality, and horror is one of her means. She exposes the relationship between sex and power, the erotic, the perverse; she digs behind the ostensibly comfortable and safe surfaces and shows up oppressions, reification, torture and dehumanisation lurking in the everyday. One way she does this is by re-examining and rewriting fairytales and myths, and another is to explore incidents in which the everyday explodes, revealing the horrors which lurk behind it.

Violence against women has long been a characteristic of much horror writing, as well as pornography. The essential powerlessness of the virginal, entrapped, victimised girl is a stock feature of pornography as it is of gothic horror which deals with taboos: 'Incest, rape, various kinds of transgressions of the boundaries between the natural and the human'.[14] Angela Carter is a clever manipulator of the techniques of horror, terror and the gothic. She takes the impetus and the structure of gothic-based romance tales for women and reappropriates them for a sexual politics which demythologises myths of the sexual powerlessness and victim role for women. She uses their structure to turn their usual denouements on their heads. As Tania Modleski argues in *Loving with a Vengeance*, gothics are 'expressions of the "normal" feminine paranoid personality' which incorporates guilt and fear, 'the paranoid individual faces physical persecution (as in dreams of being attacked by murderous figures)'.[15]

Moral and more importantly physical persecution predominate, and the reader is encouraged to wallow in the guilt and fear, and to imagine themselves as a victim, while in romantic developments of gothic fiction, persecution is 'experienced as half-pleasurable'. Romantic heroines turn their 'victimization into a triumph'. If we explore the novels which combine the gothic and the romantic there is a (for a feminist reader) tremendous disempowering celebration of this victimisation as satisfying and ultimately productive of reward. Paulina Palmer, examining Margaret Atwood's *Bodily Harm* makes comments as appropriate for Carter as for Atwood, about the reappropriation of a genre, the gothic romantic, designed very much for women,

> the Gothic genre, traditionally noted for its representation of woman as victim, becomes in Atwood's hands the perfect medium for depicting contemporary woman caught unaware in the 'rape culture' which pervades society. Motifs associated with the genre ... include: the ingenuous heroine as the victim of male manipulation and attack; an intrigue plot in which the male protagonists compete for power; the collapsing of conventional boundaries between external/internal and animate/inanimate; and the reference to certain socially taboo topics – in this case cancer, and sado-masochistic sexual practice.[16]

The resurgence in interest in horror writing by women which has produced *The Virago Book of Ghost Stories*[17] and the fiercer, more radical *Skin of Our Soul*[18] enables us to ask questions about where Angela Carter relates to other women horror writers and what might be said to be any specifically female characteristics in the horror genre. The very latest of the popular fictional forms to be reclaimed by feminist critics, investigating the operation of popular fictional characteristics in the work of women writers within the genre, horror writing might very properly be said to have originated with women, with the work of Ann Radcliffe's *Mysteries of Udolpho* or with Mary Shelley's *Frankenstein*. Great women writers throughout the centuries have produced ghost stories and horror stories, but perhaps one of the problems of reclaiming horror as a genre for women is this very equation of the female victim, the edge of the pornographic, with horror.

Lisa Tuttle argues that men and women's perceptions of fear are to some extent similar, but in others different because of their social positioning:

> Territory which to a man is emotionally neutral may for a woman be mined with fear, and vice-versa, for example: the short walk

home from the bus-stop of an evening. And how to understand the awesome depths of loathing some men feel for the ordinary (female) body? We all understand the language of fear, but men and women are raised speaking different dialects of that language.[19]

Women's contemporary horror fiction explores sexual license, alternative sexual relationships, and the power in 'normal' relationships. There are many tales which feature fear of incest, of patriarchal rape, of life-draining mother, hatred of devious, bitchy, beautiful women. There are hidden cruelties in what are 'normally' perceived as loving or nurturing relationships, and there are forbidden fantasies of lesbian partnerships or incestuous partnerships. Taboos are explored.

Angela Carter's gothic horror reappropriates women's powers. The thrills and spills of the romantic gothics are there, but the terroriser turned faithful lover is not. The main gains are self respect, liberty and equal relationships. Red Riding Hood ends up happy with the wolf, Bluebeard's wife is liberated, Fevvers settles for Walser, and retains her secret, her magic. Glittering, contradictory, intertextually familiar and playful, Angela Carter's horror brings into the clear light of the semi-realistic domestic kitchen, the nasty thoughts, fears and nightmares lurking in the cellars of our minds. And she gives us something magical too. Hers is not the horror of the abyss: it is not ultimately a black vision, it's too Rabelaisian for that, too funny and celebratory.

Notes

1. Books by Angela Carter referred to in the text: *The Magic Toyshop* (London 1967); *Heroes and Villains* (London: 1969); *Fireworks* (London: 1974); *The Bloody Chamber* (London: 1979); *The Sadeian Woman* (London: 1979); *Nights at the Circus* (London: 1984); *Black Venus* (London: 1985); *Wise Children* (1991).
2. Rosemary Jackson, *Fantasy: the Literature of Subversion* (London: 1981) p. 41.
3. Angela Carter in conversation with John Haffenden, *The Literary Review* no. v (1984) p. 37.
4. Iris le Bessiere, *Le Récit Fantastique: La Poétique de l'Incertain* (Paris: 1974) p. 62.
5. Jackson, p. 23.
6. Lee Daniells, *Fear: a History of Horror in the Mass Media* (London: 1977).
7. Martin Barker, *A Haunt of Fears: the Strange History of the British Horror Comics Campaign* (London: 1984) p. 129.
8. Roald Dahl interviewed in *Twilight Zone* (Jan–Feb. 1983).
9. David Punter, *The Literature of Terror: a History of Gothic Fictions from 1765 to the Present Day* (London: 1980) p. 130.
10. Ibid., p. 379.

11. Richard Dyer, 'Children of the Night. Vampirism as Homosexuality, Homosexuality as Vampirism' in Susanna Radstone ed., *Sweet Dreams: Sexuality, Gender and Popular Fiction* (London: 1988) p. 54.
12. Leslie Fiedler, *Love and Death in the American Novel* (New York: 1960).
13. Angela Carter, *Heroes and Villains* (London: 1981).
14. Punter, p. 19.
15. Tania Modleski, *Loving with a Vengeance* (New York: 1984) pp. 81 and 83.
16. Paulina Palmer, *Contemporary Women's Fiction* (Brighton: 1989) p. 91.
17. Richard Dalby ed., *The Virago Book of Ghost Stories* (London: 1990).
18. Lisa Tuttle ed., *The Skin of Our Soul: New Horror Stories by Women* (London: 1990) Introduction.
19. Ibid., p. 5.

13 Worlds that creep up on You: Postmodern Illusions in the Work of Clive Barker

Andrew Smith

In this account of Clive Barker his novel *Weaveworld* will be examined, as will two earlier short stories from his *Books of Blood* series, 'Son of Celluloid' and 'Human Remains'.[1] It will be argued that it is possible to see the work of Barker in terms of a postmodern aesthetic, which Baudrillard sees as characterised by the use of simulacra.[2] Barker will thus be read here in terms of how he exemplifies an aspect of the postmodern which suggests that the work of Barker is of more interest than just being, what the critic Noel Carroll called, 'The literary equivalent of slasher movies.'[3]

Initially 'Son of Celluloid' will be discussed because it introduces many of the themes which are restated in greater depth in *Weaveworld*. In particular it is Baudrillard's idea of *the simulacra* which is examined here, seeing how 'fictional' forms come to govern experience.[4] In the case of *Weaveworld*, Baudrillard's work on the theory of catastrophe in 'Fatal Strategies' will also be explored, seeing in part, how Barker's novel similarly represents apocalypse as an ambivalent moment. As both the end of the world and as creation narrative (the Big Bang).[5]

'Son of Celluloid' is an account of how a dead petty criminal's cancer comes to take on a life of its own. The criminal, Barberio, is a prison escapee who is mortally wounded in a shoot out with the police. He attempts to hide in a secret niche, which turns out to be behind the screen of a cinema. Here he dies of his wounds and the cancer comes to life. It is the energy and emotions of the movie goers which give life to this cancer. It is their emotions which are seen as being the catalyst for this life. Here is energy transformed and emotion displaced. The cancer, however, lacks any enabling form of its own, taking on the shape of various film stars in order to seduce or frighten its victims. In this sense its form is defined by the 'closed' reality of the star system which is implied in its cinema setting. One of the cinema attendants, Ricky, enters this illusory world where he is confronted by John Wayne, 'A middle period Wayne, before he'd grown fat and sick-looking'. The stars appear in their on-screen personas, as living simulacra.

In this 'closed' world of cinematic representation there can be seen a parallel with what Baudrillard sees as the 'unreal' becoming the real. He writes that, 'It is no longer a question of imitation, nor of reduplication, nor even of parody. It is rather a question of substituting signs of the real for the real itself.' Ricky thus mistakes the Marilyn Monroe that he is confronted with for the real thing, not just because of the physical similarity, but because of the attendant desire which comes with seeing this illusion. 'She' says to him, '"Am I beautiful?", "You're a goddess: whoever you are", "I'm yours: that's who I am."' Monroe, defined through the imagination of Ricky, becomes an aspect of his own desire. As simulacrum, however, the Monroe figure is a pure spectacle, a visual simulation which is essentially empty, as she says; '"I need to be looked at, or I die. It's the natural state of illusions."' (p. 26). It also becomes the state of illusions that there is an amount of image slipping. In addition to Monroe and Wayne, the cancer takes on the guises of Peter Lorre and Greta Garbo. The effect of these illusions is that they in turn fictionalise the subject. As Baudrillard proposes, the simulacra organises the 'real'. Ricky's killing is described in these terms, 'It was an appalling experience, and mercifully short. Then the feature Ricky's lived for thirty-seven years snapped in mid-reel, and he slumped in the arms of fiction.' Note the pun on mid-reel (real). What is also revealed in this process of fictionalisation and image shifting is the emptiness behind the pull of the hyperreal. In this sense this use of images in 'Son of Celluloid' approximates to what Baudrillard sees as the state of art in postmodernism. In *Fatal Strategies* he writes that, 'The more art tries to realize itself, the more it hyperrealizes itself, the more it transcends itself to find its own empty essence.'

In the story, the cancer is defined in terms of it being a living animal which has fed upon the emotions of cinema audiences. This hidden 'animal' turns itself into an object of spectacle, an amoeboid life form trying to find an acceptable persona (as a desire) in order to feed. The cancer can be seen as principally being some kind of life force, or a kind of will-to-live and it uses simulacra in order to organise experience for its own ends. What it also is, however, is an intertextual subject, its moving between simulacra, and behind these facades is revealed as a banal desire for life. It is this idea of the inter-text which will also be discussed in relation to *Weaveworld*. In this sense, the inter-text is possible to see not just as cancer but as analogous to the artist (hyperrealising himself) and creating fictions through other fictions; the appropriation of glamourous cinema iconography in order to 'seduce' the reader who is also a victim.

Illusion plays a strong part in *Weaveworld*. The plot of the novel is that a group of magic makers, the 'Seerkind' who once lived in the 'real'

(human) world, 'the Kingdom of the Cuckoo', were so persecuted
that by the end of the nineteenth century they decided to meet
together and escape from the 'Kingdom', only to be re-woken when
the Kingdom has become a safer place for them. This is effected by
having them woven into a carpet, which is a miniaturised and crude
representation of their own origins. This carpet is pursued by one of
the Seerkind, Immacolata, who has remained in the Kingdom. She is
hostile to their world and seeks to destroy it. The carpet falls into the
hands of Cal and Suzanna who attempt to protect it. The novel thus
pursues a course in which Immacolata, her sisters, and her human
associate, Shadwell the salesman, attempt to gain control of this world
which is periodically released from the carpet. Ultimately the Seerkind
are threatened by another character, Uriel (the 'Scourge') who is
defeated and their world is left intact.

As stated earlier, *Weaveworld* (as its name suggests) relies heavily on
identifying inter-textual forces and this is suggested at the beginning
of the novel.

The threads can always be traced back to some earlier tale, and to
the tales that preceded that; though as the narrator's voice recedes
that connection will seem to grow more tenuous, for each age will
not want the tale told as if it were of its own making.

This idea of inter-textuality is further carried over into the creation
of the Weaveworld, which is identified with artistic creation. Here there
is a mixing of 'fact, fiction, mind and matter'. In effect the world is
woven out of these. Here it is possible to see that what is collapsed in
this process is the 'real' with the fictional. This means that the novel's
espousal of the inter-textual is a mandate for the slippage between the
real and the fictional. There is a point in the novel when the heroine,
Suzanna, battles with Hobart, an ally of Immacolata and this takes place
in a book of fairy stories! Initially, Suzanna attempts to grab the 'real'
book of fairy tales from Hobart's grasp: 'The next moment words
seemed to rise from the book, white forms against the smoke, and as
they rose they became what they meant.' The protagonists are pulled
into the book where experience becomes fictionalised. Words themselves
are no longer seen as empty, arbitrary configurations, but rather
become lived experience, 'They'd entered the common life of words.'
It is an interweaving of thing with word which defines the experience
in this scene. The simulacrum, the fiction of the fairy story, has become
the 'real'. In fairy-land Suzanna looks at Hobart who has now changed
into a dragon. 'He was woven with the pattern of light and shade, and
so – most oddly – was the word DRAGON. All three occupied the
same space in her head: a living text of man, word and monster.'
Also, as in 'Son of Celluloid' images become prone to slippage. In one

scene, Hobart is a dragon and Suzanna a maiden, this then changes into Suzanna becoming the dragon and Hobart a naked 'Chaste knight'. Relationships are thus fictionalised to the point where the experience of the 'real' is defined by a literary trope (here the fairy story).

So then, there can be seen in *Weaveworld* a self-conscious gesture towards inter-textuality which is seen to govern experience. This is exemplified by the way in which Suzanna and Hobart are absorbed by the fantastic, and see themselves in terms of stock characters from a particular form of fiction. It is this notion of absorption which is re-translated elsewhere in the novel in terms of a bodily amalgamation with things which are external to the body, but which are later internalised and seen as intrinsic to it.

There is, for example, Suzanna's absorption by the menstrum, a powerful force of magic which is feminine. She realises that she needs to find out, 'how much it belonged to *her*, and how much she to it'. There is a similar absorption of Immacolata with her spectral sisters, and with Hobart and Uriel (wishing to take a human form) and Shadwell and Uriel. What is implied in this is a loss of self-hood to forms which are themselves fantastic: the magic of the menstrum, the ghosts of the sisters, the possession by an 'evil' force. In this process self-hood is not destroyed so much as redefined, Suzanna gains power, Immacolata repentance, Uriel a deceptive persona. Again, it is an example of the 'unreal' coming into being and becoming the real. This, it is suggested is the 'true' state of 'the Fugue' (the world of the weave) because to think otherwise is 'a Cuckoo's way of thinking, always making divisions: the viewer from the viewed; the peach from the taste it left on the tongue'. In this heavily integrated world, everything would appear to connect. It is difficult for the characters to find an outside to this world. There is however an attempt to own it and this by Shadwell the salesman. He appears to link magic to merchandise, in such a way that suggests that magic has an exchange and a use value.

Shadwell is the salesman employed by Immacolata to find the Fugue and sell it, the subsequent opening up of 'the Fugue' by the buyer would enable her to enter the Fugue and destroy it. In order to help Shadwell, Immacolata has supplied him with a jacket, the lining of which has 'raptures' or illusions which seduce the buyer into being an enforced ally. Shadwell attempts just such a seduction, unsuccessfully, early on with the hero Cal. Again, this is couched in terms of it being an absorption, a seduction for Cal.

It has become a challenge to see past the tinsel to the real treasure that lay beyond. A curious sensation attended this focusing; a restlessness in his chest and throat, as though some part of him were preparing to be gone; out of him and along the line of his gaze. Gone into the jacket.

For Shadwell, the desire to be present at the 'Sale of Sales' is over-shadowed by a desire to become its ruler. His motives become thus one of ownership rather than profit. Shadwell, by virtue of being a salesman, initially had a position outside the world of illusion, he was the purveyor of it, rather than subjected to it. As soon as he wishes to take command of this world he is forced to fictionalise himself. He takes on the disguise of 'The Prophet' (profit), to the extent that he believes himself to be the true ruler of the Fugue. The Seerkind, initially, fail to see him as the fiction which he has now become. For Shadwell, 'once he'd drawn back the veil of cloud he'd be a God'. The veil referred to here is the cloud which disguises the Gyre, or the loom which has created the world they are now in. Shadwell then, has relinquished his position of outsider to these uses of magic. He has fictionalised himself by becoming the Prophet and having expressed his desire to find the loom. It is the loom which is the centre of creation and it has formed those illusory, 'raptures' as they are termed.

In the reading given previously to 'Son of Celluloid' it was suggested that the slippage in image-making implied what Baudrillard sees as the emptiness in an art form which 'hyperrealizes itself'. This same scene is re-enacted in the Temple of the Loom where Shadwell, the salesman, is confronted by Immacolata and Suzanna. Again the inter-text is evoked in describing the building which for Suzanna, 'was built on the principle of a Russian doll, one within another, *Worlds within worlds*'. What Shadwell finds is an empty room, '*There's nothing there!*' There is an apparent absence in the centre of this creativity. However, as suggested in 'Son of Celluloid' there is a form of presence behind the image shifting, a form of crude life which manifests itself through a fictionalisation, through an analogy of the artist as inter-text story teller. Here Shadwell finds absence because he fails to discern a similar life force at work, a force which equates thought with word. It is Immacolata who ridicules Shadwell's assumption that he would find an object of some kind, rather than a controlling power, Suzanna realises that,

Magic might be bestowed upon the physical, but it didn't *reside* there. It resided in the word, which was mind spoken, and in motion, which was mind made manifest; in the system of the weave and the evocations of the melody – all *mind*.

Magic is thus an internal force manifested only when it is employed externally. Again it is another inter-text which governs creativity, an unspoken one which has for its analogy the subjectivity of the subject, a meeting of mind, with word, with motion. An idle story teller.

What this in turn comes to imply is that a story becomes real, not due to any veracity that it may contain, but due to the belief in which it is held. In 'Fatal Strategies', Baudrillard identifies this lack of the real with a decline in a concern for objective causes. He, significantly, sees this as bound-up with a problem at the level of reference which,

> becomes a fantastic burden – references living one off the other and at the other's expense. Here again we have an excrescent interpretive system developing without any relation to its objective. All of this is a consequence of a forward flight in the face of the haemorrhaging of objective causes.

This is apparent in *Weaveworld* when Suzanna visits the now contrite Immacolata at her shrine. Suzanna comments on the story of the 'madonna and christ-child' that, 'whether their story was history or myth was academic; the Fugue had taught her that. All that mattered was how loudly the image spoke.' In this meeting with Immacolata, Suzanna is told about the Scourge. It is this creature which ultimately threatens the Seerkind with destruction. The Scourge believes that it is the gate-keeper of Eden whose task it is to track down the Seerkind after they escaped from there. However, it is the Scourge, or Uriel, who is also caught up in this problem of reference identified by Baudrillard. In effect, the Scourge has become self-fictionalising. Immacolata tells Suzanna of the Scourge that, '"It *thinks* that it's called Uriel."' And again, '"It believes itself an Angel. So, for better or worse, it is."' Again it is the unreal which has come to frame and define the real. Uriel personifies this state of unreality which itself confronts the magical 'unreality' of the Fugue. Baudrillard again, 'The real does not concede anything to the benefit of the imaginary: it concedes only to the benefit of the more real than real (the hyperreal) and to the more true than true.' In this sense the 'reality' of the Seerkind can be seen as greater than the 'real' of Uriel (if for no other reason than that their's is a collective 'reality'). Immacolata confronts Uriel with this in terms which also suggest the emptiness of objective causes discussed by Baudrillard, and this is linked to the way in which the novel suggests that experience is interconnected and inter-textual. Uriel says to her,

> '*I am alone!*'
> 'No. You've forgotten yourself; and so you've been forgotten.'
> '*I am Uriel. I guard the gate!*'
> 'You are not alone. Nobody – nothing – is alone. You're part of something more.'
> '*I am Uriel. I guard the gate!*'
> 'There's nothing left to guard.' Immacolata said. 'But your duty.'

Here it is Uriel's sense of duty which is mocked as an objective cause. Later Immacolata challenges Uriel to discard the form of Hobart (who he has possessed) and reveal himself in his true identity. In the case of Uriel it can be seen that an external form has been appropriated in order to express an internal identity. Something which is extrinsic and alien has thus been used in order to simulate 'human' life. However its 'reality' is not as powerful as that of the Seerkind, and this had previously been shown by Shadwell's discovery of the Scourge in the desert. In the Fugue all is magical, but in a way which suggests its reality through its fecundity. It is a colourful world which seems to approximate to a notion of life through its constant flux and change. In opposition to this is the garden protected by Uriel, where the plants and trees echo that of the Fugue except that it is a dead world; 'It was sand. Scentless, colourless, lifeless: a dead garden.' The existence of the garden is a play on 'the Fugue', it is a crude simulacrum of an illusory world.

So then, with the character of Shadwell there exists the possibility of being on the outside of these magical worlds. He has this possibility because he uses magic in order to seduce his 'customers'. It is his coat, with its raptures, which is used by Cal in defeating Uriel. It is Uriel who has been described in terms of a fabricated self and an obsolete cause. Cal confronts Uriel with the coat, which results in a form of redemptive awakening for the Scourge; 'Unreminded of its nature it had sunk into obsession, devoted to a dead duty. But looking on itself – seeing the glory of its condition – it shed that lunacy, and shedding it; looked starward.' This can be seen as a similar process to what Baudrillard identifies in 'Fatal Strategies', 'there is something like a drive to revert to the spectacle, or to climax on stage instead of producing oneself originally. To manifest one's being is necessary; to be enraptured is absolutely vital.' Uriel is here enraptured, and in this process seems to 'manifest ... being'. Indeed, it seems to find its true self through an identification with a past conjured by the jacket. However, in terms of the hyperreal characterised by the Fugue, it is only a relative reality that the Scourge is subject to, the 'reality' of the Fugue being more powerful than its own.

This theme of being enraptured can, in an extended sense be seen as a controlling device throughout the novel. For Cal and Suzanna it takes on the form of sublimity. Cal regards the spectacle in terms which suggest the effacement of personal origins, 'I wasn't born 'til now, he thought ... I wasn't even born.' Again it is the case that the 'reality' of the hyperreal supplants the previous 'real'. It is this notion of the spectacle which will be explored in greater length especially in relation to Baudrillard's interpretation of the representation of catastrophe in 'Fatal Strategies'.

On one level *Weaveworld* can be read as a novel of the apocalypse. There are three worlds which are put under threat in the novel. The world of the Kingdom (the 'human'), the world of the Seerkind, and the closed world of the Scourge. The Scourge's world, because it is self-enclosed and encircled by a wall, with the Scourge as its only inhabitant, crumbles under its lack of resources. It is a dead world, made of sand and thus perpetually barren. In effect it crumbles into its own decay. It is, however, the clash between the Kingdom and the Fugue which takes on the form on an apocalyptic struggle. It is the Fugue, which when unwoven, literally explodes into the realm of the Kingdom. The first opening of the Fugue is described as being 'the end of the world, and the beginning of *worlds*'. It is the world of the Fugue which is nearly destroyed when Shadwell stabs Immacolata in the Temple of the Loom, the Fugue is saved by yet another use of the inter-text when it is rewritten (woven) into the book of the fairy stories for safe keeping by Suzanna. However, Cal and Suzanna are forced to watch the old Fugue disappear (the Fugue kept in the book is a re-writing of Cal's and Suzanna's remembrance of it).

> Wonderland had gone.
> The glories of the Fugue had been shredded and torn, their tatters evaporating even as she watched. Water, wood, stone; living animal tissue and dead seerkind: all gone, as though it had never been. A few remnants lingered, but not for long. As the Gyre thundered and shook, these last signs of the Fugue's terrain became smoke and threads, then empty air.

Baudrillard sees such fantasies of the apocalypse as being an 'obsession over nuclear catastrophe', but also, and paradoxically, as being 'fuelled (by) the myth of the Big Bang, of the explosion as the origin of the universe'. At one and the same moment we have the complete destruction of the world, as it is here for the Fugue, and an account of origins (the Fugue is reclaimed for rebirth in the book of fairy stories) so that,

> The sadistic irony of catastrophe is that is secretly awaits for things, even ruins, to regain their beauty and meaning only to destroy them once again. It is intent upon destroying the illusion of eternity, but it also plays with that illusion since it fixates things in an alternative eternity.[6]

It is the world of the Fugue which becomes this 'alternative eternity', kept safe through an act of remembrance which had created that world in the first place (the meeting of mind with word and notion in the Temple of the Loom). In the novel there is not just an ambivalent use of apocalyptic imagery (death as renewal) there is also something tied to this which is concerned with the importance of the spectacle. Baudrillard again, humanity can accept physical annihilation, but cannot agree to sacrifice the spectacle (unless it can find a spectator in another world). The drive to spectacle is more powerful than the instinct of preservation, and it is on the former that we must rely.[7]

The world of the Fugue is a garish place, kept alive as spectacle through an act of remembrance between Cal and Suzanna. In effect it is they who become the new loom, recreating the world of the Fugue anew.

In *Weaveworld* it is possible to see an unspoken enactment of many of the characteristics which Baudrillard sees in the postmodern condition. The world of the Fugue is a simulated one, a parodic play on the 'real'. It, literally, bursts into one reality and as a consequence undermines what had been seen as constituting that reality in the first place. Hobart, for example, thinks of the Seerkind in terms of how they manipulate the experience of the real, 'and he loved reality more than his balls'. Later, Hobart ponders on his experience of the Fugue and his meeting with Suzanna, 'Real? What *was* real? Perhaps (this thought would have been unthinkable before Suzanna) real was merely what he *said* was real.' As in Baudrillard's account of simulacra, the 'real' becomes relativised, with one version of the real being more 'real' than the others. The world of the Scourge for example, is defeated in self-recognition which destroys its grasp on its own sense of the 'real'. This is something which happens to the 'Land of the Cuckoo'. When Suzanna is walking down a high street with one of the Seerkind, Jerichau, she enters into his way of seeing and in contemplating the 'Harlot century' of contemporary life: 'she watched it afresh; saw just how desperate it was to please, yet how dispossessed of pleasure; how crude, even as it claimed sophistication; and, despite its zeal to spellbind, how utterly unenchanting'. It is through taking up another subject position that the real becomes altered, and this in turn can be related to a breakdown in 'objective' causes discussed earlier in relation to the Scourge. The 'real' has become relative, leading Hobart to believe that it may be internal projection 'real was merely what he *said* was real', rather than external recognition. It has become the world of the simulacra.

It is these ideas of Baudrillard which will now be briefly discussed in relation to another of Barker's short stories, 'Human Remains'. It will be suggested that this story offers a clearer focusing on this notion of the simulacra, which it achieves through a reliance on the motif of the *doppelgänger*.

Gavin in 'Human Remains' is a male prostitute. Through a client he discovers what appears to be a wooden likeness of himself. As time goes by this likeness takes over Gavin's life and in effect becomes a better version of him (again the hyperreal above the real). Within this transformation of the wooden dummy, there is a notion of perfectibility which is similar to the way the cancer in 'Son of Celluloid' becomes a cipher for desire. The dummy tells Gavin,

> 'I am a thing without a proper name', it pronounced. 'I am a wound in the flank of the world. But I am also that perfect stranger you always prayed for as a child, to come and take you, call you beauty, lift you naked out of the street and through Heaven's window. Aren't I? Aren't I?'

Later he tells Gavin, '"I am yourself ... made perfectible."' However, the dummy is condemned to remain a simulacrum of the human because it is only able to mimic, rather than feel, experience. Gavin goes back to the client, Reynolds, who tells him that the dummy will attempt to steal his soul in order to be completely life like. This has to be a theft of his soul because it is internal. The dummy can only imitate the external and mimic the 'human' but cannot feel for it, is denied a full 'human' existence (the 'human' remains in Gavin).

The story goes on to imply a clash between feeling and experience. At the end, both attend the funeral of Gavin's father. Here, the dummy seems to make the appropriate emotional responses. However the dummy slips up by making errors that imply that he has not become the exact simulacrum of Gavin that he had wished. The dummy cries excessively, whereas 'Gavin had seldom given in to tears, they'd always made him feel weak and ridiculous.' He puts flowers on the grave, Gavin tells him, '"He hated flowers!" the thing flinched.' The implication at the end is not that the dummy has become an exact simulacrum of Gavin, but rather that he has become more 'real' than Gavin (more 'conventionally' human). This is again the notion that the unreal not only enters the real in order to restructure experience, but that it becomes the only permissable experience. Gavin ends the story seeking his death by walking into heavy traffic.

Clive Barker has been discussed here in relation to the work of Baudrillard in order to highlight how his work can be related to postmodern concerns, in its play of surfaces and 'realities' where experience (like consumerism) has become located as a socially polymorphous promiscuity (worlds within worlds). This is not however an attempt to reclaim a 'low-brow' writer by a particular reading which suggests that it is possible to see him in 'high-brow' terms. Rather it is possible to see in this analysis a doubling of some form of postmodernism, in that a mass circulated text, consumed by a varied reading public, gestures towards (internally in the case of *Weaveworld*) the variable reading experience which postmodern mass consumerism implies. In this sense, the final words are left to Shadwell the salesman, who in some way articulates this form of consumption which is analogous to the continuing, serial, popularity of the pulp fantasy writer –

TO SELL IS TO OWN.
That was the most important lesson Shadwell had learned as a salesman. If what you possessed was desired ardently enough by another person, then you as good as possessed that person too.

Notes

1. Clive Barker, *Weaveworld* (Glasgow: 1988); Clive Barker, *Clive Barker's Books of Blood* vol. III (London: 1988); 'Son of Celluloid' in *Clive Barker's Books of Blood* vol. III.
2. 'Human Remains' in *Clive Barker's Books of Blood* vol. III.
3. Noel Carroll, *The Philosophy of Horror, or Paradoxes of the Heart* (New York: 1990) p. 21.
4. See Jean Baudrillard, 'Simulacra and Simulations' in *Jean Baudrillard Selected Writings* ed., Mark Poster (Oxford: 1989) pp. 166–84.
5. Jean Baudrillard, 'Fatal Strategies' in Poster.
6. Ibid., p. 197.
7. Ibid., p. 202.

Index